OCR
Computing
for GCSE

Sean O'Byrne and George Rouse

The Publishers would like to thank the following for permission to reproduce copyright material:

Photo credits
p.1 *T* © Pictorial Press Ltd/Alamy, *B* ©TopFoto/UPP; **p.2** © Time Life Pictures/Getty Images; **p.9** © 3d brained/Fotolia; **p.10** © www.taxdisc.direct.gov.uk Open Government Licence (OGL); **p.11** © AKSARAN/Getty Images; **p.15** © ersoy emin/Alamy; **p.18** Bruce Adams/Rex Features; **p.22** © PhotoStock-Israel/Alamy; **p.25** *C* © John Robertson/Alamy, *TR* © Science Museum/Science & Society Picture Library – All rights reserved, *BR* © PASIEKA/SCIENCE PHOTO LIBRARY **p.26** © GreenGate Publishing Services; **p.29** *T and M* © GreenGate Publishing Services, *B* Bloomberg/Getty images; **p.37** *TL* © Richard Gardner/Rex Features, *TR* © Ange/Alamy, *B* © Getty Images; **p.38** © Rob Bartee/Alamy; **p.39** © Emmanuel Lattes/Alamy; **p.40** © LINAK A/S; **p.52** *T and M* © www.canonical.com, *B* © Rob Bartee/Alamy; **p.54** *T* © Xfce Development Team, *B* KDE e.V.; **p.55** *T* The GNOME Project; **p.59** © picturesbyrob/Alamy; **p.60** © www.canonical.com; **p.61** © www.canonical.com; **p.62** © www.canonical.com; **p.81** *T* © Vasiliy Vasilyev, HHD Software Ltd, *ML* © Author's image, *MR* © Vasiliy Vasilyev, HHD Software Ltd; **p.82** © Author's image; **p.84** © Vasiliy Vasilyev, HHD Software Ltd; **p.102–8** © Libre Office; **p.114** © ACE STOCK LIMITED/Alamy; **p.127** *T* © Tony Hobbs/Alamy, *B* © Editorial Image, LLC/Alamy; **p.128** © inga spence/Alamy; **p.129** © Virgin Media; **p.141** © Hodder Education; **p.145** © Author's images; **p.149** *T* © Greek photonews/Alamy; **p.149** *B* EMILIO SEGRE VISUAL ARCHIVES/AMERICAN INSTITUTE OF PHYSICS/SCIENCE PHOTO LIBRARY; **p.158** Stephen Chen; **p.200** www.python.org; **p.224** www.bbcbasic.co.uk; **p.226** www.bbcbasic.co.uk; **p.236–44** www.bbcbasic.co.uk.

© Microsoft product screenshots reprinted with permission from Microsoft Corporation.

Acknowledgements
p.109 Shopping article © The Daily Telegraph.

Every effort has been made to trace all copyright holders, but if any have been inadvertently overlooked the Publishers will be pleased to make the necessary arrangements at the first opportunity.

Although every effort has been made to ensure that website addresses are correct at time of going to press, Hodder Education cannot be held responsible for the content of any website mentioned in this book. It is sometimes possible to find a relocated web page by typing in the address of the home page for a website in the URL window of your browser.

Hachette UK's policy is to use papers that are natural, renewable and recyclable products and made from wood grown in sustainable forests. The logging and manufacturing processes are expected to conform to the environmental regulations of the country of origin.

Orders: please contact Bookpoint Ltd, 130 Milton Park, Abingdon, Oxon OX14 4SB.
Telephone: (44) 01235 827720. Fax: (44) 01235 400454. Lines are open 9.00 – 5.00, Monday to Saturday, with a 24-hour message answering service. Visit our website at www.hoddereducation.co.uk

Cover photo © ktsdesign/Fotolia
Illustrations by GreenGate Publishing Services
Typeset in Cantoria MT Std 11 pt by GreenGate Publishing Services, Tonbridge, Kent

Printed in Italy

A catalogue record for this title is available from the British Library

ISBN: 978 1 444 17779 4

Contents

Introduction

What is computing?

Computing has become vitally important in all our lives. Computer systems affect most of the things that we do, for example doing business, controlling machinery, navigating planes, supporting administration and communicating with each other. This has happened remarkably quickly in terms of human evolution. The first programmable computer appeared in 1943, less time ago than the average lifetime of an adult in the UK. We are still inventing new ways of using computers and coming to terms with what they mean to us. We refer to 'information technology' when talking about *how* computer systems are deployed and used. But behind all this innovation, there are basic principles that form the discipline of 'computing'. Computing refers to what we have to do in order to obtain a solution to a problem by mathematical or numerical means. It underpins 'computer science' which refers to the use of computing to inform the design of equipment and processes to manipulate data.

Algorithms

Algorithms are the steps needed to carry out a task. Computing is primarily concerned with solving problems using algorithms. It is also concerned with the equipment needed to do this.

During the Second World War, a remarkable team was put together at Bletchley Park in Buckinghamshire in order to find ways to crack the encrypted messages of the German armed forces. The Cambridge mathematician, Alan Turing was a notable part of this team. He had already demonstrated that any mathematical problem could be solved by a machine if it were presented as an algorithm. Such a machine did not then exist but Turing was able to describe some of the characteristics that it would have. His thinking led to the successful decryption of enemy messages, saving countless lives and shortening the war. Turing's work also led directly to the construction of the first programmable electronic computer, Colossus. Colossus was developed by a Post Office engineer called Tommy Flowers and his team who worked for the Post Office Research Station in Dollis Hill, London. In those days, the Post Office was responsible for the British telephone system and so their engineers had much experience of working with switching circuits, using electronic valves.

Alan Turing

Tommy Flowers

Computers and information

Computers have been developed in order to make our lives easier in many ways. New ways of using computers are being developed all the time. However, computers have also changed the way we think about and understand the world and the wider universe.

We are surrounded by information in many forms, such as newspapers, signs, television, music, letters and telephone calls. Humans have always needed information but until recently no one thought very much about what information actually is. Until 1948, nobody really knew what it was that was transmitted along wires during a telephone conversation. But in that year, Claude Shannon, working in the USA, published a paper that laid the foundations of our information age. He showed the central importance of information to *everything*. He realised that information can be quantified and measured, and came up with the concept of the 'bit' as the fundamental unit of information.

Claude Shannon

We now realise that information of any kind can be reduced to bits. This has allowed the development of computers as information-processing machines, which can handle any information we like. We now understand that much of the world and life itself can be explained in terms of information. We are ourselves the products of information contained in our DNA which can be easily modelled as digital information.

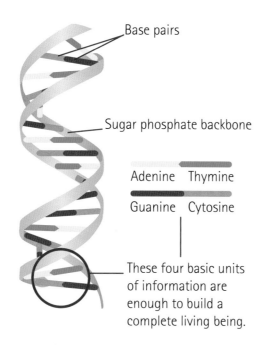

Base pairs

Sugar phosphate backbone

Adenine Thymine

Guanine Cytosine

These four basic units
of information are
enough to build a
complete living being.

The structure of DNA

So, with the powerful ideas of algorithms and the nature of information, computer science has transformed our lives and is one of the most exciting areas of study today.

OCR GCSE Computing

OCR GCSE Computing takes you a long way into understanding how to solve problems by using computers. At its heart is the understanding of algorithms and how to write computer programs based on well-planned algorithms.

The OCR GCSE Computing course is divided into three units:

Unit A451: Computer systems and programming

This unit covers the knowledge that underpins the specification. It includes the basic principles behind computer science as well as some important practical aspects. The material in this section is assessed in a single 90 minute examination worth 40% of the marks. The examination uses a mixture of long and short answer questions about basic knowledge, understanding and application of the ideas and concepts. Questions will also cover the ability to understand and create logic circuits, algorithms and simple pseudocode to solve problems.

Fundamentals of computer systems

Although there are many ways in which computers are applied, there are similarities between all of them. This part of the specification looks at some basic concepts to do with the use of a range of computer systems.

Computing hardware

The main components of any computer system are looked at in this section, together with how the basic model of a computer was developed over the years.

Software

Computers are special because they can be programmed to carry out a wide range of jobs. This section looks at some of the types of software that have been developed and how new software is commissioned and implemented.

Representation of data in computer systems

All data is stored as bits. This section explores the wide variety of ways in which data can be represented and manipulated in such a simple format.

Databases

Most practical applications of computers require databases. Databases have a huge impact on our lives – in terms of making things convenient, discovering new relationships and also changing our expectations of privacy. This section looks at the common ways in which databases are set up and used, in the context of real-life examples.

Computer communications and networking

Most computers are connected. The ways in which this is done and its implications are examined in this section.

Programming

This is at the heart of the OCR GCSE Computing specification. The principles of how to solve a problem by breaking it down into an algorithm and then turning that into program code are looked at here.

Controlled assessment

There are two parts to the controlled assessment that you need to complete as part of the course: Units A452 and A453. They are both designed to provide opportunities to solve specific problems in practical ways. They are there to back up the material studied in Unit A451 (see pages 3–4), but they also allow you to look at new areas. Computing is a fast moving part of life so these sections allow this computing course to be refreshed at regular intervals.

The OCR GCSE Computing controlled assessments are also assessed in a new way. They are not designed to be extensive pieces of reporting. They can be presented in any way that candidates find convenient. A PowerPoint presentation is as acceptable as a word processed document. Movie clips can be used where appropriate. This book shows some possible ways in which your work might be successfully presented in order to maximise your marks.

Also, the assessment is not a box ticking exercise. The assignments are designed to promote innovative approaches, so the quality of the work is judged as a whole rather than as a series of picky obstacles to overcome.

Unit A452: Practical investigation

This is a practical unit based on one of several scenarios that are made available by OCR. It is designed to go beyond the printed specification. It requires you to do some background research, perhaps learning a new skill at the same time. It requires the solution of specified problems together with an examination of how the scenario affects real-life or computing developments.

This book examines some example approaches to this unit, but it is emphasised that they are just that – examples. It is not intended that they serve as rigid models for solving the tasks set by OCR.

Unit A453: Programming project

The OCR GCSE Computing specification revolves around solving problems by writing program code. This unit requires code to be written to solve a set of three tasks. There will always be a choice of sets. The specification makes no stipulations about what programming language or development environment are used.

The examples given in the book are either independent of language – in other words you don't need specialist knowledge of a particular programming language – or they will make use of a variety of programming languages in order to show a range of possible approaches.

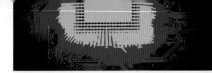

Computing in context

Throughout the book, reference is made to real-life contexts wherever possible – look out for the Computing in context feature. This is to emphasise how computing does not exist in a vacuum, but has applications to most aspects of our lives. The Computing in context feature highlights some of these real-life examples.

This is **important** because the examination and particularly Unit A452 require a demonstration that the student has a wide knowledge of the background to and the impact of computing. This specification is more than a list of topics. It is a framework around which a well-rounded understanding of computing can be built. It is the aim of this book and the specification to push the boundaries and to encourage you to explore and enjoy this most important and fascinating aspect of modern life.

Unit 1 Computer systems and programming

Chapter 1

Fundamentals of computer systems

Computer systems

Computer systems are everywhere these days. They come in all shapes and sizes, from large mainframes to small control systems that make electronic gadgets work. They are everywhere because they are:

- versatile
- cheap
- small.

What is a system?

A system is a collection of parts that work together for a common purpose. For a system to be useful, it must produce something – an output. It needs to receive and process inputs in order to produce outputs. There may be many inputs and outputs. Systems often interact with other systems. Systems may be made from many sub-systems. Interconnections between systems are called interfaces.

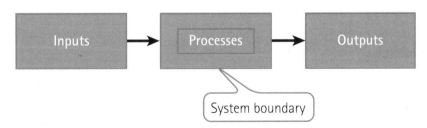

Figure 1.1 Outline of a system

A system boundary separates what is in a system from what is not. This can be difficult to define when systems form part of other systems.

Examples of systems

It is easy to think of many examples of systems, some natural, some man-made. Natural systems such as the solar system may seem not to have a purpose but all systems act together in some way and are more than just the sum of the individual parts that form them.

Specification content

(a) Define a computer system
(b) Describe the importance of computer systems in the modern world
(c) Explain the need for reliability in computer systems
(d) Explain the need for adherence to suitable professional standards in the development, use and maintenance of computer systems
(e) Explain the importance of ethical, environmental and legal considerations when creating computer systems

Underground railway system

Respiratory system

Holiday booking system

Figure 1.2 Examples of natural and man-made systems

Computer systems

Computer systems are based on processing data and producing information. They are electronic which makes them fast and the important thing about them is that they are programmable. This means that a computer system can be made to do many things depending on the instructions we give it.

Computer systems are found in most electronic gadgets. They control devices such as washing machines, cameras, burglar alarms and telephones. In each case, they have a system that has all of the basic functionality that drives a desktop PC. There are input and output devices, storage, a processor and, most importantly, software. There are more examples of these devices in Chapter 2.

Some computer systems are '**dedicated**' which means they have a fixed purpose. For example, an engine management system in a car is used to show faults and control its operation. It is not designed to do anything else.

Other computer systems are 'general purpose'. They can be used for different reasons according to what work needs to be done. PCs are 'general purpose' and can run word processors, browse the internet, and play music and movies.

Key term

Dedicated: Something which is designed for one particular purpose

Often, software is dedicated too. In other words, it is written for the particular device and situation that it controls.

For example, a computer chip controls a washing machine. It contains software that times each stage of the washing cycle, sets the water temperature and in some cases can react to sensors which detect how dirty the washing is. This software is sophisticated, but it is not useful for controlling other devices, such as operating a camera. Also, unlike with a general purpose computer, the user will not normally change the software.

Similar dedicated systems are found in many situations. For example, they:

- control the focus and shutter speed in a camera
- maintain a constant speed in a car cruise control system
- log a mobile phone onto a network
- guide a robotic vacuum cleaner around obstacles.

These dedicated computer systems that are found in most electronic devices are called **embedded systems**.

There may be a general purpose operating system such as Linux supporting dedicated software applications. This reduces the effort needed to write software for the device, because much of the functionality is 'borrowed' from the operating system. Examples of systems that make use of the Linux **kernel** are some GPS navigation systems, media players and smart phones. The Android phone operating system is based on the Linux kernel.

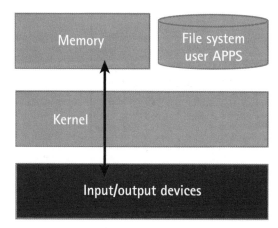

Figure 1.3 This block diagram shows how the Linux kernel can be used by embedded applications to control the hardware of a device

Key terms

Embedded system: A computer system that forms part of an electronic device

Kernel: The lowest level of an operating system that controls the hardware

Figure 1.4 GPS navigation system

Why are computer systems important?

Computer systems are involved in most human activities. The list of how computer systems affect us is endless but a few examples will show something of the extent.

Safety	guiding aircraft, controlling trains, supporting signalling systems, monitoring patient body signs
Travel	smart phone apps, GPS systems, train timetables, flight bookings
Business	orders, stock control, payroll
Retail	online ordering of more or less anything, logistics systems that control delivery of goods
Entertainment	DVDs, Blu Ray, MP3 players
Communication	email, chat, social networks, business transactions, mobile phones
Education	Virtual Learning Environments, exam marking, unlimited sources of information on the web
Politics and government	campaigns, voting (in some countries), payment of taxes
Science	number crunching, simulations, visualisations

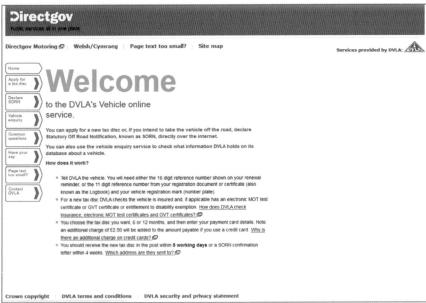

Figure 1.5 You can apply online for a new tax disc for your vehicle

Reliability

As we become more dependent on computer systems, we need to be able to trust their reliability. In fact, the computer systems that we interact with most of the time are so reliable that we do not give them much thought.

However, computer systems can sometimes let us down. Unreliable computer systems can cause very serious problems. They can be lethal, as in the case of some aircraft accidents, although modern avionic systems have made flying safer by taking some of the workload from pilots. However, it is vital that the human operators understand what the computer systems are designed to do. Pilots need to know what the computer systems are telling them. Figure 1.6 shows what happened to a new Airbus when the pilots turned off the annoying warning alarm after it was telling them that the aircraft was not properly configured for takeoff. Luckily this was a test flight and there were no passengers on board. The pilots were embarrassed but not injured.

Figure 1.6 Pilot or computer error?

Unreliable systems can result in the loss or theft of data. In 1995, the account details of 20 million credit card holders were stolen because of inadequate security systems. This type of problem is often related to poor procedures or non-compliance with procedures rather than computer system faults.

Computer systems often just don't do what was required of them. The planned NHS IT system never delivered what was hoped for after wasting £12 billion on development. This was one of the worst IT failures ever and there were many reasons behind this:

- There were far too many interested groups involved, all of which had different expectations.
- The timescale that was imposed on the developers was too tight.
- Existing systems needed to be incorporated, but this was far too complicated.
- Few users or those commissioning the system understood what it was for.
- There was little in-house expertise guiding the project – the big companies that were commissioned followed their own routes.
- Medical staff didn't want to use it.
- There were serious privacy concerns raised by some in the medical community, including some patient groups.

There have been many IT failures in the public sector and this is often caused by a lack of understanding of what a system should do.

Testing

Reliability is not easy to achieve. Any non-trivial computer system will have thousands if not millions of lines of code. There are usually limitless numbers of pathways through it. Testing systems is a vital part of development and much time and effort is devoted to this.

But, testing everything is impossible and very expensive. This means that there are bound to be errors that slip through the net and so systems need to be monitored throughout their lives. Changing systems once they have been installed is called maintenance and this often requires more effort than the production of the system in the first place.

It is important to understand what testing is and what it is for. It is also important to realise what testing is *not*. Testing is not an attempt to show that a system works. It might work in some cases but fail when unexpected data is input. Testing is carried out purposely to reveal errors. Testers try to break a system to show where its weaknesses are.

Once a system is released, it continues to be tested by the users. Sometimes certain users are given an early version of a system so that it can be tested under real-life conditions. This is called beta testing, to distinguish it from the alpha testing carried out by the developers.

A system is tested against its specification. Many unreliable systems cause problems because they were not specified correctly in the first place. Design flaws are harder to fix than faults in the coding.

Standards

One way to help make systems more reliable is to adhere to certain standards. If a new system is developed according to defined standards, it is more likely to be successful and satisfy its users. Standards also help to make sure that different computer systems can talk to each other.

Proprietary standards

These are standards that are owned by a company. For example, any software that runs under Windows must handle data in a certain way, communicate with the operating system in defined ways and work with a defined interface. Flash animations must conform to standards set up by the Adobe company. The advantages of this insistence on standards are that the system will:

- look and feel familiar to users and this will speed up learning new systems
- work in a predictable way, which in turn will improve reliability
- be maintained by one company and although there will be different versions of the software, versions that contain minor updates are usually provided free of charge.

Industry standards

Some standards are agreed across the computing industry. Many of these relate to hardware and allow easy interconnection between devices. One example is the Universal Serial Bus (USB), which has become the standard way to connect devices to most computer systems. The range of devices that use USB connectors is enormous.

De facto standards

Some standards just develop through common usage until they become the accepted way of making or doing things. Outside the computer industry, the layout of car controls has evolved to a more or less predictable form. Most cars have the indicator stalk on the left of the steering column.

HTML started life as a *de facto* standard and as it gained in popularity, it eventually became *de jure* which means that you *must* adopt it if you want to communicate with anyone else.

PDF started as a proprietary standard created by the company Adobe but the copyright was handed over to the **International Organisation for Standardisation (ISO)** in order to make the movement of digital files more open, so when free PDF readers became common, it was natural for them all to use the same file format. The Microsoft Word doc standard has become the *de facto* standard for supplying word processed documents and all word processor programs need to be able to write and read doc files.

Open standards

Open standards refer to standards that are publicly available, to an extent that software developed under them can be modified by users. They are becoming increasingly popular. In the case of software developed under open standards, the source code is in the public domain, so anyone with the time and expertise can make changes.

A further feature of software produced under open standards is that it is often updated by a community of developers who make regular updates available to anyone, usually for no or minimal cost. This software is often of very high quality because the community of developers act quickly to fix problems. However, there is no one to blame when things go wrong.

Some of the more important open standards include the world wide web, HTML, **TCP/IP**, and the C# programming language.

Key terms

HTML: Hypertext mark up language – a text based system for defining web pages

PDF: Portable document format – a file standard that displays a document accurately on any computer platform

International Organisation for Standardisation (ISO): The world's largest standards developing organisation. It produces international standards for engineering, agriculture and medicine, as well as for information technology

TCP/IP: Transmission control protocol/internet protocol – a set of standards that control how data is sent across networks including the internet

Examples of open source software are Mozilla Firefox, Libre Office, the Android operating system, Linux, the Apache web server, the Moodle VLE and the Python programming language.

Ethical considerations

Ethics refer to what is right and wrong. People may argue about individual cases, but on the whole most people agree about most things that constitute ethical behaviour. Ethics are not the same as legalities although a good legal system will be based on an ethical outlook on life.

Ethics are to some extent a personal thing, but there are codes of ethics laid down by various organisations including associations of computing professionals. The BCS (British Computer Society) has some fairly typical ethical standards that it thinks computing professionals should adhere to.

They include not undertaking work that is beyond your capability, not bringing your profession into disrepute, avoiding injuring others and not taking bribes.

Generally, most people think that they have a right to a degree of privacy concerning much of their own lives. The internet has changed this right even if many disagree with it. The use of social networking and other sites has made it harder to keep one's details private. However, it is still generally agreed by most people that privacy should not be deliberately compromised by the widespread publishing of personal details. Journalists have invaded many people's privacy in the search for stories but some would argue that this may sometimes be in the public interest, for example when exposing criminal or dishonest behaviour. It is probably impossible to impose as much privacy as one would like and it is unlikely that people will ever agree completely on what is acceptable.

Environmental considerations

Sensitivity to the environment is much debated these days. It has relevance to the computer industry in various ways.

Energy

Computer systems use energy. Data centres are particularly hungry for power. It is estimated that by 2014, computers will use more energy than the aviation industry. A lot of energy is wasted in the inefficient generation of heat which has to be removed from the equipment. Air conditioning in data centres uses yet more energy. This is of concern to us all because supplies of energy are finite and getting more expensive.

As we become more dependent on computer systems, it becomes ever more important that we do what we can to keep such systems going as economically and reliably as possible into the future.

Disposal

Old computer equipment is referred to as e-waste. Computers contain many toxic and carcinogenic components, such as dioxins, polychlorinated biphenyls (PCBs), cadmium, chromium, radioactive isotopes and mercury. In the USA, old computers are classified as hazardous waste. Much electronic waste is sent to landfill sites, where toxic materials can escape into the wider environment. Much waste is exported to countries with low standards of environmental protection. Sometimes children pick over the waste in order to extract metals that can be recycled and sold. This saves resources on a global scale but exposes the children to dangers.

Figure 1.7 Discarded computer and monitor

The safe disposal and recycling of e-waste is a problem that is not going away. Arguments rage about what to do with the hazardous waste and opinion remains divided. This can only become a bigger problem in the future.

Legal considerations

Legal issues are defined by laws. More and more laws are being passed concerning computer use. The Data Protection Act (1998) is a fairly typical law that was enacted in order to protect people's privacy. It contains a number of sensible safeguards such as demanding that those who keep personal data on computer systems should take care of it and protect it from unauthorised people. Similarly, people should be able to inspect any personal data held about them to satisfy themselves that it is accurate.

The Computer Misuse Act (1990) makes it illegal to gain unauthorised access to computer systems or to modify the data stored in them.

Both these Acts are on the UK statute book but most developed countries have similar requirements. Not all countries have the same views about what is acceptable. The USA takes a particularly unforgiving point of view about accessing data stores. The British hacker, Gary McKinnon allegedly broke into Pentagon and NASA systems and faces extradition procedures to stand trial in the USA. The international nature of the internet inevitably leads to legal confusions. Many companies will not use online storage solutions that reside on American servers because the US government is able to compel providers to decrypt and hand over data at its request.

Computing in context

Security and the cloud

Software as a service (SaaS) is an increasingly popular way for companies to implement their computing solutions, with software and data being stored remotely from a company's premises – in the so-called 'cloud'. This removes the need to employ IT staff and reduces infrastructure requirements.

In 2001, after the 9/11 terrorist attack, the US Congress passed a law called the Patriot Act as an anti-terrorism measure. It gives law enforcement officers extensive powers to search telephone, email and other records without the need for a court order or even the knowledge of the owners of such data. Providers of cloud-computing services can be required to hand over private data to the FBI, as well as IP addresses, details of web visits, and dates and times of all emails and text messages sent or received by an individual.

Microsoft admitted that data stored anywhere in the world might be accessed by US authorities under the provisions of the Patriot Act. This has led to many companies avoiding the use of US owned or based cloud-computing providers. Some European providers have advertised their services as being safe from the requirements of the Patriot Act.

But the Patriot Act is not unique in requiring providers to hand over private data. The governments of other countries can also require cloud-computing service operators to hand over data. These include the UK, Germany, France, Japan and Canada. In response to this there are now widely advertised services that will allow users to encrypt their data while in transit and when stored in the cloud.

Summary

Computer systems have developed extremely quickly in terms of human history. They have proven to be so useful that life without them would be unacceptable to most of us. Like any advance, they have generated their own special problems and we are gradually coming to terms with understanding and dealing with them.

Extension tasks

1 How would your day have been different today, if there were no computer systems?

2 Identify the inputs, processes and outputs for:
- a banking system
- a telephone system.

3 Quickly make a list of devices that are controlled by a computer system.

4 Look up 'IT disasters' online and read a few of the worst examples.

5 Make a list of devices that connect to a PC via a USB port.

6 Make a list of file format standards that are commonly in use and identify what each one is used for.

7 To what extent is it feasible for a professional writer or a school to make use of nothing but open source software?

8 To what extent would strict adherence to professional standards prevent IT disasters such as the failed NHS IT system?

9 Look up the work of the ISO. Why was the organisation set up?

Exam style questions

1 Define a system. [3 marks]

2 Explain the difference between proprietary standards and open standards. [2 marks]

3 Explain how de facto standards have helped the development of easy to use computer systems. [3 marks]

4 Define the term 'embedded system'. [2 marks]

5 Explain what the kernel of an operating system is. [3 marks]

6 State two reasons why new IT systems can fail to deliver what was intended. [2 marks]

## Chapter 2

Computing hardware

In this chapter you will learn about the hardware components that make up a computer system. This includes the central processing unit (CPU), memory, input, output and storage devices. The underlying logic that makes computers function is also covered.

Hardware is the term that describes the physical components of a computer system, anything that can be seen or touched. This includes the input, output, storage and processing devices. The range of devices available is quite staggering but this was not always the case. Colossus, the first electronic digital programmable computer, built in 1943, was never able to store programs and the operators had to enter the program each time using switches and patch cables.

But work on computers like Colossus led to the development of modern computer systems. The first computer able to store a program was Manchester University's Small Scale Experimental Machine, nicknamed 'Baby'. In 1948 Baby ran its first program, to find the highest proper divisor (that is, not 1 or itself) of 262,144. It took 52 minutes to find the correct answer – 131,072. This computer was originally able to store 1024 bits (that is just 128 bytes) and had just 7 instructions available to the programmer.

Figure 2.1 'Baby', the first computer able to store a program

In 1945, John von Neumann, who had been working on the EDVAC (Electronic Discrete Variable Automatic Computer) for the American military, published a document that would provide the way forward for the development of the modern digital computer. The concept, based on work by Eckert and Mauchley at Pennsylvania University, described a **computer architecture** in which the data and the program are both stored in the computer's memory in the same place. This is the fundamental design concept behind all modern computer systems. All instructions and data will be stored in the same place as **binary** numbers. Binary is a system of numbers using only 0 and 1 to represent all numbers (also called the base-2 system because it is based on two digits).

The central processing unit (CPU)

The processing of a computer program is carried out by the central processing unit (**CPU**). The CPU is the core of every computer system and has two main components: the **control unit** and the arithmetic and logic unit (**ALU**). The names are a bit of a giveaway:

- The control unit uses electrical signals to direct the system to execute the instructions in stored programs.
- The ALU carries out all of the arithmetic and logical operations including addition, subtraction and comparisons (for example, equal to, less than, greater than).

In order to do this the CPU needs access to two things: the main memory (we usually call this **random access memory** or **RAM**) where the programs are stored and **cache memory** which is used to store data waiting to be processed. Main memory (or RAM) and cache memory are called primary storage and are part of the computer's processing capabilities. Hard drives and other devices such as **flash memory** drives, **solid-state** drives, etc. are called **secondary storage** and these hold data to be kept when the computer is turned off.

Cache memory is fast memory that is located very close to the main CPU with dedicated connections so that the CPU has fast access to frequently used data. Cache memory is relatively expensive compared with the standard RAM used for the main memory of a computer.

One of the important features of John von Neumann's concept was that data and instructions would be stored in memory and would be indistinguishable from each other, so data and instructions look the same and are in the same place. This means that the CPU has to decide what it is looking at when it gets the binary number from memory. It could be an instruction, it could be data. In fact it can't tell and relies on the logic in the program. If it expects an instruction that is what it will assume it has and it will try to work out what it is and what to do next. If it is an instruction it will have two parts to it, an

Key terms

Computer architecture: The internal, logical structure and organisation of the computer hardware

Binary: A system of numbers using only two digits 0 and 1 (also called the base-2 system), unlike the decimal (or denary) system in everyday use that uses ten (base-10)

CPU: Central processing unit of the computer containing the control unit, ALU and cache memory

Control unit: The control unit works with the CPU to control the flow of data within the system

ALU: The ALU performs all the arithmetic and logical operations within the CPU

Random access memory (RAM): Main memory of a computer that stores data, applications and the operating system whilst in use. When the power is turned off RAM loses its data

Cache memory: Special high speed memory used by a computer

Flash memory: Solid-state memory used as low cost secondary storage in portable devices and as removable memory

Solid state: Technology based on electronics with no moving parts, for example transistors and capacitors as used in memory chips

Secondary storage: Non-volatile storage used to store programs and files that need to be kept even when the power is not on

Specification content

(a) State the purpose of the CPU

(b) Describe the function of the CPU as fetching and executing instructions stored in memory

(c) Explain how common characteristics of CPUs such as clock speed, cache size and number of cores affect their performance

instruction and possibly some data, a number or a memory location. The CPU has to decode this to work out what to do next.

In fact, when the computer is switched on the CPU starts to perform its main function, running an endless **fetch–execute cycle**. The programs that the CPU needs to process are stored in the main memory. The CPU simply fetches the next instruction it needs to process, decodes it and executes it before repeating the process.

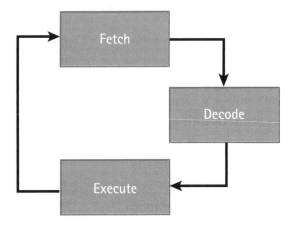

Figure 2.2 The fetch–execute cycle

Initially, after the computer is switched on, the CPU will look at a specific place in the **read only memory** (**ROM**) for the first program to load and execute. This is the boot sequence; it is always stored in ROM in a specific place so that the CPU knows where to find it. The CPU then begins the process of executing the program commands to get the computer up and running and the operating system started. After this initial boot process is completed control is handed to the operating system to provide the programs for the CPU to run.

The speed of this cycle is determined by an electronic **clock chip**. This chip uses a vibrating crystal that maintains a constant rate. The clock speed is measured in hertz (Hz) or cycles per second. The computer synchronises all processes to this clock signal. A clock speed of 500 Hz would mean 500 cycles per second. Processor speeds are generally much higher than this and a typical processor speed of 3 GHz means that the processor can complete 3 billion cycles every second. To put this into some context imagine you get a friend to ask you some simple arithmetic questions, for example they say add 4 and 5. It might take just 2 seconds for them to ask the question and for you to reply. I have just written a simple program to get my laptop to do as many simple additions as it can in 1 second and it managed 304,877. In theory, if it was doing nothing else, a single CPU running at 3 GHz could complete around 300 million simple

Key terms

Fetch–execute cycle: This is the process of fetching the instructions from memory, decoding them and then executing them so that the CPU performs continuously

Read only memory (ROM): A store for data in a computer that cannot be overwritten. Data in ROM is always available and is not lost when the computer is turned off

Clock chip: The electronic device in a computer that controls the timing of signals

calculations every second. Why are these two numbers so different? Why did my laptop only manage to complete 304,877 when in theory it could have managed to complete many more calculations?

Unfortunately main memory cannot work at the same speed and the delays in locating and transferring the data from main memory to the CPU are quite significant. While the CPU can process data very quickly, getting data from memory can be quite slow in comparison. If the CPU has to wait for main memory to supply the data it will be waiting around for much of the time and will be running well below its capacity. To overcome this, when the first instruction of a program is requested by the CPU, the remaining instructions are automatically copied into the cache memory.

Cache memory has access times similar to the CPU which means it is a lot faster than main memory. To improve performance the CPU's control unit will automatically look first in the cache for the next instruction to see if it has already been copied. If it is not there it will go to main memory to locate and fetch the data.

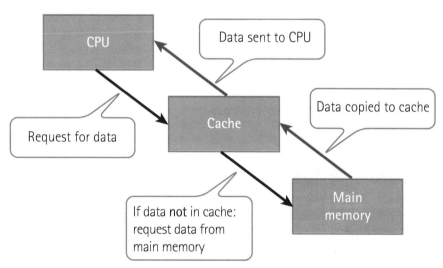

Figure 2.3 The role of cache memory in data transfer

By checking first if the required data is in the cache it reduces the time taken to access the data making the process much more efficient. The more cache memory there is, the more likely the required data has already been requested and copied to the cache memory and does not have to be fetched from main memory.

Cache memory is very fast, but also relatively expensive. Where main memory will normally be provided in gigabytes (GB), cache will be provided in megabytes (MB). 1 GB is 1024 MB so there is a big difference in size between the amounts of cache and main memory provided with a typical computer. A mid-range laptop may have 8 GB of RAM but only 2 or 3 MB of Level 3 cache.

Further information

There are three levels of cache memory in modern computer systems: Level 1, Level 2 and Level 3 (L1, L2 and L3). The numbers refer to how close each of these is to the CPU. L1 cache is often located on the CPU itself, it has a very low capacity and typically runs at the same speed as the CPU. L2 is often part of the CPU module, runs at CPU speeds (or close to them) and is usually a bit larger and slower than L1 cache. As might be expected, L3 cache is further away, on the motherboard, and it is larger and slower than both L1 and L2 cache.

The clock speed and cache memory on a computer can affect the speed or performance of the system quite significantly so a higher speed processor and more cache usually means better performance. However, this is limited by the speed data and control signals can move around the system. Data and control signals move around the system on **buses**. A bus is simply a circuit that connects one part of the **motherboard** to another. The speed of the bus, usually measured in megahertz (MHz) (millions of cycles per second), refers to how much data can move across the bus at the same time.

Key terms

Bus: A part of the computer architecture that transfers data and signals between the components of the computer

Motherboard: The central printed circuit board (PCB) that holds the crucial components of the system

Further information

The speed quoted for most computers is the front side bus (FSB) speed, typically 800 MHz. This is the bus that connects the CPU to the main memory. The back side bus (BSB) is much faster and connects the Level 2 cache to the CPU. The speed of this bus is determined by the CPU.

The core chipset on a motherboard has two chips, the Northbridge and Southbridge that manage data transfers. The CPU is connected to RAM via the Northbridge using the FSB. Other devices, such as USB, SATA, IDE, etc., are connected to the Southbridge. The Southbridge is connected to the CPU via the Northbridge.

On some later processors the Northbridge and sometimes the Southbridge are built into the main CPU module to speed up the data transfers to them.

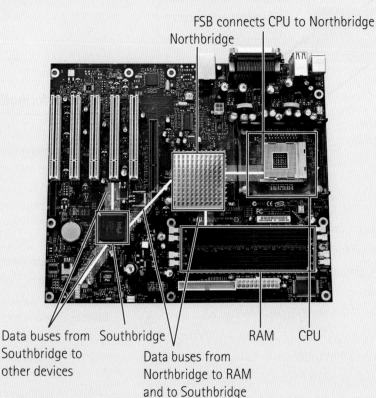

FSB connects CPU to Northbridge
Northbridge

Data buses from Southbridge to other devices
Southbridge
Data buses from Northbridge to RAM and to Southbridge
RAM
CPU

The clock speeds in use today are close to the limit for the existing technology so another way of improving performance was developed, the multi-core processor. A **dual-core** processor simply has two CPUs working together. They may both have their own cache memory or may share Level 2 or 3 cache, but since they can fetch, decode and execute instructions at the same time as one another, so the computer is able to process more instructions as a whole.

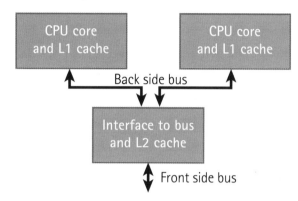

Figure 2.4 How a dual-core processor connects to the front side bus

Summary

- The purpose of the CPU is to:
  - → control the movement of data and instructions
  - → fetch data and instructions from memory
  - → decode and execute instructions
  - → perform arithmetic operations such as add and subtract, and logical operations such as AND, NOT, OR.
- The performance of the CPU depends upon the:
  - → processor speed
  - → bus speed
  - → amount of cache available
  - → number of processor cores.

Questions

A computer in a shop is advertised as having a 2.2 GHz dual-core CPU with 2 MB of L3 cache.

❶ Describe the purpose of the CPU in a computer.
❷ What is meant by 2.2 GHz?
❸ What is a dual-core processor?
❹ Describe how cache memory is used by the CPU.
❺ What are the key factors that govern the performance of the CPU in a computer?

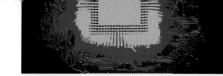

Extension tasks

1 What are the names given to CPUs with six cores? eight cores?

2 EDVAC and ENIAC were early developments in modern computing. Research
these computers and describe the main difference between them.

3 My program to count how many times a simple calculation could take place in
one second used the internal timer available in many programming languages.
I used BBC BASIC for Windows and the program was written with REMARKS to
explain how it works.

```
REM this is a system call to get the amount of time my computer has
been running in milliseconds.
SYS "GetTickCount" TO tickStart%
REM initialise x and count to 0
x = 0
Count = 0
REPEAT
  REM a simple addition
  x = 4 + 5
  REM count each time the addition is done
  Count = Count + 1
  REM check the system clock again
  SYS "GetTickCount" TO tickEnd%
REM has the value increased by more than 1000?
UNTIL tickEnd%-tickStart%>1000
REM if it has print how many times the calculation has been completed
PRINT Count
```

Find out how to do the same thing on your computer using a language you have
used and see what your results are. You will get better results by making the
program as small as possible.

4 I also wrote a small program to compare how my computer faired against 'Baby'
when calculating the proper divisors of 262,144.

```
FOR x = 1 TO 131072
  IF 262144 MOD x = 0 THEN
    PRINT x
  ENDIF
NEXT x
```

Why did I only make the loop go up to half of 262,144?

5 Write a similar program and see what it does.

6 Add a timer to this to see how long it takes.

7 Write a program to check any number for its highest proper divisor.

Memory

We have already mentioned memory in the previous section and how the CPU uses different types of memory. Let's look in more detail at the types of memory in a computer system and how the computer uses this memory.

In the 1940s, when work on the modern computer started to take shape, memory was very limited, often just a few bytes and quite unreliable. Vacuum tubes were the first devices used to store data and, originally, each one was able to store just one **bit** of data (0 or 1).

Figure 2.5 A selection of vacuum tubes from the 1940s

The first workable RAM was developed in 1948 by Freddie Williams and Tom Kilburn working at Manchester University. Later known as the Williams–Kilburn tube (or Williams tube) this device was able to store data as charged spots on the surface of a cathode ray tube and could store 512–1024 **bits** of data (that is 64–128 **bytes**).

The search for cheaper, larger and more efficient ways to store data led to the development of magnetic core memory in the 1950s. This type of memory was in use for 20 years until the mid-1970s. It used circular iron cores with wires passing in both directions through the centre of the magnet to set the direction of the magnetic field; the directions represented 0 and 1. It was possible for several of these devices to be used together but a single unit would typically be able to store 2 **kilobytes** of data.

The transistor, developed initially in 1947 by William Shockley, led to the development of the integrated circuit (silicon chip). In 1968 Robert Dennard working for IBM developed the first RAM solid-state memory

Specification content

- -

(a) Describe the difference between RAM and ROM

(b) Explain the need for ROM in a computer system

(c) Describe the purpose of RAM in a computer system

(d) Explain how the amount of RAM in a personal computer affects the performance of the computer

(e) Explain the need for virtual memory

(f) Describe cache memory

(g) Describe flash memory

(h) Discuss how changes in memory technologies are leading to innovative computer designs

- -

Key terms

- -

Bit: Binary digit 0 or 1
Byte: 8 bits
Kilobyte: 1024 bytes

- -

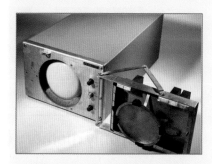

Figure 2.6 Williams tube

Figure 2.7 Magnetic core memory

chips. These devices store data as a small charge in tiny transistors etched into a circuit in the device. The charge has to be refreshed every few milliseconds or the charge leaks away. This type of solid-state memory is called **volatile** and must have power to maintain the contents.

Key term

Volatile: Data lost when there is no power

Random access memory (RAM)

RAM is the main memory in the computer. It is not unusual for a laptop to now have over 8 GB of RAM available. RAM is required for the operating system, applications that are loaded and any data currently in use. Clearly the more RAM available to the computer, the more programs and data it can load at the same time meaning better performance. When a program is loaded, it is copied from the hard disk or other device (secondary storage) into the main memory (RAM). The CPU can now access the data and instructions for the program as required. It copies the data from the secondary storage device because access to the data on these is extremely slow. Secondary storage is needed to keep copies of files and programs because RAM is volatile and the data it stores is lost when the power to the computer is switched off.

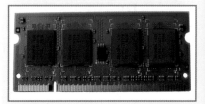

Figure 2.9 RAM chips

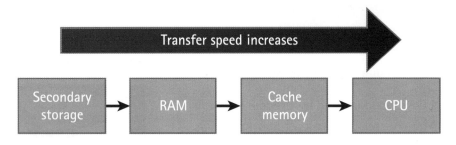

Figure 2.8 Data transfer speeds for storage, memory and CPU

Read only memory (ROM)

When you turn off a computer it loses all the data stored in RAM but it needs data in RAM in order to do anything and so there has to be some other way to get the computer to start. RAM chips use transistors to hold a charge that represents the data but require power to maintain this charge. By connecting transistors together in a specific way they can 'remember' what they are storing. This type of memory is called read only memory (ROM) and it is able to retain the information programmed in by the manufacturer – making it **non-volatile**. ROM is often used within a computer system to store the boot sequence. The boot sequence is a set of instructions that the computer needs to get started and load the operating system. ROM cannot be overwritten by the computer.

Virtual memory

Sometimes we need to run more complex programs or run several programs at the same time. The computer will start to slow down if RAM is being fully used. When there is not enough RAM to deal with all the demands on the computer it will use a section of the hard disk as a temporary store for some of the data in main memory. Data in RAM that is not currently being used will be stored on a specific area of the hard disk, while data that is needed will be loaded into RAM. Switching between programs is now significantly slower because the computer has to move data between main memory and the hard disk before it can open the second program or continue with another section of the program or data. The area of the hard disk used for temporary storage of data from main memory is called **virtual memory**.

We have already said that data transfer between hard disk and main memory is relatively slow. If the computer has to make a lot of transfers this will slow down the computer quite significantly. Also, if the computer has a relatively small main memory it means that it is not possible to run more than a limited number of programs at the same time or run programs that require lots of data, for example high definition graphics or moving images. This is because the CPU is spending a lot of time moving data about rather than processing it.

The process for using virtual memory basically combines the area on the hard disk and the main memory into a single memory space. Data and parts of programs currently being used are moved to the main memory portion of the virtual memory and those parts that are not in use to the hard disk portion. If the owner of the computer installs more main memory (a RAM upgrade) then more of the data and parts of the programs can be directly available to the CPU. The user will be able to use more programs at the same time and the performance will be improved for programs that require more data processing.

Key terms

Non-volatile: Data retained even when power turned off

Virtual memory: A section of the hard disk used as if it were RAM to supplement the amount of main memory available to the computer. Used when there is not enough main memory to run the programs required

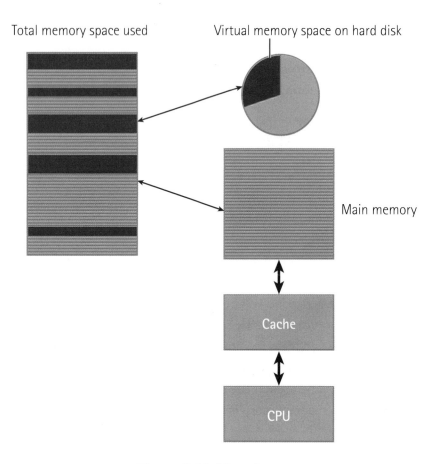

Total memory space used

Virtual memory space on hard disk

Main memory

Cache

CPU

Figure 2.10 Virtual memory

There are two main types of RAM – dynamic RAM and static RAM:

■ **Dynamic RAM** has one transistor and a capacitor that can hold a small charge for a few milliseconds to represent one bit. In order to maintain the charge in the capacitor it needs to be refreshed every few milliseconds, hence the name dynamic.

■ **Static RAM** chips are more complicated and use four or five transistors wired together for each bit but they do not lose their charge and can store the data while they have power without being refreshed. Since these chips do not need to be constantly refreshed access to the data they hold is much faster and they are used for cache memory.

It is a reasonable question to ask why we don't use static RAM for all main memory, but the answer is in the complexity of the design. Static RAM uses four or five transistors and some wiring to store each bit, this means fewer bits per chip and much more complicated manufacture. They basically cost a lot more and have a much smaller capacity.

ROM chips and flash memory

This principle of using a group of transistors wired together so that they can retain data is also used in ROM chips that are programmed during manufacture. In the early 1980s Toshiba developed a type of ROM that could be re-written by erasing the contents or part of the contents. This type of memory uses a relatively large electric current to force electrons through a barrier and trap them in a layer on the other side of the barrier until they are reset. The 'flash' of electric current used to achieve this gives us the name for this type of memory – flash memory.

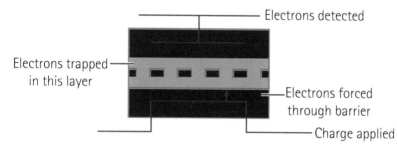

Electrons detected

Electrons trapped in this layer

Electrons forced through barrier

Charge applied

Figure 2.11 The principle of flash memory

Flash memory is used as removable memory in a wide range of devices such as cameras, removable USB memory sticks, the main secondary storage in portable devices and even as the main secondary storage on large installations. The constant writing and re-writing can cause deterioration and eventually failure so there are limitations on their uses in critical situations.

Flash memory provides low cost portable and removable storage for a range of devices such as cameras, mobile phones, portable computers and of course the USB memory stick for transferring and storing personal files. Typical capacities range up to 256 GB, though there are suggestions that larger devices may be available in the future.

Access to flash memory is not as fast as RAM even though it is a form of RAM, but it is faster than a magnetic hard disk making it an ideal choice for an additional drive to backup or supplement a portable computer.

There are a number of potential developments in computer memory that may offer significant advances including work on phase change memory (PCM) by IBM, but change in this field is often quite rapid and many research projects fail to provide a working solution. Part of the problem is the fact that current technologies have reached the limit of their development and new approaches may be required to make any significant move forward.

Figure 2.12 Examples of removable devices that use flash memory

Summary

A computer uses two types of main memory:

- **RAM** (random access memory). This is volatile memory meaning it needs a power supply to retain its content
    - → **Cache** memory is a fast form of RAM used by the computer for fast access to data.
- **ROM** (read only memory). This is non-volatile memory that retains content without the need for a power supply.

A computer also uses:

- **Virtual memory** is when a computer uses a section of the hard disk to supplement the main memory.
- **Flash memory** is solid-state memory that is used in portable devices or in removable devices to store data. It is secondary storage with slower access times than RAM, but faster access times than a magnetic hard disk.

Questions

1. Describe the difference between ROM and RAM and how these are used in a computer.
2. What is virtual memory?
3. How does installing more RAM affect the use of virtual memory and how does this affect the performance of the computer?
4. A student uses a number of different computers in school and at home. Explain how a flash memory drive will help this student to manage his/her work.
5. While a computer is working what is stored in RAM?
6. How does a computer use ROM?

Extension tasks

1 Investigate the sizes of flash memory drives available and their cost per GB of capacity.

2 Investigate new developments in memory technology and describe their benefits over existing dynamic and static RAM technologies.

3 Why do all devices using computers, for example washing machines, DVD players and televisions, have both ROM and RAM?

4 Find out how much memory a typical computer had between 1970 and now and plot this on a graph. Write some comments on the results. What is Moore's law?

Binary logic

We have already mentioned John von Neumann and the principle that all modern computers, data and instructions are based on the binary system. This follows from the ease with which we can decide between two states – off or on, true or false, 0 or 1 – using simple transistors and capacitors.

As we have said, the memory on a computer uses many small transistors and capacitors to store data and it is possible to wire these transistors together so that they can make simple logical calculations such as, for example: are both inputs 1? or is only one of the inputs 1?

These simple circuits are called **logic gates** and there are three fundamental ones we need to know about.

NOT gate

The **NOT** gate is a very simple gate – if 0 is input then it outputs 1 and if 1 is input it outputs 0.

We express this relationship between input and output as a **truth table.**

It is more usual to use algebraic variables such as A, B, C … for inputs and P, Q, R … as outputs.

A	P
0	1
1	0

We also have a diagram to represent this gate:

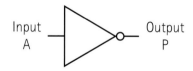

Input A — Output P

AND gate

The **AND** gate tells us if both of the inputs are 1, by outputting 1, otherwise it outputs 0.

The truth table shows two inputs, A and B, and all the possible combinations of values for A and B.

A	B	P
0	0	0
0	1	0
1	0	0
1	1	1

Specification content

(a) Explain why data is represented in computer systems in binary form

(b) Understand and produce simple logic diagrams using the operations NOT, AND and OR

(c) Produce a truth table from a given logic diagram

Key terms

Logic gate: A circuit that produces an output based on the inputs:
NOT: A logic gate that outputs the opposite value to the input
AND: A logic gate that outputs 1 if both inputs are 1
OR: A logic gate that outputs 1 if either, or both, of the two inputs are 1
Truth table: A method for recording all the possible input combinations and determining the output for each

Notice that output P is only 1 when **both inputs** A and B are 1.

The diagram for this gate is:

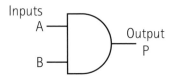

OR gate

The **OR** gate tells us if one or both of the two inputs are 1 by outputting 1, otherwise it outputs 0.

The truth table shows two inputs, A and B, and all the possible combinations of values for A and B.

A	B	P
0	0	0
0	1	1
1	0	1
1	1	1

Notice that output P is 1 when either input A or B, or both inputs A and B, are 1.

The diagram for this gate is:

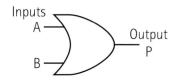

We can use these three gates to make some more complex **logic circuits**. One interesting and well used circuit is NAND, or NOT AND. This is made up from an AND gate followed by a NOT gate.

The diagram for this gate is:

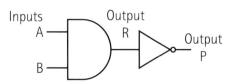

The truth table for this logic circuit can be worked out by starting with all the possible input combinations for A and B, then we use the output R from the AND gate as the input to the NOT gate.

Key term

Logic circuit: A circuit made by combining a sequence of logic gates

A	B	R = A AND B	P = NOT R
0	0	0	1
0	1	0	1
1	0	0	1
1	1	1	0

This circuit outputs 1 unless both A and B are 1.

By using truth tables and working out the outputs at each stage in the circuit to use as inputs for the next we can work out some quite complex combinations of gates. For example:

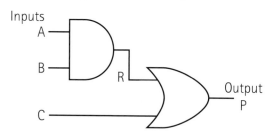

This circuit has three inputs, A, B and C so we have more possible input combinations than in the previous examples. The truth table looks like this:

A	B	C	R = A AND B	P = R OR C
0	0	0	0	0
0	0	1	0	1
0	1	0	0	0
0	1	1	0	1
1	0	0	0	0
1	0	1	0	1
1	1	0	1	1
1	1	1	1	1

We use a form of algebra to write down these circuits, called **Boolean algebra** named after the mathematician, George Boole. In the 1840s he derived the notation to express in a mathematical form the logical concepts that the early Greek mathematicians and philosophers had identified. The circuit above would be written as:

P = (A AND B) OR C

Let's look at another Boolean expression **P = (A OR B) AND C**

Key term

Boolean algebra: A method for expressing mathematically a logic circuit

The truth table is:

A	B	C	R = A OR B	P = R AND C
0	0	0	0	0
0	0	1	0	0
0	1	0	1	0
0	1	1	1	1
1	0	0	1	0
1	0	1	1	1
1	1	0	1	0
1	1	1	1	1

The diagram is:

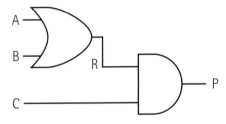

Logic in programming

We need to understand Boolean algebra in order to use many facilities within programming languages. Writing a program requires us to identify a logical process that the computer can follow and we need to be able to provide suitable Boolean expressions for the computer to use when making decisions about what to do next. There will be more about this in Chapter 7 but we might want our program to stop if one of two things happens, for example if we find a matching item in some data or we reach the end of a data file.

The computer might be given an instruction that says:

```
REPEAT
...
UNTIL data match found OR end of file reached
```

The computer's CPU will evaluate this expression using the logic:

Is there a data match?	End of file reached?	STOP
NO	NO	NO
NO	YES	YES
YES	NO	YES
YES	YES	YES

This is, of course, using the OR gate logic.

A	B	P
0	0	0
0	1	1
1	0	1
1	1	1

We will often require the computer to evaluate a logical expression in order to make a decision.

```
IF x > 10 AND y > 12 THEN …
```

This tells the computer to check the values of x and y in the program and to do 'something' if both x is bigger than 10 and y is bigger than 12.

```
WHILE x < 10 AND NOT(end of file) DO
```

This tells the computer to check if x is less than 10 and that it has not reached the end of a data file. If both things are true it carries on and does what it is asked, but if they are not both true it will stop and move on to the next instruction in the program.

Summary

- Computers use binary because it is easy to tell the state of a switch, on/off or 0/1.
- The von Neumann principle is the foundation of modern digital computing and von Neumann architecture uses binary for data and instructions which are indistinguishable from each other and stored in the same place in memory.
- Three fundamental logic gates are AND, OR and NOT.
- These gates can be combined into logic circuits.
- Truth tables are used to show what each logic gate does to the inputs.
- Truth tables can be used to work out what a logic circuit will do to the inputs by working out the values at each stage in the circuit.
- Boolean algebra is used to write down logic circuits as simple mathematical expressions.
- Boolean logic is used within programs to determine the outcome of a comparison or to determine the next step in a sequence.

Questions

❶ Draw a truth table for each of the following Boolean expressions:

a NOT(A OR B)

b NOT(A) OR NOT(B)

c A AND NOT(B)

d A AND NOT(B OR C)

❷ Draw the logic circuits for each of the expressions above.

❸ Draw the truth tables for A AND (B OR C) and for (A AND B) OR (A AND C)

   a Calculate 3x(5+6) and 3x5 + 3x6

   b What do you notice?

Extension tasks

1 Draw a logic circuit for A OR (B AND C) OR D

2 How many rows must the truth table have?

3 Complete the truth table.

4 De Morgan's law says NOT(B OR C) is the same as NOT(B) AND NOT(C). Show this is true by completing the truth tables.

5 The NAND gate is an important type of gate and is used to create a circuit called a flip-flop. Investigate what is a flip-flop, what does it do and why is it important?

Input and output devices

Without some way of getting data in and information out, a computer is of little value. Colossus, the first electronic, digital, programmable computer needed a way to get large amounts of data read into the system quickly. Using switches and patch cables was not going to be effective given how much data needed to be processed in a short time – it is physically impossible to input the data quickly enough using a manual method. A system first invented by Joseph Marie Jacquard in 1801 for reading patterns from punched cards into weaving looms and later modified by Hermann Hollerith (often regarded as the founder of IBM) for tabulating data for the US census was used. Colossus had a continuous paper tape with holes punched into it to represent the data. It read the data by recording if light passed through a hole in the tape onto an array of sensors. Output was sent to an electronic typewriter.

We often think of input and output in limited terms as applied to a modern laptop or desktop computer or the variants using touch screen technology, but input and output into computers is much more varied than that and includes specialised systems used in a wide variety of applications.

A typical home has many devices that use computer technology. A washing machine will take input from the user setting the wash program, temperature and spin speed on dials or buttons. It will also use sensors to detect the temperature of the water, the water level

Specification content

(a) Understand the need for input and output devices

(b) Describe suitable input devices for a wide range of computer controlled situations

(c) Describe suitable output devices for a wide range of computer controlled situations

(d) Discuss input and output devices for users with specific needs

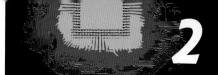

Figure 2.13 'Colossus', the first programmable computer

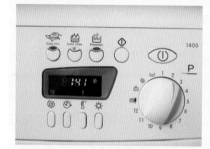

Figure 2.14 The range of programs on a typical modern washing machine

or whether the door is closed. It will output information on a digital display or with illuminated lamps and may use sounds to tell the user that the washing cycle is complete. For disabled users the washing machine may also include voice controlled input or substitute visual displays with speech output to confirm settings.

What is important is that we supply a computer system with the most appropriate input and output devices for the situation, in order for it to function effectively.

Input devices

Keyboard

A **keyboard** is used for data entry into a computer. There are standard laptop and desktop 'qwerty' keyboards, but devices such as tablet computers and mobile phones and other devices often have a modified on-screen keyboard that will adapt to the type of input expected. For blind or partially sighted users there are Braille keyboards with raised patterns instead of symbols that can be used to enter data.

Mouse

The **mouse** was invented by Douglas Engelbart in 1963 and became a common form of input to a computer. It uses sensors to track movement and translates this to a moving pointer on the screen. This pointer can then be used to select items to open, move or edit. The trackerball is often regarded as a variation on the mouse, but the invention of the trackerball, a ball that can be moved to control a pointer, pre-dates that of the mouse by more than 10 years.

Figure 2.15 The original Engelbart mouse

Touch screen

A **touch screen** is a common type of input device where the user touches an icon or symbol to select it directly on screen. These are used in tablet computers, kiosks, mobile phones, supermarket checkouts and many other situations. A touch pad is an earlier alternative to the touch screen that uses a touch sensitive pad with printed symbols to represent items. These were often found in take-away food stores or in factory environments where a keyboard or other input device would be difficult to use or subject to damage, for example when used by a garage mechanic with greasy fingers.

Microphone

It is often important to have some form of voice input and most personal computer systems have a **microphone** for inputting speech, communication or direct voice commands to the system. It is quite common now for call centres to ask the user to speak instructions so that the computer system at the other end of the telephone line can respond. These systems often only recognise numbers or basic words such as 'yes' and 'no', but they do also manage to deal with a wider range of commands. Voice input is often used by disabled users to control computer systems.

Camera

Some form of image or video input is usually found on a modern personal computer for use in taking photographs or video conferencing (for example, using Skype or social networking). **Cameras** may also be used for iris or facial recognition in security applications.

Bar code scanner

A **bar code** is a pattern of different thickness lines that can be scanned to identify an item. A light is reflected back to the scanner which detects the pattern of thick and thin lines that represent a number. This number can then be used to identify an item in a database which can then return the details.

RFID reader

Radio frequency identification (**RFID**) is an electronic version of a bar code. It uses radio frequencies to transfer information to a reader. As with a barcode the number is looked up in a database to return information about the item. Unlike barcodes these devices do not require line of sight and can be read at distances of around ten metres. They are

Figure 2.16 Smart phone with touch screen

Key terms

Touch screen: A touch sensitive surface that allows the user to select, control or move objects by touching icons and symbols using fingers

Microphone: A device for capturing sound

Camera: A device to capture still or moving images

Bar code: A pattern of thin and thick lines representing a number that can be scanned by a reader for input into a computer system

RFID: Radio frequency identification uses radio frequencies to represent a number that can be scanned for input into a computer system

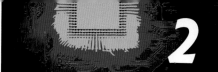

often used in shops but also to track luggage past check points in airports, as tags inside animals so that they can be scanned and identified, or issued to motorists to detect them passing through toll booths or into car parking areas to automatically collect payments or allow access.

Sensors

There are a variety of **sensors** that are used in a wide range of applications. The use of temperature and water level sensors in washing machines was mentioned earlier but other sensors include light, pressure, accelerometers (used in hand held games and mobile phones, for example) and motion sensors. Gesture based interfaces frequently use motion sensors and are a common form of input into games systems. Sensors are often found in computer control and most modern aeroplanes use a range of sensors to detect various factors and provide automatic feedback to a control system that responds by changing settings to ensure the system behaves as required.

Input devices for users with specific needs

Some people are not able to make direct use of standard input devices and there are a range of adapted input devices available for those with different requirements. There are many examples including:

- Eye-typer – for users with limited physical mobility, this device uses a camera to track the movement of the user's eye and can detect which key the user is looking at. A slow blink is used to select the key in order to type commands into a computer system.
- Puff-suck switch – this device is a switch that can be operated by blowing or sucking into a small tube and is used by those with severely limited physical mobility. The software then interprets the actions to take.
- Voice input – for those who find it difficult to operate a keyboard, spoken commands can be translated into text by software and used to communicate or instruct the computer to take actions.
- Joystick – for those with limited movement, a joystick requiring less physical movement than a mouse can guide the pointer on screen to select commands to be carried out by the computer.
- Foot mouse – for those who have limited hand movement, this device is a track ball device that can be operated with the foot.
- Braille keyboard – this keyboard has raised embossed patterns on each key that match the standard braille characters and can be used by the blind or those with visual impairment to type text and commands into a computer system.

Figure 2.17 RFID tags for various uses

Key term

Sensor: A device that can detect physical conditions such as temperature, weight, light, sound, etc.

Output devices

Monitor

The most likely output from a system will be some form of visual message, text, images or video and that requires a **monitor**. The LCD and LED type of monitor is the most common form but it was not so long ago that we used CRT (cathode ray tube) monitors and no doubt the technology will continue to advance. Hand held devices include a touch screen type of display so that input and output are through the same device.

Printer

We often require some hard copy evidence and a **printer** is a common accessory to a computer system. There are a variety of types of printer, including monochrome and colour laser printers for fast and economical output, or ink-jet printers, particularly useful for printing high quality images such as photographs. Supermarkets often have thermal printers built into their EPOS (electronic point of sale) systems because they have fewer moving parts to cause problems and are virtually silent in use. In engineering design it is now quite normal to have a 3D printer capable of producing a three-dimensional object based on a design. Architects often use large format plotters to produce plans.

Speakers

Many people use a personal computing device to play music through **speakers** or headphones. The visually impaired user often relies on speakers or headphones to obtain feedback from a computer device. Sound output is also used as a warning, for example, in hospitals, systems monitoring patients using a range of sensors will often have some audible signal to warn carers of any problems.

Actuators

A computer system being used to monitor and control a mechanical system will need some way of outputting a physical adjustment to modify the behaviour of the system. An **actuator** is a computer controlled device that can make a mechanical adjustment to a system. These are a fundamental part of an aeroplane control system – the sensors monitoring various factors will automatically apply adjustments to the flaps or engines to maintain the required performance.

Figure 2.18 Actuator

Ouput devices for users with specific needs

There are a range of output devices adapted for or designed specifically to aid those who are not able to make use of standard output from a computer system.

Some examples include:

- Screen readers – there is a range of devices used to read a computer screen to assist people with a wide range of visual impairment. For example, simple magnification software to enlarge text, speech output software that reads text and outputs through standard speakers or headphones, and devices that read text and convert this to a braille interface with raised symbols.
- Actuators – these devices create a physical movement in response to a computer command and are incorporated into a range of everyday or specialist devices so that those with limited physical mobility can operate them using a suitable input device.
- Voice synthesisers – spoken output from a computer can be used for those unable to communicate verbally. These devices can 'read' text input with other devices and output synthesised voice to communicate with others.

Summary

These input and output devices are merely a sample of the wide variety that are in use and there is a range of specialist devices tailored to specific applications that have not been mentioned. What is important is that the device chosen is appropriate to the situation.

Questions

1. A supermarket self-checkout has a range of input and output devices. Identify these and state if they are input, output or both and describe the purpose for each of them.
2. A patient in intensive care in a hospital will be connected to various sensors. Identify some of the sensors that may be used and what they are used for. There will also be various output devices; identify some that may be used and explain their purpose.
3. A physically disabled user unable to use their arms effectively will still be able to use a computer system. Explain what devices they can use and how these make it possible for the user to perform various otherwise impossible tasks.

Extension tasks

1 Identify the various input and output devices typically found on a tablet computer and describe their purpose.

2 Gesture based systems are used in various situations including movie making and medical research. Research the range of gesture based systems available and how these are used.

Secondary storage

While it is all very good that computers are able to process data to solve problems it would be quite difficult if we had to retype all the programs and data every time we needed to process anything. We have already mentioned that Colossus was not able to store any programs and the program it ran was set up using switches and patch leads. Since Colossus only ran one program and was never switched off except to fix a fault this was not a major problem. Around us there are systems that only ever perform one task and for these the use of secondary storage is not necessary because we can pre-program a ROM chip to contain the required set of instructions. However, most of our computing needs require general purpose computers capable of performing a range of tasks. RAM is volatile so we lose anything stored in RAM every time we turn off the computer; ROM is not volatile but can only store pre-programmed sets of instructions so we are unable to save any changes or results. It is clear we need to have some form of storage that we can change and that is not volatile.

Secondary storage is additional storage facilities added to a computer system to store data and programs when the power is switched off.

Magnetic hard disk

The use of magnetic media to store data goes back to 1898 when audio was stored on a magnetised wire wrapped around a drum, but it is still the most widely used secondary storage device used on modern computer systems. The **magnetic hard disk** is a magnetised rigid plate or stack of plates with heads to read the data as the platters spin around.

The hard disk was first invented by IBM in 1956 and a stack of 50 platters the size of a couple of fridges was able to store about 5 MB and cost $50,000. By 1980 the first 1 GB drive became available at around $40,000. By the 1990s hard drives were common in most personal computers and a typical 20 MB drive would cost less than £100. By 2000 drives had become much smaller (1 inch (2.5 cm) platters) and storing over 300 MB was quite common.

Specification content

(a) Explain the need for secondary storage

(b) Describe common storage technologies such as optical, magnetic and solid state

(c) Select suitable storage devices and storage media for a given application and justify their choice using characteristics such as capacity, speed, portability, durability and reliability

Key term

Magnetic hard disk: Secondary storage device using magnetised platters to store data and files

We now think of internal hard drives for systems in many gigabytes or terabytes and we can, at the time of writing, obtain a 3 terabyte drive for a little over £100. Figure 2.19 shows the approximate cost per GB of hard disk storage between 1980 and 2010.

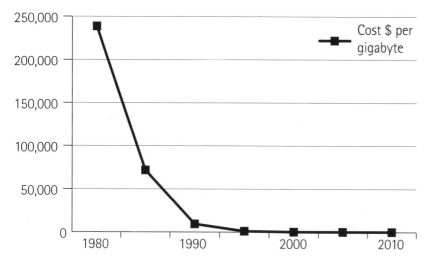

Figure 2.19 The graph shows data for the latest disk drive produced on or before 1st July in each year for the US market

The magnetic hard disk is a reliable and cost-effective solution providing high capacity at low cost. The hard disk is used in most personal and commercial computer systems. It stores the operating system, installed applications or programs and users' data. The hard disk can also be used as a portable, external device to transfer large amounts of data or to act as a backup for important data.

Optical disks

The **optical disk**, or **CD**, was invented in the mid-1980s and the **DVD** in the late 1990s. The CD-ROM and DVD-ROM are written at manufacture and are used to distribute programs, video or data that is read only. When you purchase a copy of a new program it may well be supplied on a CD-ROM or DVD-ROM. CD-RW and DVD-RW devices have the ability to be written to and are used as secondary storage to transfer files between computers. Both of these types of optical storage use light from lasers to detect reflections from the surface of the data area on the CD/DVD surface. In DVD-ROMs this is a manufactured raised area on the reflective layer in the disk. In RW media the writer is able to modify the surface of the media using a laser. The surface has a dye layer that is changed by shining a laser light at it and it is this colour difference that is detected when it is read.

Key terms

Optical disk: Secondary storage device using lasers to read (and write) data to a reflective surface. For storing files to be distributed or transferred or for backup of important files

CD: A type of optical device with a capacity of 700 MB

DVD: A type of optical device with a capacity of 4.7 GB

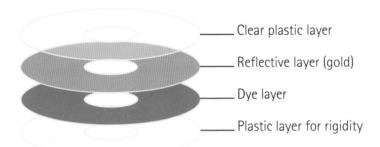

Clear plastic layer

Reflective layer (gold)

Dye layer

Plastic layer for rigidity

Figure 2.20 An expanded view of a CD-RW showing the layers

A CD will typically hold around 700 MB of data and a DVD around 4.7 GB of data. They are inexpensive and robust though data storage is not permanent as the dye layer in RW media does deteriorate over time and during the re-writing process. They are an excellent medium for transferring large files between computers and can be used for storing personal files even though transfer times are quite slow compared with other portable media such as flash drives.

Flash memory (solid-state memory)

Flash memory was discussed earlier in this chapter. It is a very common form of personal portable file storage and often uses a USB connection to a computer. Flash memory is an electronically eraseable programmable read only memory device (EEPROM for short) and in different formats it is used as memory to store images within digital cameras, as storage on mobile phones, in MP3 players and in tablet computers. Solid-state flash memory has much better access times than magnetic disks, has no moving parts to go wrong and uses significantly less power, making it an ideal choice for these devices. Flash memory is, however, not currently able to match the size of storage offered by magnetic hard disks and, while relatively inexpensive at low capacity, it becomes significantly more expensive as a replacement for higher capacity storage devices.

There are a number of things to consider when choosing what secondary storage to use:

- **Capacity** – how much data does it need to hold?
- **Speed** – how quickly can data be transferred?
- **Portability** – does it need to be portable or used to move data from one system to another?
- **Durability** – does it need to be transported and if so is it easily damaged?
- **Reliability** – does it need to be able to be used over and over again without failing?

Summary

- Secondary storage is needed to store programs, data and other files that would otherwise be lost when the power is turned off.
- Magnetic hard disks are relatively slow to access, but have a large capacity and are commonly used within personal and commercial computer systems to store operating systems, and other files and programs.
- Optical disks (CD and DVD) are used to distribute programs, video and large data files as ROM, read only devices. CD-RW and DVD-RW are used to store backup copies of personal files or software and to transfer files. They are relatively slow but also inexpensive, reliable and robust and have capacities of 700 MB (CD) and 4.7 GB (DVD).
- Flash (solid-state) memory is very flexible and can store many GB of data. It is relatively inexpensive with good access times. It is used to store data in cameras, mobile phones, portable devices and tablets computers as well as with USB interfaces for storage and transfer of personal files between systems or for backup. Portable flash memory devices are generally quite small, robust and easy to use, requiring no set up or driver software.

Questions

❶ Explain why computers need secondary storage.

❷ State which type of secondary storage is most appropriate for use in the following situations, explaining why it is the most suitable:
   a storing tracks on an MP3 player
   b transferring work from a school computer to home
   c distributing a movie
   d as the main storage area on a school network.

Extension tasks

1 What secondary storage devices could be used by a business recording and promoting new bands? Explain your choices giving reasons.

2 There is a graph on page 43 showing the cost of storage on magnetic hard disks by year from 1980 to 2010. Research the cost of storage on hard disks, CD, DVD and flash memory and draw a chart showing the relative cost per megabyte.

3 Research the access times for data from the same media and plot a similar graph showing access speeds per megabyte for each one.

Exam style questions

1 Michael's computer has a 2.2 GHz dual-core processor with 2 GB RAM and 200 GB hard disk drive. It also has 512 MB of cache memory and a DVD read/write drive.

    a What is the purpose of the CPU? [2 marks]

    b Why does the computer have both 2 GB RAM and 512 MB of cache memory? [2 marks]

    c What is meant by dual-core? [2 marks]

    d The computer is used to run several programs at the same time and uses virtual memory. What is meant by virtual memory? [3 marks]

    e How will upgrading the computer's RAM to 4 GB improve the performance of the computer? [3 marks]

2 Michael uses his computer for his school work and transfers work between home and school regularly. State what type of secondary storage he would use to do this explaining why it is the best choice. [3 marks]

3 Why do computers have both RAM and ROM? [2 marks]

4 A school wants to equip some of the computers in school to make them more accessible to students with various disabilities. Recommend some hardware the school should install explaining how this improves access for specific disability groups.

(The quality of written communication will be assessed in this question.) [6 marks]

5 What is the missing value in each of the following three diagrams? [3 marks]

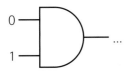 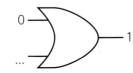 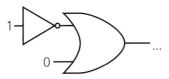

6 Complete the truth table for this logic circuit: [3 marks]

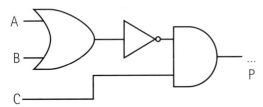

7 Draw the circuit diagram for P = (A OR B) AND NOT(C) [3 marks]

## Chapter 3

Software

In this chapter you will learn about the different types of software that are produced for computer systems. This includes system software, applications and utilities. You will also learn about different ways in which software can be sourced and supplied.

What is software?

In 1937, Alan Turing described an imaginary device that could carry out any task given to it as long as it was supplied with suitable instructions. This was a huge achievement seeing as no such devices existed at the time. It was the first time that it was seriously suggested that an **algorithm** could be given to a machine to solve multiple problems. As we have seen, this understanding led to the eventual development of electronic machines that could indeed perform different tasks according to the instructions they had been given.

Modern computers are able to do what Turing anticipated and we are all now familiar with the idea of making computing devices perform all manner of tasks for us. The **instructions** are loaded into the primary memory (RAM) from a secondary storage device and, as explained in Chapter 2, these instructions are then fetched and executed one after another by the CPU. A set of instructions to perform a task is called a **program**. Programs in general are known as **software**, to distinguish them from the hardware on which they run. The term software can also include the associated data that a program needs and the documentation that goes with it.

Nowadays, there is a vast amount of software in existence and more is being produced all the time. The popularity of smart phones has led to a huge demand for new apps (**applications**). Other new **platforms** will appear in due course. It is certain that software development will remain an important part of human achievement for a long time to come and so there will always be a need for good programmers.

Writing software

Software is written by programmers using **programming languages**. Programming languages are themselves software. There are hundreds of different programming languages and more are being developed all the time.

Specification content

(a) Explain the need for the following functions of an operating system: user interface, memory management, peripheral management, multi-tasking and security

(b) Describe the purpose and use of common utility programs for computer security (antivirus, spyware protection and firewalls), disk organisation (formatting, file transfer and defragmentation), and system maintenance (system information and diagnosis, system cleanup tools, automatic updating)

(c) Discuss the relative merits of custom written, off the shelf, open source and proprietary software

Key terms

Algorithm: A series of steps designed to solve a mathematical or other problem

Instructions: A set of commands that a processor can recognise and act upon

Program: A stored set of instructions for a computer to execute

Software: The programs that run on a computer

Application: Software designed to carry out a useful real-world task

Platform: A combination of hardware and operating system that supports the running of particular applications

Programming language: A way of writing instructions for a computer to execute

The problem is that the CPU can only recognise instructions that are given to it as binary bit patterns (see page 19). Such instructions are called **machine code**. Machine code is a **low-level language** which means it works low down at the hardware level. Each machine operation has to be written by the programmer. Writing software in machine code is notoriously difficult. This is explained in Chapter 2 and it is the reason why there are always new attempts to make writing software easier or more efficient with **high-level languages**. High-level languages allow the programmer to set out algorithms without always having to worry about every single action carried out by the CPU.

Even with a wide range of programming languages available, it is still difficult to produce robust and reliable software. Writing software is still quite a new activity for humans and there is not a long tradition about how it should be done. For this reason, various methods have been invented in order to lay down rules about how writing software should best be approached. This is the discipline of **software engineering**.

Types of software

There is software to do most things that people want a computer to do. There will be yet more in the future. Despite the huge variety of software that already exists, it can be roughly divided into two major categories.

System software is software that is written to control and make use of the hardware. It acts as an intermediary between the user and the hardware and also between applications and the hardware.

Applications are what computer users buy computers for. These are programs which do the real-world tasks that the users want. Applications need to make use of system software in order to make the hardware do what is required.

System software

This consists of operating systems, device drivers, firmware, servers, utilities and **interfaces**. System software is also often taken to include development tools such as **compilers**, **interpreters**, **linkers** and **debuggers**.

Operating systems

The **operating system** is a large collection of programs that tells the hardware what to do. When computers were first developed,

Key terms

Machine code: Instructions in binary used by the CPU

Low-level language: A programming language that is directed at controlling each machine operation

High-level language: A programming language that resembles a natural language. Each instruction translates to many machine instructions. It is problem based rather than machine based

Software engineering: Formal methods to guide the writing of software

Interface: The boundary between systems or between systems and humans

Compiler: Translation software that converts high-level source code into machine (object) code

Interpreter: Translation software that converts source code or user input into machine code which is immediately executed one instruction at a time

Linker: Software that combines together a number of separate object code files

Debugger: Software that helps a programmer track down faults in a program

Operating system: The software that controls the hardware. It acts as an interface between the user and the hardware and also between applications and the hardware

3

programmers had to work directly with the hardware. This made their job difficult and slow.

Early computers had no operating system and programmers had to enter instructions directly by setting switches or plugging in jump leads. Also, for many years, computers could only run one program at a time. The data was fed in using punched cards or paper tape and the program was run until it was completed or crashed. Operating systems were developed to help application programmers ignore the hardware to a large extent and concentrate on developing exactly what the customer wanted. Later, multitasking operating systems were developed in order to make better use of the CPU's time.

Operating systems are necessary to run all applications, except those which are **self-booting**. They are found in nearly all computing devices from mobile phones to video game consoles and **web servers**.

The operating system oversees such operations as:

- transferring data between memory locations, the CPU and the disks
- producing visual displays on the screen
- controlling peripherals
- protecting data from being accidentally overwritten.

The operating system is sometimes referred to as a **platform**. This means that it provides an environment where applications can run. Applications must be written to conform to a particular platform and this imposes a degree of consistency on them.

At the heart of all operating systems is a component called the **kernel**. This looks after the most low-level hardware operations. Applications must make use of the kernel to operate the hardware. This ensures that applications are less likely to cause problems with basic memory operations.

Multi-tasking

A **process** is a computer program that is currently being executed. Early computers could only work on one process at a time.

The CPU works a lot faster than RAM and other components of a computer system. It makes sense to keep the CPU as busy as possible so that the computer is productive. If a program is loading lots of data into RAM, such as when buffering a video, the CPU would normally be kept waiting. There may be other things that the CPU could be usefully doing while this is happening.

Also, users often want to have several processes running at the same time. For example, as this chapter is being written, the author

Key terms

Self-booting: The ability of a program to load itself. Some small devices load their applications directly without the need for a conventional operating system

Web server: A server that handles requests to a website

Platform: A combination of hardware and operating system that supports the running of particular applications

Kernel: The lowest level of an operating system that controls the hardware

Process: A program currently being executed

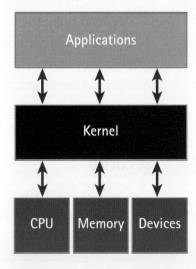

Figure 3.1 The operating system kernel connects applications to the hardware

has an email program waiting, a spreadsheet available and there is music playing on the player. Most personal computers can, in reality, still only run one process at a time, but a multi-tasking operating system is a practical way around this.

A multi-tasking operating system allows several processes to be resident in RAM at the same time. These processes are in different states – running, runnable or waiting.

While a process is running, it has the attention of the CPU. Other processes must wait.

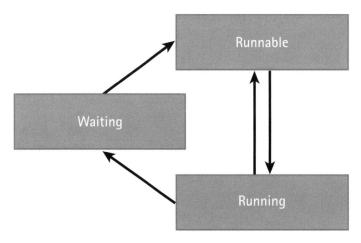

Figure 3.2 The states of a process

A process that is running will terminate if its time is up or if some external event happens. Then the runnable process can be attended to. Programs that are waiting must wait until a signal sets them to be runnable.

A multi-tasking operating system ensures that the processes get attended to by the CPU in the most efficient way. It may be that they take it in turns, or the shortest job gets done first. It depends on the policy used by the particular system. On a typical PC, the CPU usually switches between processes so fast that the user doesn't notice anything. However, we have all experienced being kept waiting while a process such as a download finishes.

Security

Operating systems must protect processes from each other. They must also protect users from each other.

If a process is using a certain part of RAM for temporarily storing data, then another process must not be allowed to overwrite that data. The operating system divides memory into pages and keeps tabs on which processes are using which pages to prevent conflicts.

Many systems are multi-user. Networks have many users, all connected to servers. Also, most individual PCs are connected to the internet. Connections mean that unauthorised users might gain access to private files.

Multi-user operating systems keep track of who 'owns' each process and each file. These are marked according to what privileges have been granted. For example, a file may be marked read-write for a particular user but read-only for others. That allows authorised users to look at the data but not change anything. These attributes are easily set up on multi-user systems such as on Unix platforms.

On home computers, firewall software can be used to take care of many permission related security issues. This is available bundled with some operating systems. Also, operating systems such as Windows allow a number of users to log in securely so that their work is kept private.

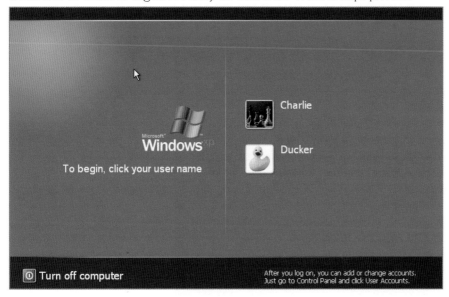

Figure 3.3 Charlie and Ducker can be logged in securely

Interfaces

Operating systems need to provide a means of communicating with them. This means making it possible for the user to issue commands and allowing applications to access their functionality.

Command line

Most operating systems allow the user to type in commands. This remains the preferred way to operate a computer for many Unix network technicians, because it allows a great deal of customisation. Batches of commonly used commands can be grouped together and run all at once. This makes administering a network less of an effort.

Key term

Command line: The place where typed commands are given to the operating system

Figure 3.4 A Linux command line session. The commands used are ls (list) and cd (change directory)

Graphical user interface (GUI)

Most personal computers and network consoles now use **graphical user interfaces**. These use **icons** (small pictures) to represent resources and actions. They reduce the need to learn commands, but they are less easily customisable.

Figure 3.5 A graphical user interface provided with the Ubuntu operating system

Smart phones make good use of GUIs, together with touch sensitive screens.

Figure 3.6 A smart phone, showing its graphical user interface

Key terms

User interface: The boundary between the computer and the user
Graphical user interface: A user interface that makes use of icons for interacting with the user
Icon: A picture on screen that represents a file, a program or an action

Voice input

In Star Trek, the characters speak to the on-board computer and it talks back. This is a difficult user interface to produce and, to date, it is still an under-developed interface. There are so many problems with different accents, ways of expression and speed of talking. However, voice input does exist and allows simple commands to be given to a system. Many call centres allow callers to speak simple inputs such as numbers and 'yes' or 'no'. Voice input will probably be an important development in the future.

Computing in context

The Apple iPhone has a voice recognition interface as part of its operating system. It allows the user to use natural language in order to ask questions such as where is the nearest Mexican restaurant or what meetings you have scheduled. It can take dictation too, so maybe the Starship Enterprise voice recognition system is not just fantasy.

Computing in context

The British catering company J. Lyons & Co. was the first company to use a computer for commercial purposes. The company contributed £3000 (approximately £80,000 in today's money) to a team at Cambridge to help them develop their EDSAC (Electronic Delay Storage Automatic Calculator). They then constructed their own computer based on EDSAC and called it LEO – Lyons Electronic Office. This was ready in 1951 to produce valuations of production runs. Later it was also used for payroll and inventory applications.

Programmers wrote applications in assembly language and also a high-level language called CLEO – Clear Language for Expressing Orders.

By 1961, Lyons had improved its LEO computers and developed a multi-tasking operating system for them.

Examples of operating systems

Many operating systems have been developed over the years. They have evolved in order to cater for different needs and also to take advantage of improvements in hardware.

The idea of what should be in an operating system has also changed a lot. Some, such as Windows have made the user interface part of the operating system. Others, such as Unix, restrict the operating system to hardware operation and a simple character based interface, leaving others to produce graphical interfaces if they so desire.

Three popular examples of graphical interfaces for Unix are Xfce, KDE and GNOME. You will notice that they all have a similarity which is increasingly common as standards tend to become accepted.

Figure 3.7 The Xfce graphical interface for Unix

Figure 3.8 The KDE graphical interface for Unix

Figure 3.9 The GNOME graphical interface for Unix

Windows

Most personal computers in the world today run on a version of Windows. This is a powerful proprietary multi-tasking operating system developed by Microsoft with a huge range of capabilities that go way beyond the original ideas of operating systems. It provides a graphical user interface (GUI) which is part of Windows itself.

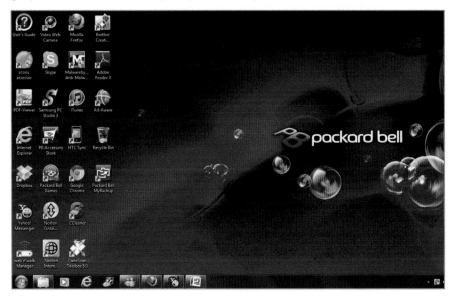

Figure 3.10 Windows desktop

The Windows GUI makes all applications running under Windows look similar. This makes learning them a lot easier than if all applications were created totally afresh. The reason why they look so similar is because the applications make use of code that is part of Windows itself. So, if a programmer wants to utilise a button or a menu, these can be called up from Windows and used in the application.

Many Windows features are stored in the Windows directory as DLL files. This stands for Dynamic Linked Library. Programmers can access routines stored in these in order to produce applications that look 'right' for a Windows environment.

DLLs are also useful in saving the application programmer effort. Routines can be linked into an application at run time, which reduces the size of the program. This also reduces the amount of coding that the programmer needs to do, and it provides code that is tried and tested.

There are versions of Windows that are used to run servers, although there is more competition for this section of the market than for desk top use.

Unix

This is a *family* of operating systems mostly found on high-end servers as well as on workstations. Some have to be purchased, but there are examples of free Unix-like systems. Some major hardware manufacturers supply their own versions of Unix that will run only on their machines. Unix was developed in conjunction with the C programming language. Unix is much valued by professionals because of its security and robustness. Many user interfaces have been developed to make using Unix easier for non-specialists. Commands have traditionally been given to Unix systems via the **command line**.

Example Unix commands are shown in the table below:

Unix command	Meaning
ps	List the processes belonging to the current user
cd	Change directory
kill	Terminate a process

Key terms

Command line: The place where typed commands are given to the operating system

Shell: Software that provides a traditional text based interface to an operating system

Computing in context

Unix is such a popular operating system that many shells have been developed for it.

The Bourne shell is available for all Unix implementations. It allows users to write shell scripts which are collections of Unix commands bundled together to save effort.

The Korn shell was written by David Korn of Bell Labs. It is an efficient shell found on all Unix implementations.

Bash stands for the Bourne-again shell – an example of programmer humour. It is a development of the Bourne shell and provides features of the Korn shell but is public domain software and written for Unix implementations.

Several programmers have written shells for Unix. These are alternative command line processors which are designed to make certain types of operation easier.

Mac OS

Apple computers come with their own proprietary operating system, which is a variant of Unix. Recent versions have included networking and internet features. The development of the iPhone and the iPad have led to new ways of thinking in how an operating systems should react to the user. The latest versions work seamlessly with cloud computing as well as having many other innovative features.

iOS

This is an operating system designed to work with the Apple iPhone. It is a proprietary system that is not permitted to run on non-Apple products. It is designed around a touch screen so that it can accept instructions from finger movements such as dragging, pointing, pinching and reverse pinching. It also interfaces to internal iPhone devices such as an accelerometer.

Linux

This is designed to behave like Unix although it was developed independently, initially by Linus Torvalds. It is open source, so anyone can have access to the source code and modify it. The Linux kernel is extremely popular. It has been adapted to run on supercomputers, mobile phones, watches and many other devices. It is not common on desk top computers but it is very popular for running servers, including many web servers.

Many versions of Linux exist and they are often packaged together with useful applications. Examples of operating system packages based on Linux are Red Hat, Debian, Ubuntu and Google's Android smart phone operating system.

One important implementation of Linux is called GNU. This is another example of programmer humour because GNU is a recursive acronym. It refers to itself. It stands for GNU's Not Unix. It includes useful applications and libraries. Ubuntu is based on GNU.

Linux is gaining ever more popularity, for similar reasons to Unix. It is a relatively small operating system which makes it fast and economical with memory. It is notably bug free and has important security features designed into it rather than added later. It is also free of charge.

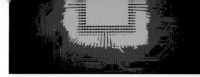

Peripheral management and device drivers

Computer systems have peripherals in order to input, output and store data. These peripherals need to be told how to communicate with the rest of the computer system. The signals that control them are provided by software called **device drivers**. Device drivers are produced for each peripheral and they are often specially written by the manufacturers of the devices. Sometimes the producers of the operating system provide generic device drivers that work with a number of devices from different hardware manufacturers.

Device drivers take care of the actions of the peripherals so that the application programmers do not need to know the hardware details of each peripheral that they will be using. They only need to pass on requests to the driver and it translates these into the codes specific to the device.

Interrupts

Device drivers are specific not only to the devices, but also to the operating system. For example, a printer needs a driver to work with a Windows based computer and a different driver to work with a Linux machine. This is because when a device is required by a program, a signal called an **interrupt** is generated. It interrupts the operating system and tells it to stop running the current program and switch the CPU's attention to a different program that is looking after the peripheral. The interrupts have code numbers and these are different for each operating system. When the job with the peripheral is finished, the CPU is directed back to the original program, to the point where it was interrupted.

Device drivers operate at a low level in an operating system and if they are badly written, they can cause serious problems with the running of the computer.

User settings

Most operating systems are supplied with **applets** that allow the user to fine tune peripherals. For example, Windows has a device manager as part of its control panel utilities. This allows the user to change settings such as the screen resolution from a printer driver for example (see Figure 3.11).

Key terms

Device driver: A program that enables communication between a computer and a peripheral

Interrupt: A signal to the operating system to stop what it is doing and perform a different task instead

Applet: A small application that performs one specific task

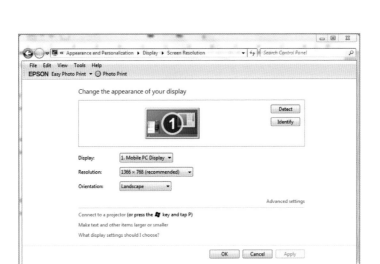

Figure 3.11 Changing the screen resolution

Firmware

The software we use on computers is usually loaded from a disk when required and then run from RAM. This is not practical for small devices running **embedded systems** (see page 9). There is no room or need for a disk drive on a mobile phone or a camera. Also, when a computer is switched on, it can't get its first instructions from the disk because the disk drivers have not yet been loaded into RAM.

In these cases, software is stored permanently on ROM or flash memory chips. Software that is stored on memory chips is called **firmware**. It typically consists of small programs that are used to control an electronic device such as a TV remote control or a camera. Larger computers also have firmware to take care of boot up operations.

Servers

A server is software that responds to the requests of other programs, known as **clients**. A good example is a web server, such as Apache. This software handles web pages so that remote internet users can communicate with a website. The server accepts and processes these requests and supplies the resources required from the website. Apache is the most popular web server in the world and has many hundreds of millions of websites depending on it. It typically runs on Unix or Linux machines.

Server software is also important in running smaller networks. When a network user logs on to a network or wants to access a

Figure 3.12 A satellite TV remote control. Its functionality is provided by firmware on a chip

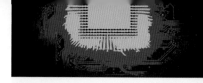

resource such as a printer or a file, the server software processes the request and delivers what is required to the client.

Server software also provides security on a network. It handles login requests, verifies passwords and ensures that users have access only to allowable resources.

The word **server** has also come to mean the computer that runs the server software. Hardware servers are high-end machines that are capable of handling many simultaneous requests at high speed.

Utility software

Most personal and large-scale computer systems have many utility programs installed with the operating system. They are usually installed with the operating system, but many users like to install their own favourites as well. **Utilities** are generally small-scale programs that perform a limited range of functions.

Standard utilities are handy to have because if you need to carry out simple maintenance, you know that there will be tools available to do the job.

Security utilities

Some operating systems provide a simple **virus detection** utility. This is unlikely to be particularly useful unless it is regularly updated. New threats are always appearing and it is important to have the latest counter-measures.

- **Spyware** is a common threat. A **Trojan** is harmful software that is disguised as something useful. Criminals often download Trojans to users' PCs which log key strokes and send them back. This can be used to steal passwords and other sensitive data. There are plenty of free anti-spyware utilities available online. You have to be careful to download only from trusted sites because some Trojans masquerade as anti-spyware.
- **Firewalls** can be set up by software utilities. They restrict outgoing and incoming access to certain network addresses. Windows comes with a firewall utility, but most users buy alternatives that have more features.

Maintenance utilities

Operating systems always come with **disk organisation** tools. They let you format new disks, move files from place to place and carry out jobs as such renaming or copying files.

Figure 3.13 A typical virus scanner interface

3

After a period of use, the files on your hard disk get broken up into fragments. This is because files get deleted and this leaves holes of varying sizes. If a new larger file is saved, it will have to be split across the available spaces. This slows down loading because the read-write heads have to make lots of disk accesses to load the complete file.

Defragmenting utilities (**defragmenters**) reorganise files so that individual files and all the free space are put together.

Various tools are available that detect errors on your system. Some of these are third party, in other words, they do not come with the operating system. The operating system will usually supply one, for example ScanDisk on Windows systems. This checks for and fixes bad links between file fragments and bad sectors on a disk.

Many programs leave temporary files or cached copies of data. These can take up huge amounts of disk space. There are plenty of utilities such as CCleaner that clear away unused files.

Operating systems are always being updated. Sometimes there are important bug or security fixes. Most operating systems regularly check for updates and install them. This can be set to be automatic or manual.

Other examples of common utilities include:

- calculation of free space on a disk
- calendars
- change the clock settings
- email clients
- finding files that contain particular search strings
- image editing
- providing help from a manual
- simple text editing
- simple word processing.

Development software

Sometimes software development tools are regarded as system software although they are not usually provided with operating system distributions.

Editors

To write programs, you need an **editor**. This is like a cut down word processor but it does not save formatting along with your text. Examples are Notepad for Windows or gedit for Linux.

Although any editor will do for writing programs, there are enhanced editors that give extra features such as **pretty printing**.

Key terms

- - - - - - - - - - - - - - - - - -

Defragmenter: A utility that brings together file fragments on a disk and collects all the free space in one area
Editor: Software used for entering source code when writing a program
Pretty printer: An editor that automatically sets out program code in an easy to read way

- - - - - - - - - - - - - - - - - -

Figure 3.14 A typical update manager interface

This detects programming constructs such as loops and automatically indents them and uses different colours to show key words. Line numbering can be added automatically by some of them.

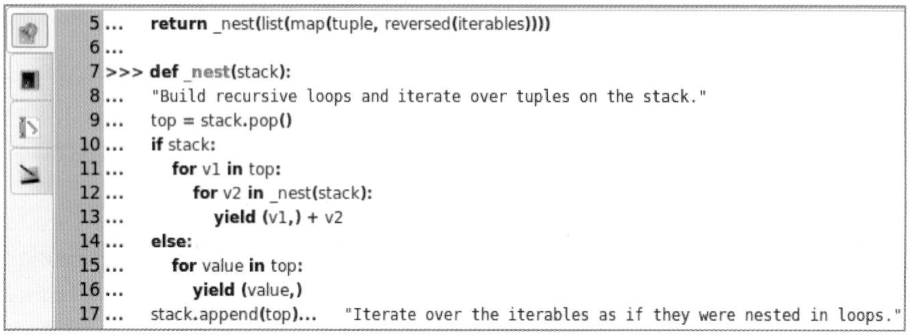

```
 5 ...   return _nest(list(map(tuple, reversed(iterables))))
 6 ...
 7 >>> def _nest(stack):
 8 ...     "Build recursive loops and iterate over tuples on the stack."
 9 ...     top = stack.pop()
10 ...     if stack:
11 ...         for v1 in top:
12 ...             for v2 in _nest(stack):
13 ...                 yield (v1,) + v2
14 ...     else:
15 ...         for value in top:
16 ...             yield (value,)
17 ...     stack.append(top) ...    "Iterate over the iterables as if they were nested in loops."
```

Figure 3.15 Pretty printing feature in Eric (a Python text editor)

Compilers

High-level languages are programming languages that look rather like normal English. They are designed to make programming easier. Each statement in a high-level language is turned into many machine instructions, which reduces work for the programmer. The high-level statements are more related to the task that the programmer wants to carry out instead of being focused on how the machine functions. The code written by the programmer is called source code.

Compilers are translator programs that convert high-level source code into machine code that the CPU can run. They do not often come supplied with an operating system, but they are still regarded by some as system software because they are not applications designed to do a specific task for a user. Compilers are available for most programming languages.

Interpreters

Interpreters also translate high-level code into machine code, but they do so a line at a time and execute the code as they go. They are useful for debugging programs because they give an instant result. The problem with interpreters is that they have to be resident when the application written with them is run. This uses more RAM and also restricts who can run the software to those who have the correct interpreter. Also it is slower to translate and run every time a program is executed. Examples of interpreted languages are Logo, Forth and many versions of BASIC.

Assemblers

Assembly language is a more convenient way to write machine code programs than writing binary bit patterns. Assembly language uses a set of mnemonics to represent the possible machine operations. Both assembly language and machine code are low-level languages, which means that the programmer is directly controlling every step that the processor takes. It is a slow way to program, but sometimes it is necessary to keep complete control over the action of the program. Assembly language is completely specific to the processor that will run it. An assembly language program for an Intel processor will not be the same as one written for a Motorola chip.

Assembly language is not machine code. But, each assembly language instruction translates to just one machine instruction, which is why it is called a low-level language. Just as with high-level languages, programs written in assembly language have to be translated to machine code before they can be run. The software to do the translation is called an **assembler**.

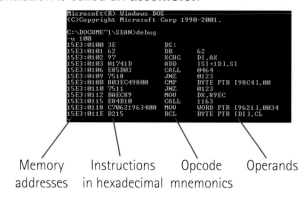

Memory   Instructions   Opcode   Operands
addresses   in hexadecimal   mnemonics

Figure 3.16 Memory dump showing machine code and equivalent assembly instructions

Linkers

A program is usually built from many subprograms. Often these parts are produced by separate teams, sometimes using different programming tools and languages. This results in a collection of object code modules which need to be combined together to make the finished application. The software that does this job is called a linker. It makes sure that there are no conflicts between the modules and 'glues' them all together to make a complete application.

Key terms

Assembly language: A low-level programming language that uses more memorable mnemonic codes and labels to represent machine-level code. Each instruction corresponds to just one machine operation

Assembler: Software that translates assembly language code into machine code

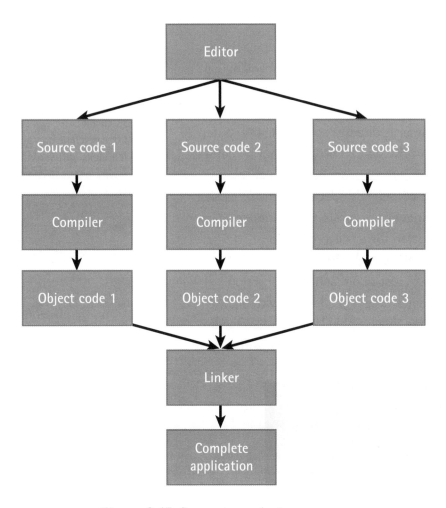

Figure 3.17 Stages in producing a program

Applications

We buy computer systems to run applications, which are often referred to as apps. These are the programs that do the real-world jobs that we want. There is a huge range of applications already in existence and more are being produced all the time. Applications exist for all computing devices and many are not at all obvious to their users.

Applications are normally purchased from a developer or free ones may be downloaded from websites. Users often produce their own; for example, it is easy to set up mail filters, which is another form of application software.

Examples of applications

Office software consists of a bundle of applications such as a word processor, a spreadsheet, presentation software, a drawing package and sometimes a database management system. Examples include Microsoft Office and Libre Office.

Enterprise software is often specially written for a company and includes a wide range of business applications such as stock control, payroll and customer management. There are also many examples of applications that are designed to help IT staff do their work, such as managing the help desk, organising network security and database applications.

Much software these days is designed to help people work together. Email is a classic example, but increasingly, applications are made available online – in the cloud – so that many users can easily access the same files using the same software.

Internet access requires its own specialist software, such as a browser and many media players.

There is much educational software available, such as VLEs (virtual learning environments), teaching and simulation packages.

In the entertainment world, many movies make use of special media software for creating special effects and software is used to control lighting and make bookings in theatres.

Software is used to control most electronic devices and other embedded systems such as engine management systems in cars and avionic control systems in aircraft.

Nowadays, thousands of apps are being written all the time for smart phones, allowing all sorts of functions from finding your way with GPS systems to accessing social network sites.

Procurement

Off the shelf and custom written software

With so much software available, it is a big decision to choose the best examples, especially when organisations require expensive systems. In some cases, there are existing software systems that can be bought more or less 'as is' which reduces their cost because the development costs have been met already. The more customers that buy a product, the cheaper it can be sold for because the costs are spread more widely. Office suite software packages are much cheaper than one-off systems.

Software that exists already is sometimes called '**off the shelf**'. It has the advantage of being available straight away. Also, many users have worked with it and most of the bugs should have been discovered and fixed. There is a wide community of users who can help each other.

Key term

Off the shelf: Software that is aimed at many users and sold 'as is'

Custom written software has the advantage of being specially made for a particular client. If a company has a particular requirement, it can work together with the developers to produce something that fits its requirements exactly. If there are problems, the developers can be contacted and if there is a maintenance contract, bug fixes can be organised after delivery.

The problem with this is that all the development costs are borne by one customer. Also, it takes time to develop and test the product. With only one client, there are likely to be more faults because the product has not been tried out by other users.

Smart phone apps are aimed at millions of users and many of them are quite small, so developers can often afford to give them away or make only a small charge.

Proprietary and open source software

Software can be developed as a commercial undertaking. The developer owns it as 'intellectual property' and licenses it to clients to use. The source code is a trade secret and only the compiled programs are released to customers. Software that is owned by its developers is called proprietary software. The advantage of this arrangement is that there is someone 'out there' who can take responsibility for the quality of the software. If the software is custom written, there will usually be contracts that ensure that updates are produced or maintenance is provided. The disadvantage is that custom written software can be expensive.

Much software is produced on an open source basis. It is normally developed by a community which is often worldwide. They do it either to improve their skills or because they want to do something useful for the public good. The source code is publicly available, so, in theory, anyone can adapt it and recompile it. The disadvantage of open source software is that it comes with no guarantees or contracts. Often, this is not an issue because the quality is usually extremely high. The developer community is quick to spot errors and fix them and much open source software is exceptionally well written and reliable. Well-known examples are the Linux operating system, Libre Office, the Apache web server and the Mozilla Firefox web browser.

Key term

Custom written: Software developed specially for one or a few customers

3

Computing in context

Choosing enterprise software

Information system managers have a responsibility to choose systems for their organisations that help deliver the business strategy at an acceptable cost. This might mean adopting a mix of proprietary and open source software. They also have to take into account the abilities and experience of the staff who will be using the systems. Factors that must be considered include:

- Security – the software must not compromise the safety of the organisation's data.
- Support – there should be ways to get users trained and problems fixed. Possibly this can be done in-house.
- Integration and conformance testing – the software will have to work with existing systems. It must connect with them. Testing needs to be carried out to ensure this.
- Scale – software that works well on a small scale might not cope if it has to handle larger quantities of data or work with many users.
- Future-proofing – the software needs to be upgradeable as needs change. If many people are already using the software, there are likely to be fewer problems in recruiting trained staff in the future.

Summary

- Software can be classified as system software and applications.
- Operating systems control the hardware and provide an interface for humans and applications.
- Applications do the real-world jobs that we require.
- Software is produced using other system software.
- Software may be proprietary and paid for, or open source and freely available.

Extension tasks

1 Look at the utilities available on your computer. How many of these do you use? Do they duplicate actions that other software on your system performs?

2 Find out how to set the firewall on your computer.

3 Run an antivirus check on your computer.

4 Go online and make a list of several anti-spyware utilities.

5 Use your system utilities to rename a file.

6 Find out how to defragment a disk on your system.

7 Find out how your system updates itself.

8 Make a list of software available on your computer that is specially designed to work on the internet.

9 Think of any commercial activity that you know about. Make a list of some of the types of software that are needed to carry out its activities.

10 Look up three Unix commands and explain what they do. Find out how you would do the same things in Windows.

Exam style questions

1 Explain how a pretty printer helps a programmer to produce source code. [2 marks]

2 Fred is a systems manager of a large insurance company. He is choosing general purpose office software for the staff to use. He is considering installing open source software.

    a State what is meant by open source software. [2 marks]

    b Describe two reasons in favour of choosing open source software in this situation and two reasons against. [4 marks]

3 Describe the following types of common utility programs:

    a Editor

    b Disk defragmenter

    c Firewall. [6 marks]

4 a Explain what is meant by off-the-shelf software. [2 marks]

    b Explain why off-the-shelf software can be cheaper than custom-written software. [2 marks]

## Chapter 4

Representation of data in computer systems

I n this chapter you will learn about the importance and versatility of binary numbers and how binary is used to store data in computer systems. Numbers, text, images, sound and instructions are all stored in binary and we will look at how this is done.

We have already mentioned how important the work of John von Neumann was – it was he who proposed the principle used in all modern computers that data and instructions should all be stored in binary. It is easier to see how numbers are stored in this way, but what about images, text and sound? The principle is, of course, to convert images, text and sound into numbers before storing them. In order to understand how the computer stores all these forms of data in binary we need to first understand the concept of binary numbers and how values can be converted to binary.

The computer uses electronic circuits to store one of two values using a switch – the switch is either on (1) or off (0). Using a number of these switches provides us with many possible combinations of 1s and 0s which we can use to represent numeric values.

In the common **denary** (or decimal) (base 10) system we all use there are 10 different symbols – 0, 1, 2, 3, 4, 5, 6, 7, 8, 9. We use these symbols to write numbers, so 573 means 5 lots of 100, 7 lots of 10 and 3 1s. In primary school we may have seen this written in a table:

100	10	1
5	7	3

The column values are simply 10 times the previous value as we move from right to left.

In **binary** (base 2) we only have two symbols – 0 and 1. We can use a similar table, but this time we multiply the column values by 2 rather than 10.

128	64	32	16	8	4	2	1

So the binary number 10101 can be put into the table starting from the right-hand column.

Key terms

Denary: A system of numbers using ten digits, 0 and 1–9 (also called the base-10 system)

Binary: A system of numbers using only two digits, 0 and 1 (also called the base-2 system)

128	64	32	16	8	4	2	1
			1	0	1	0	1

We can now use the same approach we did for our base-10 system and say we have:

1 lot of 16, no 8s, 1 lot of 4, no 2s and 1 lot of 1.

So we have 16 + 4 + 1 = 21

This means that 10101 in binary is the same as 21 in base 10.

Units

In base 10 we have some important numbers we give names to: for example 10 × 10 × 10 is 1000 which we call a thousand; and 1 thousand multiplied by 1 thousand which we call 1 million; and so on. In base 10 we are also used to the metric system which uses kilo to mean a thousand, for example kilometre or kilogram. In binary we also have names to describe key values.

The basic unit is 0 or 1 – this is a **b**inary dig**it** or **bit**.

A group of 8 bits is called a **byte** and half a byte (4 bits) is called a **nibble**. (Computer humour!)

We also use the kilo prefix to represent the same sort of scale as we do in base 10. But 1000 is not a very tidy binary number so we go to the closest 'tidy' value in binary which is 2^{10} or $2 \times 2 \times 2 \times 2 \times 2 \times 2 \times 2 \times 2 \times 2 \times 2 = 1024$. Using this approximation to 1000 we can now define a whole set of names commonly used to describe binary numbers.

8 bits	1 **byte**
1024 bytes	1 **kilobyte**
1024 kilobytes	1 **megabyte**
1024 megabytes	1 **gigabyte**
1024 gigabytes	1 **terabyte**

Numbers

In the introduction to this chapter you were shown the connection between binary and denary numbers. Converting binary integers into their base 10 equivalent is a relatively straightforward process. You simply write the binary number under the binary column headings and add up those columns where there is a 1.

Let's look at another example:

What is the denary (base 10) equivalent of 11011001 in binary?

Specification content

(a) Define the terms bit, nibble, byte, kilobyte, megabyte, gigabyte, terabyte

(b) Understand that data needs to be converted into a binary format to be processed by a computer

Key terms

Bit: Binary digit 1 or 0
Byte: 8 bits
Nibble: 4 bits or half a byte
Kilobyte: 1024 bytes
Megabyte: 1024 kilobytes
Gigabyte: 1024 megabytes
Terabyte: 1024 gigabytes

Specification content

(a) Convert positive denary whole numbers (0–255) into 8-bit binary numbers and vice versa

(b) Add two 8-bit binary integers and explain overflow errors which may occur

(c) Convert positive denary whole numbers (0–255) into 2-digit hexadecimal numbers and vice versa

(d) Convert between binary and hexadecimal equivalents of the same number

(e) Explain the use of hexadecimal numbers to represent binary numbers

128	64	32	16	8	4	2	1
1	1	0	1	1	0	0	1

128 + 64 + 16 + 8 + 1 = 217

The process to convert from base 10 to binary can also be quite straightforward. There are other methods, but a simple approach is to divide by 2 repeatedly noting the remainder value each time until the answer is 0.

The answer is the remainder column starting at the last value

11011001

Further information

Another method is to search for the largest column heading that we can subtract from the number, take it away and repeat with the remainder until we get an answer of 0.

217 (largest column heading that we can subtract from 217 is **128**), so 217 − 128 = 89

89 (largest column heading that we can subtract from 89 is **64**), so 89 − 64 = 25

25 (largest column heading that we can subtract from 25 is **16**), so 25 − 16 = 9

9 (largest column heading that we can subtract from 9 is **8**), so 9 − 8 = 1

1 (largest column heading that we can subtract from 1 is **1**), so 1 − 1 = 0

Using the values we subtracted (**128, 64, 16, 8, 1**) we get the column values for the binary equivalent.

We get the answer:

128	64	32	16	8	4	2	1
1	1	0	1	1	0	0	1

This method is much easier to use if you want to convert these values in your head, but don't forget to double check by converting the answer back to base 10.

The examples are all limited to 8 bits but the computer uses much larger values than this. While the arithmetic is a bit harder the process for dealing with larger values remains the same.

Adding binary numbers

Adding binary numbers is very similar to the way we add base 10 numbers:

For example let's add 367 to 284

```
3   6   7
2   8   4
6   5   1
1   1
```

7 + 4 = 11, so we write down 1 and carry the 1
6 + 8 + 1 = 15, so we write down 5 and carry the 1
3 + 2 + 1 = 6
These are carried over values from the previous column.

When adding binary numbers we follow the same process, but 1 + 1 = 2, which is written as 10 in binary. The first few numbers in binary are:

Base 10	Binary
1	1
2	10
3	11
4	100
5	101
6	110

Let's look at an addition in binary, 1011 + 1101

```
    1   0   1   1
    1   1   0   1
1   1   0   0   0
1   1   1   1
```

1 + 1 = 10 (in binary)
  so we write down 0 and carry the 1
1 + 0 + 1 = 10 (in binary)
  so we write down 0 and carry the 1
0 + 1 + 1 = 10 (in binary)
  so we write down 0 and carry the 1
1 + 1 + 1 = 11 (in binary)
  so we write down 1 and carry the 1
0 + 0 + 1 = 1 so we write down the 1
These are carried over values from the previous column.

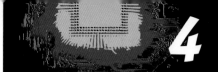

More examples

Add 101 and 1001

```
          1   0   1
      1   0   0   1
      1   1   1   0
              1
```

Add 11000010 and 10111010

```
    1   1   0   0   0   0   1   0
    1   0   1   1   1   0   1   0
    0   1   1   1   1   1   0   0
  1                   1
```

In this case when we add the two numbers we find that we need a ninth column. If our computer only had 8 bits to store numbers this would mean the carry from the eighth column would be lost. This is called **overflow**; the calculation has overflowed the available space. In 8 bits the largest number we can store is 255.

Key terms

Overflow: When a number becomes too large to fit into the number of bits allocated it is said to 'overflow' and some bits are 'lost' leaving an incorrect value

Hexadecimal: The base-16 number system

Hexadecimal numbers

Large binary numbers are quite difficult to remember and when programmers work with these values they need something that is easier to recognise and appreciate. Converting everything from base 2 to base 10 and back is quite complex and we need something that still uses base 2 but is easier to understand. Since a byte has 8 bits it easily splits into two equal sections, nibbles with 4 bits each. If we look at our column headings for a 4-bit number we see that we can represent the range of numbers 0 to 15.

8	4	2	1	
0	0	0	0	= 0

8	4	2	1	
1	1	1	1	= 15

If you recall, in base 10 we have the 10 symbols, 0 to 9, if we use the 16 symbols for 0 to 15 we can use a system based on place values of 16 rather than 2 or 10. We call this **hexadecimal** (or hex for short).

We do, however, need to have symbols for the numbers 10, 11, 12, 13, 14 and 15 because in base 16, 12 would mean 1 lot of 16 and 2 lots of 1 (or 18).

We use the letters A, B, C, D, E and F to represent these values so in hexadecimal we have the set of symbols:

Base 10	Base 2	Base 16
0	0	0
1	1	1
2	10	2
3	11	3
4	100	4
5	101	5
6	110	6
7	111	7
8	1000	8
9	1001	9
10	1010	A
11	1011	B
12	1100	C
13	1101	D
14	1110	E
15	1111	F

Converting from hex to base 10 is the same process we have used before with column values, using the values 1 and 16. For example, 23 in base 16 is:

16	1
2	3

$2 \times 16 = 32$ $3 \times 1 = 3$ **32 + 3 = 35 in base 10**

Some more examples

Convert 3C from base 16 to base 10

16	1
3	C

$3 \times 16 = 48$ $12 \times 1 = 12$ **48 + 12 = 60 in base 10**

4

Convert 5F from base 16 to base 10

16	1
5	F

$5 \times 16 = 80$ $15 \times 1 = 15$ **80 + 15 = 95 in base 10**

Converting from base 10 to base 16 can be done using the same methods we identified for converting base 10 to base 2:

Divide by 16 repeatedly and record the remainders.

Converting 45 in base 10 to base 16 is:

45	÷ 16	= 2	Remainder	**13 = D**
2	÷ 16	= 0	Remainder	**2**

Therefore **45** in base 10 = **2D** in base 16.

Converting 235 in base 10 to base 16 is:

235	÷ 16	= 14	Remainder	**11 = B**
14	÷ 16	= 0	Remainder	**14 = E**

Therefore **235** in base 10 = **EB** in base 16.

This may seem quite tricky but when we look at converting between hexadecimal and binary we will see some useful features.

Using the examples above.

45 in binary is 32 + 8 + 4 + 1 (using mental arithmetic method)

128	64	32	16	8	4	2	1
0	0	1	0	1	1	0	1

Split this into two nibbles and treat each as a 4-bit binary number

8	4	2	1	8	4	2	1
0	0	1	0	1	1	0	1
		2		8	+ 4		+ 1
		2		13	= D		= 2D

235 in binary is 128 + 64 + 32 + 8 + 2 + 1 (using mental arithmetic)

128	64	32	16	8	4	2	1
1	1	1	0	1	0	1	1

Split this into two nibbles and treat each as a 4-bit binary number

8	4	2	1	8	4	2	1
1	1	1	0	1	0	1	1
8	+ 4	+ 2		8		+ 2	+ 1
	14	= E		11		= B	= EB

From this we can see that hexadecimal numbers are related to binary very closely. To convert a binary number to hexadecimal we split it into nibbles and convert each nibble to its hexadecimal equivalent.

For example

Convert 10100011 to hexadecimal

Split into two nibbles:

8	4	2	1	8	4	2	1
1	0	1	0	0	0	1	1
8		+ 2				2	+ 1
	10	= A			3		

So 10100011 in binary is equivalent to A3 in hexadecimal.

To convert from hexadecimal to binary we convert each digit to its binary equivalent and join these together to form the binary equivalent.

For example

Convert A5 in hexadecimal to binary

A (10 in base 10) is 8 + 2 or 1010 in binary

5 is 4 + 1, which, using 4 bits, is 0101 (we need the leading 0 here)

Joining these together we get the binary equivalent of A5 in hexadecimal: 10100101

Another example

Convert 3B in hexadecimal to binary

3 = 0011
B = 1011
3B = 00111011
(We shouldn't really use the leading 0s in the final result so the correct answer is 111011).

This close relationship between binary and hexadecimal is why hexadecimal is used so extensively by programmers. The data on the computer is in binary, if the programmer needs to examine this data then pages of 1s and 0s are not much help, but the hexadecimal equivalents are much easier to work with. One example of this is the HTML coding of colours. Light blue on an HTML page has the hexadecimal value ADD8E6, and brown is A52A2A. Working with these hexadecimal numbers is much easier than working with the binary equivalent 101011011101100011100110. (Can you tell which of these two colours this binary number represents?)

4

Summary

- Computers use switches to represent data, since switches can be either 'off' or 'on', data is represented as binary values, 0 or 1.
- The basic unit is a bit (binary digit) which takes the value 0 or 1.
- 8 bits is a byte.
- We have a set of named key values based on 2^{10} which is 1024 to define: kilobyte, megabyte, kilobyte, gigabyte and terabyte.
- We convert between binary and base 10 by adding the column values where there is a 1.
- We can convert from base 10 to binary by: dividing repeatedly by 2 and recording the remainders; or by subtracting the highest column heading from the number, repeating with the remainder and recording the column heading subtracted to get the binary equivalent.

Questions

1. Convert 28, 72, 131, 235 and 255 from base 10 to binary.
2. Convert 1011, 11011, 10001010 and 11001000 to base 10.
3. How many kilobytes are there in a gigabyte?
4. How many megabytes are there in 3 terabytes?
5. Add the following numbers in binary showing the working:
   a 1010 + 101
   b 10001 + 11001
   c 111001 + 100011
6. Convert the following binary numbers to hexadecimal:
   a 10010011
   b 10101000
   c 111011
   d 1010101
   e 11111111
7. Convert the following hexadecimal numbers to binary and to base 10.
   a 1A
   b 35
   c BC
   d 4D

Extension task

What are the names used for units larger than a terabyte?

Characters

When you press a key on a computer keyboard a code is generated that the computer can convert into a symbol for display or printing. It is clear that it is important that systems agree on the codes being used if the data is to make sense. In 1960 the American Standards Association agreed on a set of codes to represent the main **character set** used in telegraph systems, **ASCII** (American Standard Code for Information Interchange). This system was agreed to deal with basic textual messages and included codes for:

All the main alphabetic characters, upper and lower case	52 characters
All the numeric symbols, 0–9	10 characters
32 punctuation and other symbols, and 'space'	33 characters
32 codes reserved for non-printable control codes	32 characters

In total, 127 codes (95 printable and 32 non-printable) plus the 'null' code (represented by the binary 00000000) which is used as a control character in certain applications but has no associated symbol.

In binary, 127 is 1111111, so this system uses 7 bits.

Some ASCII codes are:

Binary	Hex	Decimal	Character	Binary	Hex	Decimal	Character
0100000	20	32	'space'	1100001	61	97	a
1000001	41	65	A	1111001	79	121	y
1000010	42	66	B	1111010	7A	122	z
1011010	5A	90	Z	1111111	7F	127	'delete'

If you look at a complete table of ASCII values on the internet you will see that the character values increase from 'A' to 'Z' and from 'a' to 'z'. This means it is possible to sort these characters based on their numeric value. For example, A is less than B, B is less than C, etc. Note that 'a' is larger in value than A and Z, so when you sort words 'Zebra' comes before 'apple'.

ASCII was very useful for transmitting textual messages but it fails to deal with the range of other characters we often need, such as those used in various non-English languages and mathematical symbols. As 8-bit computers became the norm the ASCII character set was extended to use 8-bits rather than 7, this meant another 128 characters could be included. It also conveniently uses just one byte to store each character.

Specification content

(a) Explain the use of binary codes to represent characters

(b) Explain the term 'character set'

(c) Describe with examples (for example ASCII and Unicode) the relationship between the number of bits per character in a character set and the number of characters which can be represented

Key terms

Character set: The characters available to a computer

ASCII (American Standard Code for Information Interchange): 7-bit system to code the character set of a computer

Unicode: Up to 32-bit system to code the character set of a computer (usually 16-bit or 32-bit versions)

The **Unicode** system for encoding characters uses up to 32 bits (4 bytes) providing more than 4 billion possibilities. Within the Unicode system the original 128 ASCII characters still occupy the same values, so ASCII could now be considered a subset of the Unicode system for coding characters.

Summary

The characters available to a computer are called its character set and, depending upon the system it uses, the more bits the character set uses to code the symbols, the more symbols the computer system has available. ASCII was one of the first agreed standards using 7 bits and containing codes for 127 characters. Unicode can use up to 32 bits to code the character set and provide over 4 billion possible character codes. Many of the possibilities in the 32-bit system remain unused and the 16-bit version, providing over 65,000 possibilities, is sufficient for most needs. There are various versions of Unicode using different numbers of bits to code the character set, but they each contain subsets of agreed values to maintain compatibility.

Questions

❶ What is meant by the character set of a computer?

❷ Explain how ASCII represents the character set of a computer.

❸ What happens if you sort the list 'Apple, bear, Charlie, dog, elephant' in a program using ASCII or Unicode to represent the character set?

❹ Explain the difference between using an ASCII character set and a Unicode character set.

Extension tasks

1 There are not enough keys or combinations of keys to make use of a full Unicode character set. How do we enter these extra characters when using a computer?

2 The definition of a byte is usually considered to be 8 bits but what was the original definition of a byte?

3 What do we mean by 'word length' in a computer?

Images

This simple image based on the sort of graphics in the Space Invaders video game can be represented in just eight bytes by representing each row as a byte with white as 0 and black as 1.

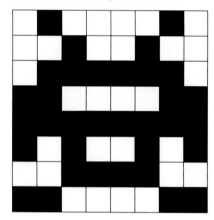

0	1	0	0	0	0	1	0
0	0	1	0	0	1	0	0
0	1	1	1	1	1	1	0
1	1	0	0	0	0	1	1
1	1	1	1	1	1	1	1
1	0	1	0	0	1	0	1
0	0	1	1	1	1	0	0
1	1	0	0	0	0	1	1

In reality images are often more complex than this and this simple small drawing of a cat has 100 × 123 pixels or dots. That is just under 2 kilobytes.

This image is made up of dots and when enlarged we can see that the image becomes less defined and we can clearly see these dots or **pixels**.

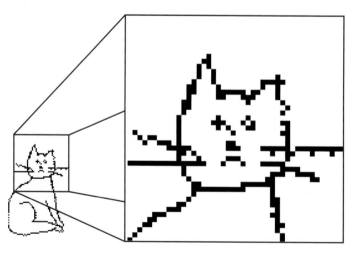

Specification content

(a) Explain the representation of an image as a series of pixels represented in binary

(b) Explain the need for metadata to be included in the file such as height, width and colour depth

(c) Discuss the effect of colour depth and resolution on the size of an image file

Key term

Pixel: The smallest element of an image. Pixels are the dots that make the image on screen

The screenshot below shows what the computer has stored for just a small section of this image.

```
00000000   00       01       02       03       04       05       06       07       08       09       0a       0b       0c
00000000   01000111 01001001 01000110 00111000 00111001 01100001 01111011 00000000 01100100 00000000 11110111 00000000 00000
00000010   00000000 00000000 00110011 00000000 00000000 01100110 00000000 00000000 10011001 00000000 00000000 11001100 00000
00000020   00110011 00000000 00000000 00110011 00110011 00000000 01100011 01100110 00000000 00110011 10011001 00000000 00110
00000030   11111111 00000000 01100110 00000000 00110011 01100110 00110011 00000000 01100110 01100110 00000000 01100110 10011
00000040   00000000 01100110 11111111 00000000 10011001 00000000 00000000 10011001 00110011 00000000 10011001 01100110 00110
00000050   10011001 11001100 00000000 10011001 11111111 00000000 11001100 00000000 00000000 11001100 00110011 00000000 11001
00000060   10011001 00000000 11001100 11001100 00000000 11001100 11111111 00000000 11111111 00000000 00000000 11111111 00110
00000070   00000000 11111111 10011001 00000000 11111111 11001100 00000000 11111111 11111111 00110011 00000000 00000000 00110
00000080   00000000 01100110 00110011 00000000 10011001 00110011 00000000 11001100 00110011 00000000 11111111 00110011 00110
00000090   00110011 00110011 00110011 01100110 00110011 00110011 10011001 00110011 00110011 11001100 00110011 00110011 11111
000000a0   00110011 01100110 00110011 00110011 01100110 01100110 00110011 01100110 10011001 00110011 01100110 11001100 00110
000000b0   10011001 00000000 00110011 10011001 00110011 00110011 10011001 01100110 00110011 10011001 10011001 00110011 10011
000000c0   11111111 00110011 11001100 00000000 11001100 00110011 01100110 00110011 11001100 01100110 00110011 11001100 10011
000000d0   00110011 11001100 11111111 00110011 11111111 00000000 00110011 11111111 00110011 00110011 11111111 01100110 00110
000000e0   11111111 11001100 00110011 11111111 11111111 01100110 00000000 00000000 01100110 00000000 00110011 01100110 00000
000000f0   10011001 01100110 00000000 11001100 01100110 00000000 11111111 01100110 00110011 00000000 01100110 00110011 00110
00000100   01100110 00110011 10011001 01100110 00110011 11001100 01100110 00110011 11111111 01100110 01100110 00000000 01100
00000110   01100110 01100110 01100110 01100110 10011001 01100110 01100110 11001100 01100110 01100110 11111111 01100110 00110
00000120   00110011 01100110 10011001 01100110 01100110 10011001 10011001 01100110 10011001 11001100 01100110 10011001 11111
00000130   01100110 11001100 00110011 01100110 11001100 01100110 01100110 11001100 10011001 01100110 11001100 11001100 01100
00000140   11111111 00000000 01100110 11111111 00110011 01100110 11111111 01100110 01100110 11111111 10011001 01100110 11111
00000150   11111111 10011001 00000000 00000000 10011001 00000000 00110011 10011001 00000000 01100110 10011001 00000000 10011
00000160   10011001 00000000 11111111 10011001 00110011 00000000 10011001 00110011 00110011 10011001 00110011 01100110 10011
00000170   00110011 11001100 10011001 00110011 11111111 10011001 01100110 00000000 10011001 01100110 00110011 10011001 01100
```

http://www.hhdsoftware.com/free-hex-editor

When we examine what the computer is storing for this far more detailed and complex picture of some flowers we see the same sort of data, lots of 0s and 1s.

```
00000000   11111111 11011000 11111111 11100001 01001101 10010100 01000101 01111000
00000010   00001000 00000000 00000000 00000000 01001001 00000000 00001111 00000001
00000020   00000000 00000000 00010000 00000001 00000010 00000000 00101001 00000000
00000030   00000011 00000000 00000001 00000000 00000000 00000000 00000000 00000000
00000040   00000000 00000000 11011010 00000000 00000000 00000000 00011011 00000001
00000050   00000000 00000000 00101000 00000001 00000011 00000000 00000000 00000000
00000060   00000010 00000000 00101001 00000000 00000000 00000000 11101010 00000000
00000070   00000000 00000000 00000010 00000000 00000000 00000000 01101001 10000111
00000080   00000000 00000000 01010000 00110101 00000000 00000000 00000101 01000001
00000090   01000100 01000001 01001011 00100000 01000001 01001111 01001101 01010000
000000a0   00000000 00000000 00000000 00000000 00000000 00000000 00000000 00000000
000000b0   00000000 00000000 00000000 00000000 00000000 00000000 01001011 01001111
000000c0   01010011 01001000 01000001 01010010 01000101 00100000 01000011 00110111
000000d0   01000100 01001001 01000111 01001001 01010100 01000001 01001100 01000000
000000e0   00000000 00000000 00000000 00000000 00000000 00000000 11100000 00000001
000000f0   00000000 00000000 00000001 00000000 00000000 00000000 01001011 01001111
```

http://www.hhdsoftware.com/free-hex-editor

How does the computer know what to do with the binary numbers in order to display the right image?

The cat drawing uses only black and white, whereas the flower image has a large number of colours. If a pixel is to be able to represent more than one colour then we need to use more bits to make a range of colours available.

With 1 bit we can have just 2 colours, black or white for example.

With 2 bits we can have 2^2 or 4 colours.

With 3 bits we can have 2^3 or 8 colours and so on.

8 bits will give us 2^8 or 256 colours.

16 bits will give us 2^{16} or 65,536 colours.

This is the same image with the **colour depth** reduced to:

16 bits   4 bits   2 bits

So the more bits per pixel (bpp), the greater the colour depth or range of colours in the image, we achieve.

16 bpp is often regarded as high colour, 24 bpp as true colour and 32 bpp, or more, as deep colour.

The greater the colour depth the more bits we need to store the image data.

Another factor affecting the size of the file needed to store the data is the **resolution** of the image. The resolution of an image is the number of pixels per unit, for example pixels per inch (often referred to as dots per inch, dpi – but strictly speaking dpi refers to the density of dot placement in a printed output). The more pixels per inch the larger the file storing the image data will be.

Since the data is all stored in binary, for the computer to be able to make sense of it and display the image as intended it needs to know something about the data. It needs to know the size of the image in terms of height and width in pixels, and the colour depth of the image. With this information the computer is able to make sense of the binary data. This data about data is called **metadata**.

The screenshot above is a section from the properties for the original flower image. You can see the size is 3056 × 2292 pixels, the colour (or bit) depth is 24 bpp and the resolution is 480 dpi (dots or, more correctly, pixels per inch).

Further information

Image files are stored in a variety of formats but basically either as a set of pixels in a bitmap form or as a vector form. In vector graphics formats, images are made up from a set of primitive components such as lines, arcs, circles, ellipses, in fact a whole range of geometric shapes. Vector graphics are stored as a shape with further information including a set of control points that the shape must pass through. When enlarged, bitmapped images become pixelated, that is we can see the blocks that make up the image. Vector graphics do not become pixelated since the primitive shapes, control points and other information simply needs to be recalculated to create the new shape. Therefore vector images do not suffer from loss of resolution when enlarged and they also do not suffer from the file size issues that affect large, high-resolution bitmapped images. Since the definitions for the shapes and control points remain unchanged the file size is not affected by the size of the image. Ultimately, though, displays and printers are **raster** devices that use pixels to display or print the image regardless of the graphic type and in order to display or print vector images they must be converted to bitmapped ones.

Key term

Raster: Graphics format consisting of a matrix of dots

Summary

Images are stored as binary data on a computer. So that the computer can make sense of this data the file is stored with some data about the data, or metadata, to tell the computer the image size in pixels and the colour depth used for the image. Using this information it can read the binary data and recreate the image. The size of an image file is determined by its size in pixels, the colour depth and resolution of the image.

Computing in context

When images are taken using a mobile phone with GPS location, the image files is saved with metadata that identifies the location where the image was taken as well as the time it was taken. This means that the image file can be used to locate exactly where and when the image was created. This raises some concerns about privacy and, while it is possible to turn off this extra information, most people do not do so.

Questions

❶ How does the resolution of an image affect the size of the file?

❷ What do we mean by image size?

❸ What metadata is stored with an image file?

❹ If an image has its colour depth decreased what is the effect?

❺ How many colours can be represented using a 4-bit colour depth?

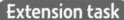

Extension task

The colours of an image file using 2-bit colour depth are defined in binary as 00 (white), 01 (red), 10 (green) and 11 (blue). The metadata for the file is given in the order: height, width, colour depth (as 8-bit binary numbers) followed by all the data for the image in binary numbers. (The data should be used to create the image by working across the rows starting in the top left-hand corner).

Draw the image defined by this set of data.

```
00000111,  00010001,  00000010

00 00 00 01 00 00 00 00 00 10 10 00 00 11 11 11 00
00 00 01 00 01 00 00 00 10 00 00 10 00 11 00 00 11
00 01 00 00 00 01 00 10 00 00 00 00 00 11 00 00 11
00 01 00 00 00 01 00 10 00 00 00 00 00 11 11 11 00
00 01 00 00 00 01 00 10 00 00 00 10 00 11 11 00 00
00 00 01 00 01 00 00 00 10 00 00 10 00 11 00 11 00
00 00 00 01 00 00 00 00 00 10 10 00 00 11 00 00 11
```

Create some images and convert them to binary using this method and see if others can recreate them accurately. If you change the colour depth don't forget to say what colour each binary value represents (the colour palette).

Sound

This is what the computer file for a music track looks like. Once again it is just binary numbers like our images. The metadata tells the computer what type of file it is so that it doesn't try to display it as a picture, but it still looks just like any other computer data.

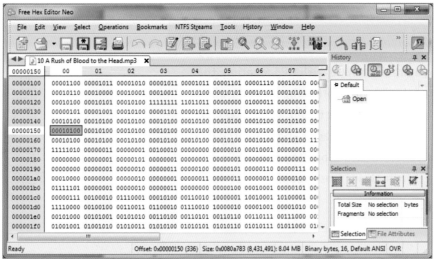

http://www.hhdsoftware.com/free-hex-editor

Sound is often continuously varying data (**analogue**) but the computer needs to have this in a digital form as a set of binary numbers. To convert sound from an analogue form into a digital form

Specification content

(a) Explain how sound can be sampled and stored in digital form

(b) Explain how sampling intervals and other considerations affect the size of a sound file and the quality of its playback

Key term

Analogue: Refers to continuously changing values

we sample the sound wave at set intervals and record the values. This set of values is saved and replayed by the computer.

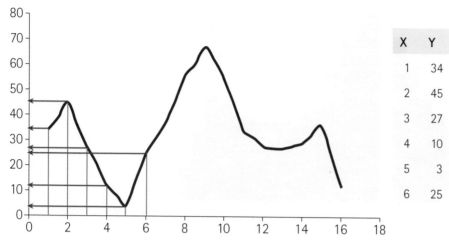

X	Y
1	34
2	45
3	27
4	10
5	3
6	25

In this case we are sampling every 1 unit on the x-axis (time) and from the graph we can read the corresponding values for the curve at each of these points on the y-axis. The first few of these are shown in the table above.

When the computer uses these values to recreate the curve we get something like this:

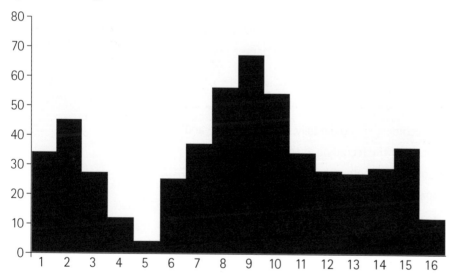

This is approximately the same shape as our curve though not as smooth and the sound produced will not be the same quality as the original.

If we sampled every 0.5 units instead we would need more data but our bar chart would start to look a lot more like our original curve and the sound would be closer to the original.

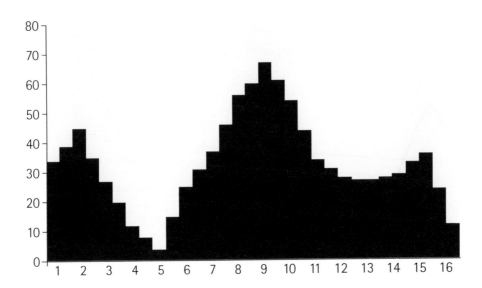

The **sample rate** affects the quality of the sound recorded so a high sample rate (or sampling at smaller time intervals) improves the quality of the sound recorded, but needs more data and creates a large file.

The **bit rate** used to store the sampled data also has an effect on the quality of the recording. The bit rate is the amount of space available to store the sampled data per second. A typical MP3 track will be stored at 128 kbits per second whereas an audio CD will use a bit rate of 1411.2 kbits per second, 12 times as fast. Once again a high bit rate will produce better results but will require more space to store.

Key terms

Sample rate: The number of times the sound is sampled per second, measured in Hz (100 Hz is 100 samples per second)

Bit rate: The bit rate is the space available for each sample, measured in kilobits per second (kbits/s). (128 kbits/s is 128 kilobits per second of sampled sound)

Summary

There is a trade-off to be made when recording sound digitally. The sample rate and bit rate both have an effect on the quality of the recording. If the sample rate and bit rate are higher the quality of the sound will improve, but higher sample rates and bit rates both require more storage space and increase the size of the file.

Questions

1. Why are there so few tracks on a typical audio CD?
2. How does the sample rate affect the quality of the playback for an MP3 sound track?
3. What effect does a high bit rate have on the number of sound files that can be stored on a CD?

4

1 Without breaking any copyright laws it is possible to copy sound files at different bit rates and sample rates. Experiment with these and try to determine at what levels these have a noticeable effect on the quality of the sound.

2 By experimentation try to find out how many minutes of sound you can record onto a CD at different sample rates and bit rates.

Instructions

Program instructions and data are stored by the computer in binary in the same place. When a computer is instructed to run a program it is directed to the start **address** for these data and instructions. The CPU fetches the first instruction from this start location and **decodes** it to find out what to do next. In the meantime it has already updated a **register**, the **program counter**, to point at the next memory location so that it is ready to fetch the next instruction if necessary.

How does the computer know that the binary it is fetching is an instruction and not data? It doesn't, they look the same, but it finds what it expects to find. If it is told to run a program at a certain location it expects the first item it fetches to be an instruction and it deals with it accordingly.

A program instruction has two parts – the instruction part or **operator**, and a data part or **operand**. A typical instruction may be to add the data in a memory location to data in another register, the **accumulator**.

If we take a simple example where the add instruction is the binary 1001 then 10011101 means add the number you find in memory location 1101 to what is already in the accumulator.

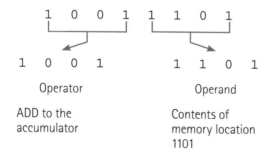

1 0 0 1	1 1 0 1
1 0 0 1	1 1 0 1
Operator	Operand
ADD to the accumulator	Contents of memory location 1101

If the program has any mistakes in it then it is possible the CPU could fetch what was meant to be data, but it thinks to be an instruction, decode it and it all goes wrong. The CPU will just do what it is told to do and has no way of knowing if the binary number it has just fetched is meant to be an instruction or data.

Key terms

Address: A location in main memory used to store data or instructions

Decode: An instruction is decoded by the CPU into two parts – the operator and the operand

Register: Special fast access part of the CPU that stores data in use by the CPU

Program counter: A register in the CPU that keeps the address of the next instruction

Operator: This is the part of the instruction that tells the CPU what to do

Operand: This is the part of the instruction that tells the CPU what to apply the operation to

Accumulator: A register in the CPU that stores data currently being used by the CPU

Further information

The CPU has a number of special registers or stores including the program counter to store the address of the next instruction it expects to fetch. When an instruction is fetched it automatically adds one to this register but if the program does not require this then it can be changed by the program to point at the right memory location. The accumulator stores the data currently being worked on by the CPU, data to be used and the results of any calculations.

Summary

At machine level the instructions in computer memory are stored in binary. Each instruction is represented by a different bit pattern that the CPU recognises as an instruction. When the CPU fetches data from memory it cannot tell the difference between instructions and data and finds what it expects to find based on the program it is running. An instruction is in two parts – the operator which tells the CPU what to do and an operand which tells the CPU what data or memory location is the subject of the operation.

Questions

❶ Explain how instructions are coded in binary in a computer.

❷ Explain how a computer distinguishes between instructions and data.

Extension tasks

1 If in an instruction set:

- 1001 x means ADD the data in memory location x to the accumulator
- 1010 x means STORE the data in the accumulator in memory location x
- 1011 x means SUBTRACT the data in location x from the accumulator
- The memory location 1100 has the value 0111 in it and memory location 1101 has the value 0100 in it.

What will the following sequence of instructions do?

1001 0011

1011 1101

1010 1110

2 Write a sequence of instructions that will add three numbers together using this instruction set.

Exam style questions

1 Add the binary numbers 110111 and 10001 showing working. [2 marks]

2 Add the binary numbers 11010011 and 11000101 showing working.

Explain what would happen if the result was stored as an 8-bit binary number. [3 marks]

3 Convert the binary number 10110101 to:

a base 10 [2 marks]

b hexadecimal. [2 marks]

4 Convert the decimal number 57 to:

a binary [2 marks]

b hexadecimal. [2 marks]

5 Convert the hexadecimal number AF to:

a binary [2 marks]

b decimal. [2 marks]

6 Explain how the resolution of an image affects the size of the file. [3 marks]

7 Explain how sample size and bit rate affect the quality of a sound file. [4 marks]

## Chapter 5

Databases

In this chapter you will learn about what databases are and why they are so important. You will also learn about how relational databases are constructed and used.

The database concept

A database is a persistent organised store of related data on a computer system. It is organised so that computer programs can easily select or edit data items. Persistent simply means that it is stored in secondary storage so that it can be accessed later.

A database is handled by software. Database software has to be able to create, retrieve, update and delete the data in a database. This is sometimes referred to as CRUD.

Most computer systems store, process and retrieve data. This is what they are good at and the main reason why organisations buy them. In your programming controlled assessment, you will probably write a program in order to handle stored data on a disk file.

Here is a simple program, written in Python, that writes some numbers to a file.

```
# program to write ten values to a disk file

f = open('workfile.txt', 'w')

for x in range (1,11):
 f.write(str(x))
 f.write('\n')

f.close()
```

Figure 5.1 Program to write 10 values to a disk file

What this program does is to open a text file called workfile.txt for writing (w). The program will refer to the file as f. Then it counts from 1 to 10. It converts each number as it counts into a string (str(x)), so that the text file will accept it, writes the value to the file with the write method, then writes a new line character (\n). Then the file is closed.

We can do the reverse process to read the data back and display the contents in the Python shell using the print function.

```
# program to read ten values from a disk file

f = open('workfile.txt', 'r')

for x in range (1,11):
 f.read(x)
 print(x)

f.close()
```

Figure 5.2 Program to read 10 values from a disk file

You can also look at the data file in workfile.txt using a text editor such as Notepad.

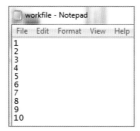

So far so easy. It would also be a simple matter to change the program to add new data to the file or write different data. If you wanted to write ten names to a file instead of ten numbers, then it would be easy to arrange that. Or ten addresses as well. Maybe this could work as a customer file in an online e-commerce business, or could it?

It would be easy to write a program to find an item in the file too. This is called a **serial file** because the items are stored as a series, one after another. All you need to do is to start at the first data item, examine it, if it is what is looked for then print it, otherwise move on to the next one. A simple loop can be written to do this.

Expressed as an algorithm, that would be:

```
input search item
go to first item in file
repeat
if item = search item then output item: end
else
move to next item
until item found or no more data
endif
output item not found
```

When searching a serial file, the items are looked at one after another in order to find a particular item. It would not take very long to search through ten data items. But imagine a million data items. Even with a fast processor, this would take too long. There are better ways to do this.

Sequential files

If the data in a serial file is in some sort of order, perhaps based on an account number, the file is a **sequential file** – the data is in some sequence. It can be a lot faster to find data in a sequential file. There are various well-known algorithms such as the binary search that can quickly find items in an ordered file. The binary search works not by starting at the beginning but by looking at the middle record and deciding whether the wanted item is before or after it, then repeating the process. At each step, the amount of data looked at is halved. It doesn't take too many steps before the data is found or it becomes clear that the data is not there.

Another way to search a sequential file is to use an index. This is like an index in a book. The software looks up the position of the item in the index, goes straight to the part of the file where the required data is, then does a serial search there.

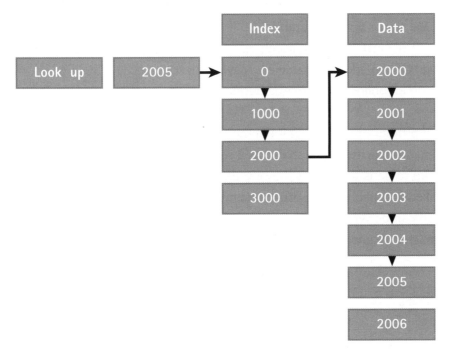

Figure 5.3 Searching for data in an **indexed sequential file**

Flat file databases

Think of a personal address book. It is likely to be fairly small and it will only need to store a few things such as names, addresses and phone numbers. A **flat file database** such as the one in Figure 5.4 is fine for this. It is made up from **fields** and **records**. A field is some characteristic about the people, such as a surname. A record is all of the data about one person. A flat file database can easily be set up in a spreadsheet. Spreadsheet software is quite capable of sorting and searching the data, so it may be enough for simple purposes.

5

First Name	Last Name	Telephone	Street	City	Post Code	DOB
Claire	Pate	1 55 791 7964-8421	1434 Aenean Road	Iowa City	K3I 1RF	28/06/1999
Virginia	Landry	1 61 306 9087-9418	404 Morbi Road	Rock Island	EI30 7QR	23/01/1974
Orli	Goodwin	1 51 119 4068-1665	704-6375 Varius St.	Lynwood	CG12 9LQ	26/09/1984
Callie	Hodge	1 70 829 9014-9968	P.O. Box 362, 5198 Vulputate, St.	Wichita Falls	D1Z 9AN	05/07/1978
Rhonda	Pugh	1 44 202 4884-7705	P.O. Box 250, 7653 Fusce Road	West Covina	S5 9OD	23/06/1984
Dara	Goff	1 70 115 3175-0607	844-4722 Felis St.	Knoxville	KE9C 7XR	03/10/1999
Susan	Carney	1 15 217 7394-9919	3235 Vel Rd.	Manassas Park	T8M 6ZF	20/02/1996
Leila	Moreno	1 17 669 7461-3103	220 Mollis Avenue	Altoona	M3 2IV	26/01/1999
Yasir	Fitzgerald	1 15 912 6723-2845	2168 Sed Rd.	Kokomo	MX9A 3JH	04/08/1988
Noelle	Cline	1 30 289 4151-3931	8089 Nullam Avenue	Hannibal	I8Q 3VA	30/01/1981
Maya	Bush	1 78 470 3633-2571	831-739 Eget Avenue	Hilo	TI7 5ZB	22/11/1981
Laurence	Wong	1 75 759 5511-9535	221-9359 Luctus Road	Cumberland	V60 1JQ	01/07/1980
Briar	Hewitt	1 91 258 6422-5420	269-1587 Consequat Ave	Kearns	Q4 1HN	17/04/1994

1 field

1 record

Figure 5.4 A flat file database

A file like this could form the basis of a customer database for an online vendor. But suppose that the company decides that it needs to add customers' email addresses or credit limits to the database. Then the software would need to be rewritten and the data files completely changed to process the additional data. That's OK if the company has programmers who are not too busy but it's not the greatest way to develop a database. With larger stores of data, it would be impractical to have to rewrite software every time the nature of the data is changed.

Things get difficult when there is a lot of data or when the data consists of many different things. Businesses such as one dealing with online sales, where details of customers, products, suppliers and orders all need to be stored and organised need a more carefully planned database than this simple flat file address book.

Further information

An **entity** is something in the real world that we store data about. In this case it is a person or a group of people. An entity can be anything, such as a car, an invoice, an order or an exam subject. An entity becomes a table in a database. One instance of an entity, such as one particular person, is stored as a **record** in a database.

An **attribute** is something about an entity. It becomes a **field** in a database. An example of an attribute is a surname, an invoice number or a car's colour.

Key terms

Entity: Something that we store data about in a database

Record: All the data about one item in a database

Attribute: A characteristic of an entity. It becomes a field in a data table

Field: A characteristic of something stored in a database

Data redundancy

Suppose we used the address book file in Figure 5.4 to record orders that these people had made. We have names, addresses and telephone numbers. Might it be a good idea if we added a field to take order details? But each person might make lots of orders. How could that be recorded? You could copy the details of a person every time an order was sent in. Here, we can see that Callie Hodge has so far made three orders.

First Name	Last Name	Telephone	Street	City	Post Code	DOB	Order Item	Date
Claire	Pate	1 55 791 7964-8421	1434 Aenean Road	Iowa City	K3I 1RF	28/06/1999		
Virginia	Landry	1 61 306 9087-9418	404 Morbi Road	Rock Island	EI30 7QR	23/01/1974	Printer	23/11/12
Orli	Goodwin	1 51 119 4068-1665	704-6375 Varius St.	Lynwood	CG12 9LQ	26/09/1984	Screen	12/11/12
Callie	Hodge	1 70 829 9014-9968	P.O. Box 362, 5198 Vulputate, St.	Wichita Falls	D1Z 9AN	05/07/1978	Paper	23/11/12
Callie	Hodge	1 70 829 9014-9968	P.O. Box 362, 5198 Vulputate, St.	Wichita Falls	D1Z 9AN	05/07/1978	Toner	30/11/12
Callie	Hodge	1 70 829 9014-9968	P.O. Box 362, 5198 Vulputate, St.	Wichita Falls	D1Z 9AN	05/07/1978	Antivirus software	12/12/12

Figure 5.5 Redundant data

Already, this is getting difficult. We probably want more information about each order. How many of each item? Reference number? Size? We might need to add lots of new fields that will sometimes, but not always, be required.

Also, suppose Callie Hodge gets married and changes her name. Or moves address. We would have to change every single occurrence of her details in the database and there will be one entry for each order she has ever placed. We might update some and miss others. When an invoice clerk is sending the bills, which address would be the right one? Also, we are taking up more storage space than we need. These problems result from having **data redundancy** in the database. Data redundancy is where data is needlessly repeated. This inevitably leads to complex processing problems because each instance of the repeated data has to be updated. This is inefficient and will probably lead to mistakes.

Key term

Data redundancy: The unnecessary repetition of data

Data integrity, validation and verification

Data integrity is when data reflects reality – it is what is expected. There are many ways in which data integrity can be compromised and redundancy is just one of them.

If data is entered incorrectly, then integrity is lost. **Validation** is the process where data is checked as it is entered into a system. This checking is done by the data handling software and it can be set up to reject any data that does not conform to specified rules. These rules can be whatever the database administrator wants. Here are some common examples. They can be useful when data is being copied into a computer system by human operators.

Validation check	Explanation
Check digit	A calculation is performed on a number that generates another digit which is appended to the number. This is common on account numbers, bar codes and book ISBNs. When the data is entered, the calculation is repeated and if the same check digit is not generated, the input is rejected.
Format check	The data might have to conform to a particular pattern. For example, modern UK car registration numbers are all in the format LLNNLLL where L = letter and N = number.
Length check	The data must be within certain limits. A telephone number might be set up to be no longer than 12 digits.
Lookup check	Some fields might be looked up to see if they are from an allowed range. Postcodes can be checked to see that they do in fact exist.
Presence check	This is to ensure that all important information has been included. An application for a bank account must have a surname, for example.
Range check	A number must fall within limits. For example, for a popular theatre event, each applicant might be limited to two tickets only.
Type check	The data type might be restricted. For example, a person's surname might be restricted so that no numerals are accepted.

These are just a few common examples of validation checks. The software can be set up to check for many other potential errors. It is important to realise that validation does not prevent all errors, it only detects any breaking of the rules.

Verification is a process that is used to ensure that data is correct. In other words, data in the database is the same as in reality. Often, the only way to ensure this is by human inspection. Simple verification can be just a matter of carefully comparing what is entered into a database with the source material, such as a form that someone has filled in. But, humans make errors too easily. A slower but more reliable method is to enter the same data twice, using two operators. The software can compare the two versions and highlight any differences.

It is more accurate and faster to enter data by machine, so there are numerous ways in which data entry can be automated. Some examples are:

- Bar codes
- Magnetic strips
- OCR
- OMR
- RFID
- Smart cards.

Data models

There are several common ways of organising large databases so that data redundancy is limited and so that data is kept separate from the applications that process it. The way in which a database is constructed is called a data model. Examples of data models are flat file, hierarchical and relational. A flat file was described on pages 92–93.

Hierarchical databases

In some situations, items are composed of other items. An example is a door, which has many components making it up. When storing data about such entities, which might be stored in different sections of a factory, it could make sense to link related items in a tree. That way, by searching through a tree, the correct components would be found.

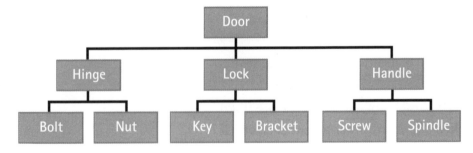

However, most data storage situations are not like that and by far the majority of data handling situations make use of the relational model.

Relational databases

- A relational database stores data in tables.
- Each table contains data about just one **entity**.
- A table is called a relation.

Key term

- - - - - - - - - - - - - - - - - -

Entity: Something that we store data about in a database

- - - - - - - - - - - - - - - - - -

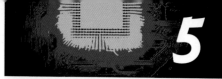

- A table has **attributes**, arranged as columns, which are identified by their names. A single instance of an attribute is called a field.
- A table has rows which are equivalent to records.
- Tables must have a primary key. In other words, each row must be uniquely identifiable.
- Each row of a table has the same data structure. You cannot have one row containing just a surname and a date of birth and another row containing extra fields. All rows are the same size.
- Tables are linked by primary and foreign keys.

Entity relations

When designing a relational database it is important to keep data about different entities separate. Tables are linked together so that data duplication is kept to a minimum. To avoid data redundancy, it is best to have tables that are related in a **one to many** way. Here is an example. Suppose you are storing data about cats and fleas (well someone might want to!). Each cat has many fleas, but each flea has only one cat. This can be shown on a diagram like this:

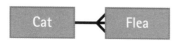

This is called an **entity relationship diagram**. In this case, we have used connections with 'crows' feet' because one end of the link looks a bit like a bird's foot. The three prongs mean 'many'. The one prong at the other end means 'one'.

Case study – a hotel booking system

Now let us look at a more realistic example. Suppose we have a hotel room booking system. We shall look at how it can keep track of room bookings using a database application. Clients contact the hotel with their requirements and if a booking can be met it is recorded in the database. As well as looking after the bookings, the system can also produce many useful management reports.

We need three entities: a room, a client and a booking. In reality there would be more to it but this is the basic requirement.

Here is the entity relationship diagram for this situation:

It shows that each room can be booked many times and each client may make many bookings. But a particular booking is for just one room and one client. This translates into actual tables like this.

Key terms

Attribute: A characteristic of an entity. It becomes a field in a data table

One to many: A relationship where one record in a table may have links to many records in another table

Entity relationship diagram: A diagram that shows how different entities used in a database are connected

The key symbol indicates a primary key (see page 97).

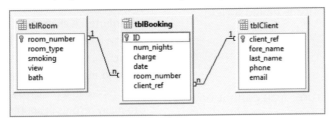

The one to many relationship is represented by the software as 1 to n.

Database design

When designing a database, you have to make decisions about each field.

Data type	The software needs to know how to handle the data. The choice made will affect what processing can be done. If you define a field as text or a string, the software will not be able to perform calculations on it without doing some conversions.
Field size	There is no point in reserving more bytes for each field than are necessary.
Validation	Rules can be set up to filter out some types of mistake.
Key field	Choose at least one field to make a primary key.

Here is the structure of the tables:

tblRoom

Field name	Field data type	Size in bytes	
room_number	integer	2	Primary key
room_type	text	20	
smoking	boolean	1	
view	boolean	1	
bath	boolean	1	

tblBooking

Field name	Field data type	Size in bytes	
ID	integer	2	Primary key (could use room_number and date combined as a compound key)
num_nights	integer	2	
charge	double	8	
date	date	8	
room_number	integer	2	
client_ref	integer	2	

tblClient

Field name	Field data type	Size in bytes	
client_ref	integer	2	Primary key
fore_name	text	25	
last_name	text	25	
phone	text	20	
email	text	50	

The description of the database is called the **schema**. It includes the table structures and the rules that will be followed. The complete database not only has to store the data required by the user, but also the schema. The schemata are stored in a data structure called the **data dictionary**.

Key terms

Schema: Definition of a database
Data dictionary: The stored schema of a database

Key fields

Notice that each table has a primary key. It has to be a unique value so that a record in the table can be identified without any mistake. Most tables use some sort of reference number as a primary key but, sometimes, a combination of fields can also be unique. For example, it would be possible to define a particular booking by room number and date combined to make a compound primary key.

Primary keys are often used to link a table to a foreign key in a different table. A foreign key does not have to be unique. So, in this example, a unique room can be linked to many different booking records. This linkage allows the data for a room to be held just once. It can be looked up when a booking is made.

Notice that every field in the booking table is to do with a booking and nothing else.

Sharing data

A large organisation is likely to have a store of data that needs to be seen and worked on by many people. It is not good enough for one person to open a data file and work with it if no one else can get access to it at the same time.

The importance of a corporate store of data has led to the development of databases which are used by a whole enterprise. Most organisations are totally dependent upon their databases these days. Without them, there would be no business. With large 'mission critical' stores of data, database software needs to do far more than just read, write and change data. It needs to be able to:

- protect data from damage and unintended deletion
- protect data from unauthorised access
- make sure that all who need to access it can, whenever they need it
- supply users with no more than they need to work with
- make sure that as far as possible, the data is accurate and up to date.

For all these reasons, much work has gone into making the design of databases as robust and flexible as possible. In most cases, this means using a DBMS – a database management system.

Questions

1. Define the term database.
2. The words 'one', 'two', 'three', 'four', 'five', 'six' are saved one after another in a data file. What type of file is this?
3. Explain how an indexed sequential file is searched to find a particular data item.
4. What is a flat file database?
5. What is an entity?
6. Define the term 'data redundancy'.
7. Define the term 'data validation'.
8. What is data integrity?
9. What is a data model?
10. What is a primary key?

Database management systems (DBMS)

Most database systems are handled by a database management system (DBMS). This is software that handles the data directly and provides an interface to the applications. The whole point of a DBMS is to separate application programs from the data. This is to prevent applications from conflicting with each other and compromising the integrity of the database. Programmers who write applications do not handle the data directly, but have to work through the DBMS.

Specification content

DBMS

(a) Describe how a DBMS allows the separation of data from applications and why this is desirable

(b) Describe the principal features of a DBMS and how they can be used to create customised data handling applications

Relational databases

(a) Understand the relationship between entities and tables

(b) Understand the components of a relational database, such as tables, forms, queries, reports and modules

(c) Understand the use of logical operators in framing database queries

(d) Explain the use of key fields to connect tables and avoid data redundancy

(e) Describe methods of validating data as it is input

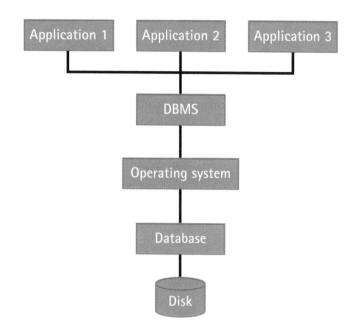

Figure 5.6 Layers in a database system

The DBMS provides a number of protections and features:

- It allows different applications to access the data at the same time.
- It controls access to the data. Security features are provided to limit who can do what.
- It provides backups and the ability to restore from a backup if a disaster occurs.
- It supports a query language and other languages which can be used to extract, add and amend data and to alter the structure of the database. New applications can be written using supported languages.
- It can force referential integrity. This means that it prevents any operation that could damage the relationships. For example, deleting an exam subject would not be possible if there were students linked to that subject.
- It controls concurrency. That means it can lock data while someone is working on it so that someone else cannot change it at the same time.

Separating data from applications

One advantage of having a DBMS instead of writing stand-alone applications is that if there is a need to change the data structure or the processing, this can be done without making big changes throughout the database. Databases are at the heart of most businesses. Businesses change. Suppose the company that owns the database needs a new program module to search for customers who have particular preferences. This can be done with a query language without having to alter the underlying data. The DBMS will not allow a new module to violate integrity rules so the data will remain safe.

Suppose that a company needs to add new fields to a database. This could be due to changes in business activity or perhaps because of new legislation. Governments often require more information from companies and the database might need to be changed to allow this. When changes are necessary to the data structures, this can be done without having to worry about changing all the applications that use other parts of the database.

Database views

External (user) view

One particularly important aspect of DBMSs is that they can provide 'views' of the database. That is they can present a subset of the data to those who need it. Staff in the accounts department will get a different subset of the data to work on than staff in human resources. But, the data all belongs to the same enterprise-wide database and, importantly, each data item is stored just once, so everyone always gets a view of the one up-to-date version.

The external view is the user friendly face that users of the database see. It is typically designed as a set of forms containing form objects to make work easier.

This example shows a form for the selection of an existing client so that details can be checked or changed. It has five text boxes, a drop down box and a command button.

Conceptual (logical) view

This view of a database is for the database designer. It shows how the component parts of the database are constructed and fit together. It can be used to create the database in a visual way.

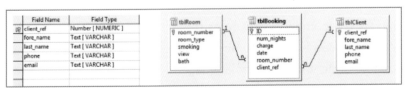

Alternatively, a query language can be used to achieve the same result programmatically. Here are some examples of how structured query language (SQL) can create or alter data tables or select data from an existing table.

```
CREATE TABLE customer                  ALTER TABLE customer ADD
(First_Name char(50),                  Gender char(1);
Last_Name char(50),
Address char(50),
City char(50),                         SELECT store_name
Country char(25),                      FROM
Birth_Date date)                       Store_Information
                                       WHERE Sales > 1000
```

Internal (physical) view

The stored data is, of course, a stream of bytes, like all other data stored in a computer system. The DBMS makes it possible for most designers and users to ignore this detail and work more easily with what interests them. Here is a dump of data from one part of a database.

memory addresses | Bytes of data – each takes 2 hex digits

```
1385:0000      20 FF 9F 00 9A EE FE-1D F0 4F 03 E9 0D 8A 03
1385:0010   E9 0D 17 03 E9 0D 11 04-01 01 01 00 02 FF FF FF
1385:0020   FF FF FF FF FF FF FF FF-FF FF FF FF 8D 0D 4E 01
1385:0030   A9 12 14 00 18 00 85 13-FF FF FF FF 00 00 00 00
1385:0040   05 00 00 00 00 00 00 00-00 00 00 00 00 00 00 00
1385:0050   CD 21 CB 00 00 00 00 00-00 00 00 00 00 20 20 20
1385:0060   20 20 20 20 20 20 20 20-00 00 00 00 00 20 20 20
1385:0070   20 20 20 20 20 20 20 20-00 00 00 00 00 00 00 00
1385:0080   00
```

Concurrency

In most large data handling operations, it is necessary for a database to be accessible to many users at the same time. Imagine if the hotel booking system were available online. Hundreds of potential customers could be looking to make bookings at the same time. This availability to many is called concurrency. This could be a source of problems. Imagine that Fred is looking at booking a room on 20 May 2013 and so is Bridget. Suppose there is just one room left for that day. Fred makes a booking but doesn't confirm it because he's still thinking about it. Bridget does the same thing. If they both confirm while the room record is open, there could be a double booking.

To avoid concurrency problems, most DBMSs use a record locking mechanism. That means that when one user is looking at a record, the record becomes locked to any other user. Others may look at the record but not change it. When the first user has finished, the record becomes unlocked again. This prevents conflicting updates.

ACID

A change to a database is called a transaction. Transactions must be controlled in order to prevent conflicting changes being made. To ensure this, every transaction must conform to what are called the **ACID** rules. ACID stands for:

Atomicity

This means that the transaction is either completely carried out or not at all. A transaction might involve several steps. A bank transfer will involve debiting one account and crediting another. It must not be possible to do just part of this. If any part of a transaction fails, the whole transaction fails and the database remains in its original state.

Consistency

A transaction must take the database from one valid state to another. It must not break any rules such as those of referential integrity.

Isolation

No transaction may interfere with any other transaction. So, it should not normally be possible for two transactions to be operating at the same time on one record because the results could be unpredictable.

Durability

Once a transaction has been committed, it must remain so, even in the case of an error or power failure.

Features offered by a DBMS

Queries

Queries are objects that extract data from a database. They are used to select the fields required and the conditions that need to be met. One common way to create a query is to use an interactive graphic tool called 'query by example' (QBE). This allows you to drag in the tables you want to query and enter the criteria you need to select the data.

The following query shows how details of bookings of rooms with a view can be selected.

Key term

ACID: A set of rules that protects a database from errors during a transaction

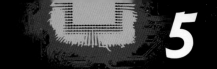

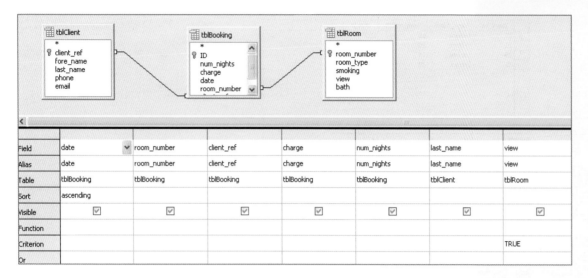

Field	date		room_number	client_ref	charge	num_nights	last_name	view
Alias	date		room_number	client_ref	charge	num_nights	last_name	view
Table	tblBooking		tblBooking	tblBooking	tblBooking	tblBooking	tblClient	tblRoom
Sort	ascending							
Visible	☑		☑	☑	☑	☑	☑	☑
Function								
Criterion								TRUE
Or								

Here is a query that makes use of more than one criterion to extract data. It is looking for who has made bookings after 20 September 2011 for rooms with a view. The lower part of the query screen shows the selection criteria and the top part shows the output.

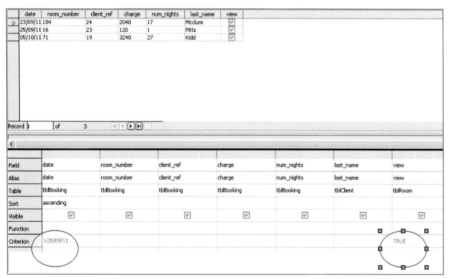

date	room_number	client_ref	charge	num_nights	last_name	view
23/09/11	184	24	2040	17	Mcclure	☑
25/09/11	16	23	120	1	Pitts	☑
05/10/11	71	19	3240	27	Kidd	☑

Record 1 of 3

Field	date	room_number	client_ref	charge	num_nights	last_name	view
Alias	date	room_number	client_ref	charge	num_nights	last_name	view
Table	tblBooking	tblBooking	tblBooking	tblBooking	tblBooking	tblClient	tblRoom
Sort	ascending						
Visible	☑	☑	☑	☑	☑	☑	☑
Function							
Criterion	>20/09/11						TRUE

The following query selects the fields client_ref, last_name, num_nights and charge for the client whose reference number is 25.

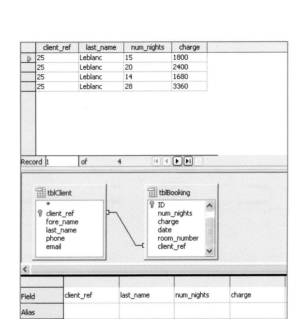

QBE is an easy way to create a query, but it is not always the best. Programmers have more control over what they do by writing a query using a query language. SQL (Structured Query Language) is a popular one and some DBMSs have their own integral SQL capability.

The query above could be programmed like this in SQL:

```
SELECT "tblClient"."client _ ref", "tblClient"."last _ name",
"tblBooking"."num _ nights", "tblBooking"."charge" FROM "tblBooking",
"tblClient" WHERE "tblBooking"."client _ ref" = "tblClient"."client _ ref"
AND "tblClient"."client _ ref" = 25
```

Notice the use of the linking word AND in this statement. We want details of clients who made bookings AND only for client number 25. If we want to select data based on two conditions being true, we link them with AND. If we want to select data based on either of two conditions, we use the linking word OR.

Here is a QBE query that asks for client_ref, last_name, num_ nights and charge, for anyone who spent more than 5 nights at the hotel **or** spent more that £3000.

Field	client_ref	▼	last_name	num_nights	charge
Alias					
Table	tblClient		tblClient	tblBooking	tblBooking
Sort					
Visible	☑		☑	☑	☑
Function					
Criterion				> 5	
Or					> 3000

Notice that the second condition is placed on a row marked OR.

The same query in SQL also shows the OR condition.

```
SELECT "tblClient"."client _ ref", "tblClient"."last _ name",
"tblBooking"."num _ nights", "tblBooking"."charge" FROM
"tblBooking", "tblClient" WHERE ( "tblBooking"."num _ nights" > 5 OR
"tblBooking"."charge" > 3000 )
```

Forms

The average database user does not want to use SQL queries directly to find or change data. This would require programming expertise and would take a lot of time. On-screen forms are usually provided for users so that the information needed is easy to see and modify. Forms can be made very user friendly and they sit on top of hidden program code that does the work of finding or changing data. This form shows what a clerk would see when booking in a new customer.

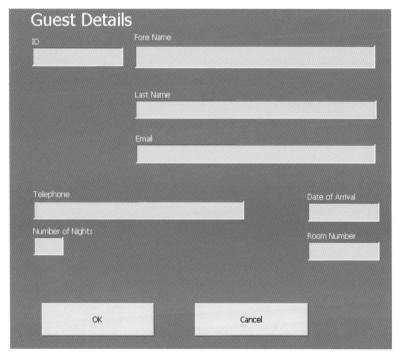

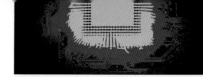

Reports

These are often the printed output of data from the database. They can be tables of data or fully formatted and well-presented reports for management. They are usually based on queries that have done the work of extracting and collating the fields required.

Here is part of a report for the hotel management about room usage.

Room Number	16			
	Date	*Client Ref*	*Number of Nights*	*Name*
	25/09/11	23	1	Pitts
	07/06/11	26	13	Kelly
Room Number	**20**			
	Date	*Client Ref*	*Number of Nights*	*Name*
	03/02/11	27	14	Sullivan
Room Number	**24**			
	Date	*Client Ref*	*Number of Nights*	*Name*
	16/08/11	11	10	Barber

Data mining

When a company has a very large collection of data, it can represent a valuable resource in ways that the company might never have anticipated. Imagine a chain of hotels with huge amounts of historical data about clients, bookings, room use, functions, staffing, catering and many other aspects of running the business. They will probably have good systems to look after each of these aspects of their business.

However, the business might want to look at connections between the data, such as are certain types of meal popular at certain times of the year or what types of rooms are booked during holiday periods. It is probable that the database applications don't have this sort of ability built in. Also, the managers might not even know what questions to ask when they are looking at the effectiveness of their business.

Data mining is using software to trawl through data from many sources, looking for connections. It is at its most useful when it shows up surprising things.

Computing in context

Shopping

Supermarkets have always kept track of how people shop, but in the last few years the extent to which retailers collect data has rocketed. Tesco owns a majority stake in Dunnhumby Ltd, which carries out data mining and analysis for a large group of retailers including Coca-Cola, BT, Mars, Vodafone and other leading brands. Dunnhumby operates the Tesco Clubcard scheme. Using data collected from the scheme, Tesco can predict when people will shop, how they'll pay for their items and even how many calories they will consume. Dunnhumby recently reported a 32 per cent rise in operating profits to £53.4 million, and has grown from 300 employees at the start of 2007 to nearly 1,250 in 2012. The data collected by Dunnhumby has changed the way we shop.

Source: *The Daily Telegraph.*

Summary

- Databases are at the heart of most computer applications.
- Databases provide up-to-date data for many users.
- Databases are usually managed by a Database Management System (DBMS).
- A DBMS separates data from the applications that use the data.
- Most databases are relational.
- Relational databases are designed to reduce data redundancy and to protect data from harmful transactions.

Questions

1. Data handling applications usually work through a DBMS. Explain why this is a desirable practice.
2. What is the purpose of a query in a database?
3. What is meant by the physical view of a database?
4. Why is record locking used in multi-user databases?
5. Explain why a supermarket might make use of data mining.

Extension tasks

1 Look at the program in Figure 5.1.

   a Identify the variables.

   b Identify two functions.

   c Identify two methods.

   d Identify a loop.

   e Describe how the loop is terminated.

2 Here are some methods of automated data entry:
   Bar codes, OCR, OMR, RFID, Smart cards.

   ■ For each method, identify a situation where it is used.

3 Describe the binary search algorithm in pseudocode.

4 Using the hotel room booking database described in this chapter:

   a Construct a query using QBE to show the last name and the number of nights for all customers who spent more than 20 nights at the hotel.

   b Show the same query in SQL code.

Exam style questions

1 Here are two tables in a relational database, used for recording students and the examinations they will take.

   TblStudent

   student_number

   surname

   forename

   date_of_birth

   gender

   TblExam_entry

   exam_number

   subject_name

   level

   exam_organisation

   a   State the primary key of TblStudent.   [1 mark]

   b   An extra table is needed in order to allow the recording of exam entry information. State the fields needed in this table.   [3 marks]

   c   Draw a diagram to show the links between all three tables.   [4 marks]

d State the data types needed for the following fields:

   i   surname   [1 mark]

   ii   date of birth   [1 mark]

   iii gender.   [1 mark]

2 Here is some data from TblStudent:

student_number	surname	forename	date_of_birth	gender
1564	Pate	Claire	28/06/1999	f
1787	Landry	Virginia	23/01/1974	f
1897	Goodwin	James	26/09/1984	m
1978	Hodge	Callie	05/07/1978	f
1979	Pugh	William	23/06/1984	m

a State the names of the students who would be shown if the following queries were run. [4 marks]

- SELECT surname WHERE date_of_birth<01/01/1984 AND gender="f"
- SELECT surname WHERE student_number>1897 OR gender="f"

b Describe a query that would show the exams entered by all students with a date of birth earlier than 20 March 2008. [4 marks]

3 Describe how **a** a form and **b** a report might be used in the development of this database. [4 marks]

## Chapter 6

Computer communications and networking

In this chapter, you will learn about the great importance of computer networking and how networks are put together. We shall look at the components of a network and different ways of arranging them.

What are networks?

A stand-alone computer is any computer that is not connected to another. This used to be normal when there were fewer computers than there are today. Computers were fed the data that they needed and they gave back the processed information to the user. This applied to large mainframes as well as to personal computers. It became clear that data processing could be far more efficient if computers were linked together. After all, they all used the same binary representation of data. They moved around bytes of data inside themselves as electrical pulses. It is not that big a step to connect computers together so that they can share signals. What was needed was the infrastructure, the cabling, the software, shared ways of doing things and of course the human expertise. The advantages of linking computers were so great that ways were devised to make it possible for computers to 'talk' to each other.

A network is a set of connected computers and other devices in order to share resources.

The resources are information, application software and hardware. Networks also make it a lot easier for people to communicate.

Imagine two computers connected together. This can be by wire, radio, infrared or any other feasible means. With a connection, it is possible to send data between them. All networking stems from this idea: from a simple Bluetooth upload, to a mobile phone, to the entire internet. Nowadays, most computing devices are networked, even if only some of the time.

Advantages and disadvantages of networks

Advantages of networks

Networks have become vital to businesses because they allow groups of users to share and exchange information very easily. Networks bring people and data together, which improves productivity.

Workgroups

Groups of users can easily send data to each other over networks. It is easy to work collaboratively if you and your colleagues have connected computers. Databases can be interrogated and updated by teams of people working at the same time. Documents can be passed between workers who can edit and update them. The production of this book was made easier because the authors, editors, designers and publisher all sent files back and forth in order to polish up the product and to share ideas. Without networking, it would have taken much longer to put it all together.

Shared databases

Centralised databases are made possible by networking. As we have seen in Chapter 5, if a single master copy of data is maintained on a central **server**, then all those who work with it will have access to the latest correct version of the data. Without networks, such everyday activities as making bookings, checking bank accounts, making phone calls and placing orders for goods would become less reliable and much slower.

Distributed systems

With networked computers, it is possible to hold data and software anywhere. It is possible to divide a problem into parts and solve the parts independently on different computers, then share the results. This makes sense if a particular problem is best solved by a number of low-end computers rather than investing in a more expensive and powerful computer. Also, there is no single point of failure; there can be spare capacity in the distributed system in case of individual computers failing.

It may also make sense for certain activities to be handled in different places. In an international company, it might make sense if the payroll for each country is processed locally, to take account of the special conditions in that location. Connecting the systems then allows managers to see the whole picture when making strategic decisions.

The following diagram shows how data and processing can take place at multiple sites with data sharing across a WAN (see page 126). In this case, it is concerning processing image data from satellites using Picture Transfer Protocol (PTP). Each site has its own special activities to carry out so that it makes sense to concentrate the data and software for an activity locally.

Key term

Server: Software that provides services to a client, or the hardware that is running it

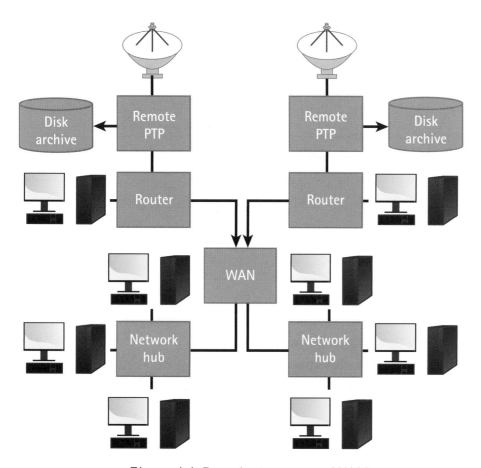

Figure 6.1 Data sharing across a WAN

Communications

Networks are good for sharing data. This data can be about anything. It is as easy to send an email across the world as it is within an office. Networks have made all this possible. Using networks for communication can go much further than that. Speech is easily converted into digital signals, as we saw in Chapter 4. So is visual information. This allows networks to be used for video conferences, which can save a lot of time and money that would otherwise be spent on travelling. Anyone can use the internet for live voice and visual communication with applications such as instant messaging or VoIP (Voice over Internet Protocol) telephony services such as Skype.

Device sharing

There is no need to buy a laser printer for everyone in an organisation. With networks, it is possible to position a printer and other peripherals at strategic places so that print jobs can be sent to them from many **client** machines.

Figure 6.2 Video conferencing

Key term

Client: Software or hardware that requests services from a server

Software sharing and maintenance

It is usually possible to store software on the hard disk of any station on a network. Many users like to have their own choice of software installed on their own computers. But it makes sense to install common software on a server so that when it is updated, there is no need to go around updating many computers.

Networks help in providing a service to users. If an individual suffers a problem on a client machine, it is an easy matter to reinstall the whole hard disk image from a server rather than build the configuration from scratch.

Security

With all workers in an organisation connected to a network, it becomes possible to fine tune the resources that they can access. This central control can ensure that a company has a standard security policy about who is allowed to do what. If any security breaches occur, it is easier to track down the problem if all activities are handled centrally in a network.

Disadvantages of networks

In most cases, the advantages outweigh the disadvantages, which is why networks are so widespread. But, there are still some issues that have to be taken into account when setting up a network:

Expertise

Building and maintaining a network requires know-how. In a large organisation it may be necessary to employ teams of analysts and technicians in order to design the right networks and keep them running all the time without problems. This can be expensive. One way around this is to outsource the running of the networks. It is possible for an external company to do the maintenance work remotely (from any distance) so that the organisation does not need to employ as many staff.

Outsourcing can go much further. Some companies now offer software as a service (SaaS). This means that the software is located and run remotely and the company using the service no longer has to worry about updating software on its own network as well as other network maintenance problems.

Computing in Context

Here is an advertisement for a remotely run SaaS maintenance scheme:

Good News for Service Management Departments
You no longer have to worry about finding skilled practitioners to support your enterprise-wide IT. No more expensive courses to make sure that your team members are all ITIL qualified. Cloud Nine Services will take care of all your service management requirements for a fraction of your present costs.

- ITIL based approach ensures that solutions are tailored for your business and meet all accepted standards.
- Services available immediately.
- Training and support of your on-site help staff.
- Fully automated help desk solutions.
- Upgrades included and automatically installed.
- Easy to use intuitive interface.
- Greatly improved problem resolution.

www.cloudninesaas.co.uk

Security

Networks can help unauthorised people gain access to data because their connections can provide a pathway to what they are looking for. Network managers have to be vigilant in protecting company data from prying eyes. They must ensure that the users follow company policies which might include:

- using strong passwords – this means them being long enough, using characters other than just letters and choosing difficult to guess passwords
- changing passwords often
- not installing software from unknown sources – it may contain Trojans
- not visiting certain websites – this can be enforced by suitable firewall rules
- logging out after use.

If a company has wireless networking facilities, there must be even more security measures because there is no need to be physically connected in order for intruders to access the network.

Networks and modern life

Much of modern life would be impossible without computer networks. Anything at all that involves going online to the internet immediately makes use of many networks. All schools and universities have networks that help their students to do work, as well as handling administration. Most companies have networks to allow their workers to collaborate and access the information they need.

Networks allow business and other organisations to share information. For example, it is possible to renew car tax online. When someone does this, several networks are involved:

- The telephone network connects the taxpayer to the DVLA (Driver and Vehicle Licensing Agency).
- The DVLA has a network so that its staff can carry out their work.
- The DVLA computers are connected to the insurance company networks to check that the vehicle has valid insurance.
- The DVLA computers contact MOT records to see if the car has a valid MOT certificate.
- The DVLA computers contact the taxpayer's bank to collect the payment.

A lot is going on, but the taxpayer only has to make a few clicks to complete the transaction.

This is just one example of how networks make life more convenient.

Computing in context

Every time you use an automated teller machine (ATM) you are immediately using a number of networks. At the very least, there is the telephone network, much of which is digital. This connects the various devices involved in a transaction. The banks maintain host computers that interact with the cash machines from various banks. These may be owned by a number of banks or by a third party. The host computers then connect to the relevant servers of each bank.

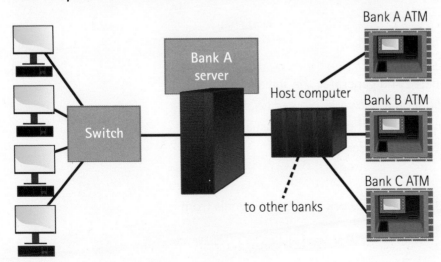

Computing in context

Networked computing devices are found in all sorts of places. A modern car may have up to 50 microprocessors in it. They carry out such jobs as:

- engine management
- airbag control
- cruise control
- climate control
- controlling anti-lock brakes
- power distribution
- emissions monitoring.

The main computer is called the engine control unit (ECU). This gathers data from dozens of sensors around the car. It can vary the engine performance by doing such things as changing the spark plug timing in order to maximise efficiency in changing conditions. The sensors and other devices communicate on a bus (no not a car!) and form a CAN, that is a controller area network.

If a sensor detects an abnormal condition, a code is generated and stored. A mechanic can then connect a laptop to the bus and download what are called trouble codes, which can help in diagnosing faults.

Car computers have helped to simplify wiring as well. When operating a switch from the driver's position, for example to lower the passenger window, it is no longer necessary to run a wire to take power to the relevant motor. A signal can be sent along the bus to the passenger door controller and the job is handled locally.

Network infrastructure

Network hardware

Network interface card (NIC)

This is the circuitry that prepares and generates the signals that are presented to the carrier medium on a network. Nowadays, because most computers need to be networked, the circuitry is usually integrated onto the motherboard of the computer.

Terminator

A device attached to the end of a bus network to prevent signals from bouncing.

Repeaters

Any signal transmitted along a medium, will lose integrity because of what is called attenuation. In other words, the signal weakens and the information it carries may become corrupted. A repeater cleans up a message and then sends it on to the next segment of the network.

Hubs

Hubs are effectively repeaters, but they have more than one output port. They can boost a signal but they then send it onto all the devices connected to the output ports. Only the intended receiver of the data will actually process it. If a network is extended by adding more hubs, the network may slow down because with the extra traffic, there will be more collisions.

Hubs and repeaters can also be useful in connecting different network media, such as a copper wire cable with a fibre optic line.

Key term

Hub: A device for connecting multiple network devices in one segment

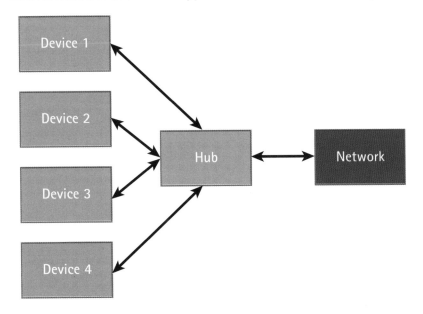

Figure 6.3 Devices connected to a network via a hub

Bridges

Bridges are devices that can connect different network segments as well as different media. They can operate on data packets and send them to the right segment. Bridges can help to speed up a network's performance. When they receive a packet, they check the MAC address of the sending device against a list of addresses that they hold. If it is for a different segment, they forward it. If it is for a device on the same segment, they assume it has been delivered and discard it. This reduces the amount of unnecessary traffic.

Switches

A **switch** is a high speed bridge. It is high speed because it has a dedicated CPU that is designed purely to perform switching operations. A bridge has a general purpose CPU and it uses software to route packets to segments. A switch can create and connect different segments of a network. This reduces network traffic because much of the data is confined to the segment where it is needed instead of being broadcast across the entire network. Switches are described as Level 2 if they identify computers by hardware MAC addresses and Level 3 if they use IP addressing.

Routers

Routers work with data packets. They are important when there are completely independent networks such as with different departments in a university or with internet connections. A department may have its own network with hardware and facilities designed especially for their needs. Another department may have a totally different set up. A router allows data to be sent between them.

Types of network

There are several common classes of network. They differ in terms of performance, security, ease of set up and expense.

Peer-to-peer

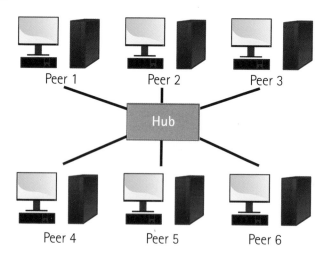

Figure 6.4 A peer-to-peer network

In a **peer-to-peer** network, all computers are equal. No computer has priority over any other. Every user is a network administrator and has to control their own machine. Access can be given to anyone else on the network. You just give them a password. There are no

Key terms

Switch: A device for connecting multiple network devices and multiple segments

Peer-to-peer: A network arrangement where all computers are equal

restrictions on how a peer-to-peer network is organised. It is up to the owner to decide what software and files go on what computers. Printers and other devices can be attached to any of them.

A peer-to-peer network will often make use of a hub in order to connect the computers.

Most operating systems make it easy to set up a peer-to-peer network. They can be very flexible. But they have many disadvantages and can quickly become chaotic:

■ No network-wide security is in place – security is up to each user.
■ They soon become unworkable because the users have too much to worry about.
■ A machine slows down when being accessed by another.
■ A user might restart a machine when someone else is accessing it.
■ It is difficult to keep track of who has what information.
■ Backup becomes complicated.

However, if the requirements are simple and there are ten or fewer users, they can be a workable solution. They might be suitable in a home or small office.

Client-server

This is the commonest network model in medium to large organisations. One or more computers are designated as servers. These provide services to the rest of the machines on the network, which are called clients.

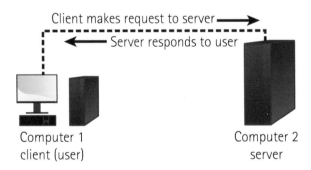

Client makes request to server ⟶
⟵ Server responds to user

Computer 1
client (user)

Computer 2
server

Figure 6.5 A client-server relationship

A client-server network has advantages over a peer-to-peer network:

■ Central control of security.
■ Easier to supervise network performance.
■ Easier to perform software upgrades.
■ Faster performance because of fewer data collisions.
■ Client machines freed up to perform their jobs.
■ Easier to perform backups.

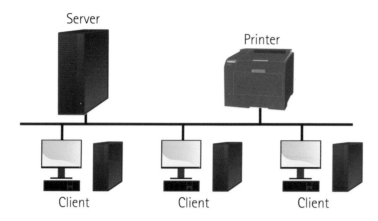

Figure 6.6 A client-server network

There are some disadvantages of a client-server network, mostly to do with expense:

- A knowledgeable administrator is needed.
- Only the administrator can set up access and enforce security rules.
- The administrator normally has enough work to do to justify paying a separate person to carry out this role.
- There is more infrastructure to set up with wiring cabinets to install and building work may be necessary.
- If a server malfunctions, it will have more impact on work than if one peer is lost on a peer-to-peer network.

Servers

You should remember that the word server can refer to the software that provides services to clients or the computer which runs it. Most people think of servers as hardware, but this is only part of the story. Hardware servers are typically high-end machines that are capable of handling multiple requests at high speed.

Application servers

A server can be the location of a database and the software that handles it. The querying and analysis of data is carried out by DBMS software on the server such as Microsoft SQL server or MySQL. Applications are written to run on the servers and work with the DBMS.

Usually the client machines will have special client software that sends requests to the database handling applications. The client software receives the data that it has requested and formats it for the user.

6

Communication servers

These provide an entry point to a network for external users. These are useful for workers who are travelling or are working from home.

File and print servers

These are the most common servers that are found on most networks. They allow users to work and run software from their local workstations, but store their data centrally on the server. They usually provide access to central print facilities, so that there is no need for each workstation to have a range of printers connected directly.

Mail servers

Users of web mail such as Hotmail, Yahoo and Gmail make use of someone else's servers which are situated remotely. When you log on to one of these services, you are connecting to servers which are storing your messages. Your browser acts as a client and you can use it to request messages to be forwarded to you.

Large organisations commonly have their own email facilities which are stored and processed on their own email servers. These act in the same way as web mail but the company has total control over what can be stored and sent.

Web servers

Increasingly, large networks run on TCP/IP. This allows them to be set up as **intranets**, using the same features as the wider internet. This is particularly helpful because it becomes easier to integrate services with the internet and also because users will be familiar with the tools to access it. Users need no special software to interact with the stored data as they will have browsers on their client machines.

Network server operating systems normally provide the web server software that is needed to make use of web technology. Web server software delivers HTML pages, images, style sheets and scripts to the remote user's browser.

Windows Server software is one common example. It includes FTP software to allow the uploading of data to reside on the server disks. The Apache web server is widely used on many platforms including Linux.

Web servers are also embedded in many devices such as webcams, routers and printers so that they can make use of TCP/IP networks.

Key term

Intranet: A private data resource using the same technology as the internet, such as browsers and protocols

Topologies

All computers communicate in the same way. They prepare a
signal to send to an address and place it on a transmission medium.
However, the way in which the computers are laid out varies and can
have effects on the cost and performance of a network. There are
three topologies that you need to know about – bus, ring and star.

Bus

A bus network has a single backbone cable and all the devices are
attached to it.

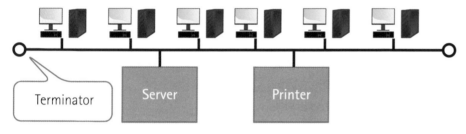

Figure 6.7 A bus network layout

When a message is sent, it is divided into chunks and sent in both
directions along the cable. All the computers on the network
receive it. Only the one addressed accepts it. On a bus network, all
computers share the medium. Only one can transmit at a time. They
might have to wait if the network is busy. With enough users, the
wait can make the network unusable.

The signal passes along the cable in both directions until it
weakens or is absorbed by a device. If it reaches the end, it bounces
back. Bounces also affect the performance of a network, because
they add enormously to the traffic and cause data collisions.
Terminators are attached at the cable ends in order to prevent the
signals from bouncing. If the cable breaks, there will be bouncing from
the broken end and the network breaks down.

Bus networks are very simple to set up, but they are only suitable
for very small network installations.

Ring

The devices are arranged in a circle. Each computer is responsible
for passing the message on. One way to implement a ring network is
by token passing. With this, a packet called a token passes from one
computer to the next. If a computer has data to send, it modifies it.
When received at the intended destination, the receiving device sends
a message back to the sender acknowledging safe delivery. A ring

topology guarantees that a computer can send a message because there is no need to wait.

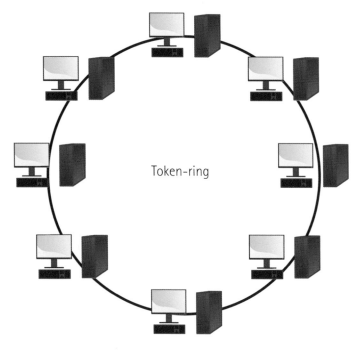

Figure 6.8 Token passing layout

Star

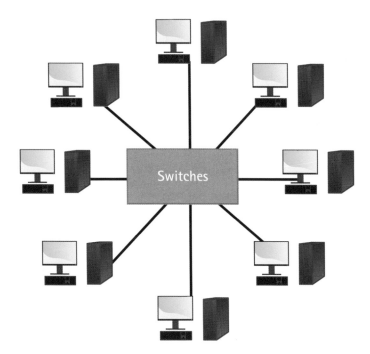

Figure 6.9 A star network layout

This is the most common way to set up a network. All connections are to a central device such as a wiring cabinet with switches.

Installation of a star network is labour intensive as the cable often has to go through walls and ceilings or under floors. It is a skilled job to wire up the cabinets and all the connecting leads, but the network performance is faster than a bus. Also, if one part of the network is damaged, it does not necessarily affect the entire network.

Classification of networks

There are other ways to categorise networks. The extent of a network is another way of looking at them.

LAN

A **LAN** is a local area network. It is still the commonest configuration of a network for most businesses, although this is likely to change gradually. A LAN is a network located at one site. The site might be one building or it might be several buildings such as a single university campus. The infrastructure is normally owned by the organisation that uses the network. In other words, the cabling and the hardware are the owner's responsibility.

WAN

Sometimes a LAN needs to connect to other LANs. An organisation may have several branches, anywhere in the world and it is an advantage to connect the networks together. That way, all the employees can access a common data source, with all the efficiencies that entails.

Widely spread LANs that are connected make up a **WAN** or wide area network. These differ from a LAN, not only in geographical spread, but also in the ownership of the connecting media. The different parts of the WAN are connected by telecom companies who own the infrastructure and charge for its use.

MAN

A MAN is a metropolitan area network. It covers a wide but defined area such as a city. It normally uses public communication links, is owned by more than one organisation and is often provided as a public utility.

PAN

A PAN or personal area network is usually also a wireless personal network (WPAN). It is set up by and for one or a few individuals to connect a range of devices such as a:
- phone to car radio system for hands-free operation
- PC to a phone to synchronise address books
- laptop to a portable printer so that a tradesman can print an invoice at any location.

Key terms

LAN: Local area network – confined to one location
WAN: Wide areas network – covers large geographical area

There are various technologies in use for WPANs such as Bluetooth, which is a short range wireless standard. Infrared radiation networks use the same technology as television remote controls, but unlike Bluetooth it cannot penetrate walls.

Figure 6.10 A network interface in a car

VPN

Physical networks can be costly and difficult to maintain, so some organisations outsource their whole network operation. A VPN (virtual private network) is a secure simulated network that uses insecure public facilities such as the internet to provide connectivity. Security is the main challenge with a VPN. Enhanced encryption is used to prevent data falling into the wrong hands.

A VPN provides exactly the same services as a physical network, such as access to company data, printers and websites. It saves money because there is no need to invest in special network hardware and cabling.

Network media

Network media connect the devices on a network. There are several common technologies:

Copper cable

Most large-scale LANs use copper cable. For this, the devices need a network interface card (NIC). The cabling is usually configured as an unshielded twisted pair (UTP). This is fairly thin and this makes it quite easy to install as it can easily be passed through conduits.

Coaxial cable is used in some networks because it is easy to install over a short distance and protects signals from outside interference.

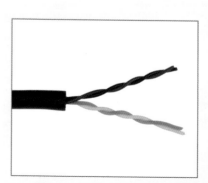

Figure 6.11 UTP cable

This is achieved by shielding the conductor with a layer of metal braid. It is quite bulky and can be unsuitable for wiring up large buildings.

Plastic jacket

Metal shield

Dielectric insulator

Centre core

Figure 6.12 Coaxial cable

Fibre optic cable

Signals can be sent between devices using light which can be modulated in order to carry a signal. It is transmitted along glass fibres and is totally internally reflected in the fibre so it can travel long distances. Fibre optic cable has the advantage of not being subject to interference and its signals lose less strength than those in metal cables.

Fibre optic cable, unlike metal cable, does not deteriorate in open air locations. It also carries a wider bandwidth than metal. On the other hand, it is more expensive to buy and requires more expensive associated hardware.

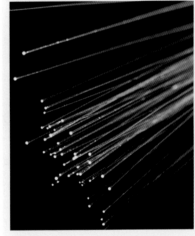

Figure 6.13 Optical fibre

Wireless

Wireless networks – otherwise known as Wi-Fi – are often used as part of a wider installation. They allow flexible additions to the network. If visitors need to access a network, it is a simple matter to provide permission so that they can connect to it using their own laptop.

Wireless poses extra security problems because any Wi-Fi enabled computer (and these days that is most) can 'see' the wireless signals. In order to reduce these risks, network managers protect the wireless access by:

- Hiding the wireless broadcast service set identifier (SSID). This prevents anyone knowing that there is a wireless access point and may discourage snoopers.
- Restricting access to authorised MAC addresses.
- Using Wi-Fi protected access (WPA) encryption so that the signals cannot be read by outsiders.

Wi-Fi gives slower access to a network than cable connections but its flexibility often outweighs this disadvantage.

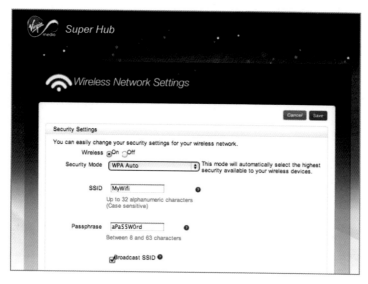

Figure 6.14 A Wi-Fi configuration screen

Summary

Networking is one of the most commercially important aspects of modern business. Considerable resources go into making it as reliable and safe as possible. Networking provides highly skilled and rewarding employment for many computing professionals. There are many ways to construct a network which vary in cost and effectiveness. The biggest network in the world is the internet and that continues to change all our lives.

Questions

1. Describe the type of network that is suitable for ten or more users.
2. State three resources that are commonly shared on a network.
3. What are computers that can provide services but also request services off other computers called?
4. What is a star network layout?
5. Two colleges are three miles apart in the same city. They each have a LAN. When these are connected, what is the resulting network called?
6. A small company has a tight budget and four workers. Describe the type of network that is suitable for them.
7. What is the difference between a LAN and a WAN?
8. Explain what is meant by a client computer.
9. What hardware is needed to connect any device to a network?
10. What is a network switch?

Extension tasks

Think about making a booking for a flight. What networks are likely to be accessed during the process? What servers might be needed?

Networks in action

Protocols

For computers to communicate, they need to be able to:

- interpret signals
- identify themselves
- identify others
- initiate an exchange
- end an exchange
- manage information exchange.

Protocols are the rules used for devices to communicate. There are many protocols that have been developed over the years. They are generally known by acronyms such as TCP/IP, NetBEUI and IPX.

TCP/IP is the one we need to look at here. It stands for Transmission Control Protocol/Internet Protocol. TCP/IP is a set of rules that looks after data transmission on the internet. Many LANs make use of the same set of rules. It is important to have a common protocol for the internet, even if the connected LANs have their own. Imagine a French speaker trying to speak to a German who does not speak French. If they can both communicate in English, they have to use that when they talk to each other. TCP/IP allows networks of different types to communicate with each other.

Other protocols are used for particular purposes on the internet:

Protocol	Meaning	Application
DNS	**Domain Name** System	Translates domain names such as ocr.org.uk into **IP addresses**
TLS/SSL	Transport Layer Security/ Secure Sockets Layer	Cryptographic protocols designed for secure communications
FTP	File Transfer Protocol	For copying files from one host to another
Gopher	–	An early means of searching for files on the internet
HTTP	Hypertext Transfer Protocol	For distributing hypermedia files – essentially web pages
IMAP	Internet Message Access Protocol	One method for accessing emails
POP3	Post Office Protocol (version 3)	Another method for accessing emails, used by most webmail services
Telnet	–	Allows bi-directional text communications on a network

Specification content

(a) Explain the terms IP addressing, MAC addressing, packet and protocols

(b) Explain the need for security measures in networks, such as user access levels, suitable passwords and encryption techniques

(c) Describe and justify network policies such as acceptable use, disaster recovery, failover, backup, archiving

Key terms

Protocol: A set of rules or standards that control communication between devices

Domain name: A human readable name for a resource on a network. It is changed to a numerical IP address by a DNS server

IP address: A number that identifies a device on a TCP/IP network

IP address

Each computer on a TCP/IP network has an IP address. This is a 32-bit numerical identifier, for example, 10000011 01101011 00010000 11001000. Each group of eight bits is called an octet. Each octet can store numbers ranging from 0 to 255. Binary digits are hard for a human to work with, so the address is normally quoted in four groups of decimal numbers, for example, 131.107.32.200. IP addresses can be permanently allocated to a device (static addressing), but they can alternatively be allocated as needed (dynamic addressing), so a particular computer will not always have the same IP address each time it connects. This saves the network administrator effort and makes efficient use of the addresses available. Most switches are what is known as level 3 switches. These can locate a resource on a network by its IP address.

Because of the huge growth of the internet, in order to make sure that there are enough addresses, there has been a move towards 128-bit addresses.

When you access a web page on the internet, you have to tell your browser the address to go to. Long numbers are hard to remember, so we normally use domain names like ocr.org.uk instead. There are special servers called DNS servers that convert domain names such as ocr.org.uk into numerical IP addresses.

MAC address

MAC stands for Media Access Control. Each physical interface connected to a network, such as a network card, has a unique number written to the device by the manufacturer. The MAC address is used to identify a device on a network. Some switches, known as level 2 switches use MAC addresses to identify devices on a network.

A MAC address is usually given as six pairs of hexadecimal numbers, for example, 01:1F:33:69:BC:14.

Packets and packet switching

The internet is a packet switching network. This means that data is sent as bundles of data called packets. Suppose an application wants to send a message, say a file, to another computer connected to the internet. The message is broken down into units. These units are packaged together with control information – where they have come from, where they are going to and extra information such as a checksum that allows them to be checked for accuracy.

The data is like a letter and the control information is a bit like the envelope with address.

Source address	Destination address	Packet sequence number	Data	Checksum

In a packet switching network, the packets are sent from one router to the next. Decisions are made about which route to take according to traffic conditions, so the data may arrive at the destination in a different order from when it was sent. The receiving device uses the packet numbers to reassemble the complete message. The availability of many routes is one of the reasons why the internet is so reliable. If one route is interrupted, there are usually more that can be used.

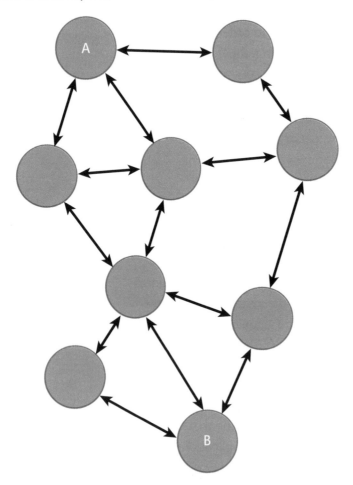

Figure 6.15 Sending a message from A to B, using many routers

Network software

Computers need special software to access a network. Network operating systems provide this capability by managing the resources of the network such as users, groups, files and services. They provide log on controls, so that each user is recognised by a user id. The operating system keeps a database of allowed users and what resources each user can access.

The resources that a user can access are controlled by what is known as an access level. Access levels are assigned by the network administrator and are designed to allow users to get what they need for their work, but no more than that. The highest access level is the network administrator, who can look at and change files throughout the network.

Most common operating systems provide features for some simple networking, but high performance servers will run dedicated server operating systems.

Bandwidth

Data is carried on a network by electrical signals on carrier waves. Bandwidth refers to the difference between the highest and the lowest frequencies that are carried on a transmission medium. However, the term bandwidth has also come to mean the data capacity or availability of a network. This affects the speed at which data can be moved. Bandwidth is measured in bits per second or multiples of it (for example, kilobits/s, megabits/s).

Bandwidth is important because a network can become unusable if the data transmission is too slow. If many users are using a single wireless access point, then the available bandwidth of the access point is shared among the users and can cause a significant loss of performance.

Security

Because organisations depend so much on their networks, it is vital that they are protected against failure or malicious acts. To gain access to a network, a user must enter a user id and a password. The user id determines what level of access will be available. The password should be strong, that is hard to guess. Most network managers insist on certain rules to ensure that users choose strong passwords. A strong password:

- contains letters and numbers
- contains other characters
- is long enough to be hard to guess

- should not be obvious like a pet's name
- should be changed regularly
- should be kept secret.

There are simple online checks that assess the strength of a password.

Figure 6.16 An online password strength checker

One way that can be used to gain unauthorised access to a network is to use what is called a brute force attack. In this, a program tries out every possible password until it gets the right one. Another common way to get a password is to ask for it! Many people quite innocently hand over passwords to someone who pretends to need it to do some work to a network.

Computing in context

In April 2011, intruders broke into Sony's PlayStation network services and stole personal details from 77 million account holders. The network was also put out of action for 23 days while the security problem was sorted out.

Encryption

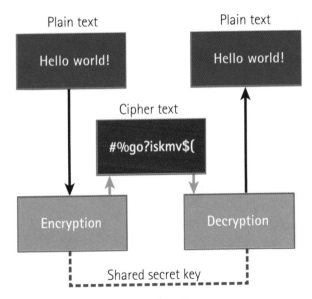

Figure 6.17 Use of an encryption key

Traffic that is sent over a network is usually encrypted so that if it falls into the wrong hands, it will not be usable. Encryption means transforming the message so that it cannot be understood except by someone who has the correct key – the information needed to decrypt the message.

Wireless network access is a problem for security because the broadcast signals can be picked up by anyone. There are plenty of cracking tools available online to help get past security features.

Wireless transmissions should be encrypted by using at least the 256-bit key that works with WPA (Wi-Fi Protected Access). A further safety precaution is to restrict network access to specific MAC addresses.

Network policies

Network security is most often breached because of human carelessness. It is common to find passwords written on Post-it notes stuck to filing cabinets. To avoid this, most companies have an acceptable use policy that all employees must sign up to. Most acceptable use polices include rules such as:

- using polite language online
- not revealing personal details
- not using the network for sending unsolicited mail
- not sending offensive documents or images
- not using the network for personal commercial purposes
- not defaming anyone
- not downloading programs.

Most such policies also include penalties that are imposed for any violations, such as suspending an account or dismissal.

Disasters

Disasters can and do happen. Networks can go wrong, earthquakes and fires happen. The loss of network services or data can be crippling for an organisation. Because of this, most have disaster recovery plans. These are policies, procedures and plans that are kept in readiness should the worst happen.

Disaster recovery plans usually contain three elements:

- prevention
- detection
- correction.

Prevention is often just a matter of staff using common sense. Locking doors, using strong passwords and employing security guards are all useful steps to take. Many procedural rules can be put in place to guard against data loss or theft. Firewalls must be used to restrict which external networks can connect to the company resources. They can also be set to restrict outgoing traffic and to detect unauthorised communications.

Detection can often be done automatically. Software can log accesses and report suspicious activity.

A full set of steps needs to be laid down concerning what to do to recover from a disaster. This includes who is responsible for what, as well as the action that must be taken.

Any disaster recovery plan must make use of backups. Data should be copied regularly and stored somewhere safe, normally off site. Backups can be of different types, depending on the needs of the business. Complete backups of all the company data are usually carried out regularly, but they may take a long time. Incremental backups are quicker and they are just backups of data that has changed.

More often these days, data is replicated off site as it is stored. The growth in cloud computing has made it easy and safe to use a third party provider to keep live copies of important data. Individuals can do this too, with simple online backup services.

Keeping IT running is another issue. Many companies have duplicate systems that kick in if there is a problem. Software keeps track of the health of the system and, if it detects a problem, it can instantly transfer control over to the mirror system, a process called **failover**.

Archiving is different. When data is no longer in regular use, it is copied and stored somewhere safe, just in case someone needs it one day. Then it is deleted from the working environment. A good example of archiving is the school records of pupils who have left. They may want a reference one day, but there is no need to have their details on the live system.

Key term

Failover: Automatic switching to a backup computer system in the event of system failure

Summary

Networks require rules for communication so that devices can understand each other. They also need to be expertly managed to avoid security and reliability problems. Security depends on policies as well as the common sense of all their users.

Questions

❶ What is meant by a network protocol?

❷ What is an IP address?

❸ What is the purpose of a router on a network?

❹ Explain what the term encryption means.

❺ What is an encryption key?

Extension tasks

1 Find out for your own school, college or home network what hardware is used to link devices together.

2 Find out if your school or college has a disaster recovery plan. Comment on how effective you think it would be.

Exam style questions

1 Which two of these are possible IP addresses?

   a 122.3.45.6

   b 256.34.55.7

   c 126.35.22.67.4

   d 126.57.68.33

   e 22.55.77

2 Explain why a web developer might use:

   a FTP

   b HTTP

3 Explain the purpose of a MAC address.

4 Identify four components of a data packet.

5 George wants to watch movies streamed from the internet on his computer. Explain why he needs a connection with high bandwidth.

6 Here are four user passwords. For each one explain how strong it is.

   a united

   b henry123

   c A3zY$x4r

   d secret

7 State two requirements of users that would be likely in an acceptable use policy.

8 Explain what a disaster recovery plan is.

The internet

In this section, we shall take a look at the most important and biggest network of them all. We shall look at some of the technology behind it and the file standards associated with it.

Nature of the internet

The internet is a network of networks. These networks are worldwide and can be very different from each other. The success of the internet is in no small way because it uses a standard set of protocols, allowing computers to communicate with each other. These protocols are all part of a family of protocols called TCP/IP (see page 130).

The internet is an infrastructure – a facility for sending data between computers. It is often confused with the world wide web, which is the collection of web pages hosted on the internet. The internet can be used for email, file sharing, telephone conversations and many other purposes in addition to looking at web pages.

Clients and servers

A typical surfer on the internet is using a computer as a client machine in order to access data from a server. On p.59 we saw how clients are systems that request services. Servers are systems that provide these services.

Clients and servers can be software or hardware or both. For example, a web browser is client software. The computer that is running it becomes a client machine while it is running the browser. There are many web browsers available and most people have their own favourites. They are usually supplied free and often bundled with an operating system. Windows installations supply Internet Explorer. Some users prefer to use the open source Mozilla Firefox. Google supplies Chrome. All browsers have certain features in common. They all retrieve information from the world wide web which they present to the user. They also allow the user to navigate around and between websites, using **hyperlinks**. Ideally, all browsers should present web pages in the same way; the way the web designer intended. In reality, there are sometimes differences. These may be caused when a website has not been tested with each of the browsers that are intended to display it.

Specification content

(a) Describe the nature of the internet as a worldwide collection of computer networks

(b) Describe the hardware needed to connect to the internet including modems, routers, etc.

(c) Explain the need for IP addressing of resources on the internet and how this can be facilitated by the role of DNS servers

(d) Explain the importance of HTML and its derivatives as a standard for the creation of web pages

(e) Describe common file standards associated with the internet such as JPG, GIF, PDF, MP3, MPEG

(f) Explain the importance of compressing files that are transmitted via the internet

(g) Describe the differences between lossy and lossless compression

Key term

Hyperlink: An item on a web page that directs the user to another location when clicked

6

Hardware needed to connect to the internet

Modems

Modem is short for modulator/demodulator. Computers process digital data, in other words, signals that are either 'on' or 'off'. Standard telephone systems are still mainly analogue – their signals vary in voltage between certain limits. This means that a computer's signal has to be converted to analogue if it is to use the standard telephone system (POTS – plain old telephone service). The incoming signal has to be converted in the other direction.

Originally, modems could only transmit data at fairly low rates – up to 300 bps (bits per second) but at their best they could sometimes manage 56 kbit/s (56 kilobits per second). Even this is not fast enough for comfortable internet connectivity.

ADSL allows a great improvement on these speeds. ADSL stands for asymmetric digital subscriber line. This takes advantage of the fact that most home users will download far more data than they upload. So, the system can be made asymmetric – with most of the bandwidth in the download direction. ADSL makes use of unused bandwidth in a POTS system and provides a fast broadband service. Broadband is considered to be a channel that delivers data at a minimum of 4 Mbit/s.

If a subscriber already has cable TV, it is possible to share the TV channel with data transmission. A cable modem is attached to the single cable and uses the same frequency band as the TV. Usually, 'up' and 'down' signals are kept separate.

Many broadband modems include the functions of a router with Ethernet and Wi-Fi ports.

Router

Large networks connect to digital transmission media using routers. The job of routers is to decide where a data packet should go. It uses a **configuration table** that contains information about:

- which connections lead to particular groups of addresses
- priorities for connections
- rules for handling traffic.

The router has to:

- Ensure that information doesn't go where it's not needed. This is to prevent large volumes of data from clogging the connections.
- Make sure that information gets to the intended destination.

Key term

Configuration table: A store of information about devices on a network

Routers are useful for joining two networks and they can sometimes translate different protocols used by them. The internet relies upon routers to ensure that data packets get delivered by the most efficient routes available at any given time.

Broadband routers make use of Ethernet standards in a home network. They usually include Wi-Fi access and reduce the need for cable connections.

IP addressing

Every network adapter on a network has a unique address, so that data can be delivered to it. This applies to the internet just as much as to a LAN. IP addresses are typically made of four 8-bit numbers (octets), for example 192.168.0.1. To allow many computers to be addressed, there will often be more than one IP address used to locate a particular computer. So, the computers on a LAN may each have a private IP address, whereas the router through which they connect to the internet has its own public IP address.

Routers make use of IP addresses in order to deliver data to the right place.

Because humans are not very good at remembering sets of numbers, many of the resources on the internet are given easily remembered names such as bbc.co.uk. Domain name servers translate the names into IP addresses.

HTML

We have seen how the success of the internet is very much because of the adoption of uniform standards. This allows communication between devices of different specifications and from many different manufacturers. The world wide web has its own standards and **HTML** (Hypertext Markup Language) forms the basis of all web pages. At its most basic level, each web page is a text document which could be written in any text editor. In addition to the text, there are instructions embedded which tell browsers how to display the text. Many of these instructions are in the form of tags which are mostly arranged in pairs, within angle brackets. So, `<h1>` tells the browser to display what follows in a top level (large) heading type and `</h1>` indicates to turn that type off again.

Here is a web page that has:

- a heading
- a table
- an image
- three links.

Key term

HTML: Hypertext mark up language – a text based system for defining web pages

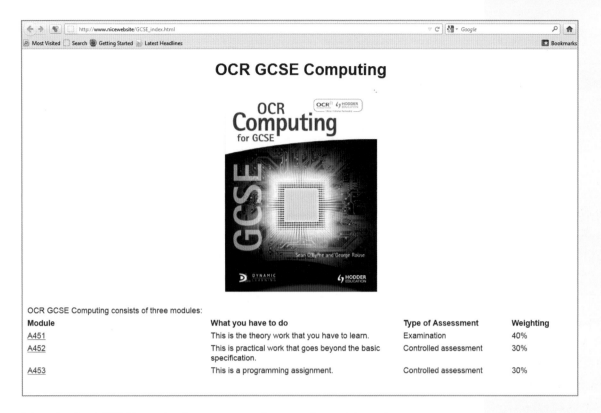

Here is the HTML code that was used to produce this web page. Notice that each feature on the page is enclosed between tags. These are markers enclosed in angle brackets. For example, `<h1>This is a heading</h1>` makes the text 'This is a heading' appear in large letters (h1 or heading 1), when interpreted by a browser.

```
<!DOCTYPE html PUBLIC "-//W3C//DTD HTML 4.01//EN" "http://www.w3.org/TR/
html4/strict.dtd">

<html><head>

<meta content="text/html; charset=ISO-8859-1" http-equiv="content-
type"><title>GCSE</title><style type="text/css"></style></head><body>

<h1 style="color: rgb(0, 0, 153); font-family: sans-serif; text-align:
center;">OCR GCSE Computing</h1>

<div style="text-align: center;"><img style="width: 348px; height: 452px;"
alt="Hodder GCSE Computing book" title="This is the book that you need"
src="book _ cover.PNG"><br style="font-family: sans-serif;">

</div>

<br style="font-family: sans-serif;">

<table style="text-align: left; width: 100%; font-family: sans-serif;"
border="0" cellpadding="2" cellspacing="2">

  <tbody>

    <tr align="left">
```

```
    <td colspan="2" rowspan="1" style="vertical-align: top; color: rgb(0,
    0, 153);">OCR GCSE Computing consists of three modules:<br>
    </td>

    <td style="vertical-align: top; color: rgb(0, 0, 153);"><br>
    </td>

    <td style="vertical-align: top; color: rgb(0, 0, 153);"><br>
    </td>

</tr>

<tr>

    <td style="vertical-align: top; font-weight: bold; color: rgb(0, 0,
    153);">Module<br>
    </td>

    <td style="vertical-align: top; width: 35%; font-weight: bold; color:
    rgb(0, 0, 153);">What you have to do<br>
    </td>

    <td style="vertical-align: top; font-weight: bold; color: rgb(0, 0,
    153);">Type of Assessment<br>
    </td>

    <td style="vertical-align: top; font-weight: bold; color: rgb(0, 0,
    153);">Weighting<br>
    </td>

</tr>

<tr>

    <td style="vertical-align: top; color: rgb(0, 0, 153);"><a href="A451.
    html">A451</a><br>
    </td>

    <td style="vertical-align: top; width: 25%; color: rgb(0, 0,
    153);">This is the theory work that you have to learn.<br>
    </td>

    <td style="vertical-align: top; width: 20%; color: rgb(0, 0,
    153);">Examination<br>
    </td>

    <td style="vertical-align: top; color: rgb(0, 0, 153);">40%<br>
    </td>

</tr>

<tr>

    <td style="vertical-align: top; color: rgb(0, 0, 153);"><a href="A452.
    html">A452</a><br>
```

```
        </td>
        <td style="vertical-align: top; color: rgb(0, 0, 153);">This is
        practical work that goes beyond the basic specification.<br>
        </td>
        <td style="vertical-align: top; color: rgb(0, 0, 153);">Controlled
        assessment<br>
        </td>
        <td style="vertical-align: top; color: rgb(0, 0, 153);">30%<br>
        </td>
      </tr>
      <tr>
        <td style="vertical-align: top; color: rgb(0, 0, 153);"><a href="A453.
        html">A453</a><br>
        </td>
        <td style="vertical-align: top; color: rgb(0, 0, 153);">This is a
        programming assignment.<br>
        </td>
        <td style="vertical-align: top; color: rgb(0, 0, 153);">Controlled
        assessment<br>
        </td>
        <td style="vertical-align: top; color: rgb(0, 0, 153);">30%<br>
        </td>
      </tr>
  </tbody>
</table>
<br>
</body></html>
```

Web pages can be written by simply using a text editor such as Notepad to write text like that shown here. However, it is usually easier to make at least some use of special web page editors where you can assemble the components of the web page and the software translates this into HTML.

HTML has been extended many times so that web pages could become ever more complex and interactive. Images and various other objects can be embedded in the HTML based page and forms can easily be constructed for users to fill in.

Links can be embedded which allow the user to click on objects or text and navigate to other places in a page or to other websites.

Various scripting languages such as Javascript are supported in order to make web pages more dynamic.

Cascading Style Sheets (CSS) can be applied to HTML pages in order to control the overall appearance of pages. These are designed to separate format from content and thereby make the web pages less complex.

XML (Extensible Markup Language) is an open standard for encoding structured information. It is human- and machine-readable and has become a widely-used format for sharing information between programs, people and computers.

Compression

In order that as much content as possible can be successfully displayed in browsers, various file standards have become common for documents, visual and sound files. Some of these involve **compression**. This is necessary in order to reduce download times for what might otherwise be very large files. A single colour image taking up a typical computer screen can be 1 MB or more. A reasonable quality movie will display 25 images per second. It is easy to see that files can become extremely large. Even with fast broadband, downloads can take a long time and be unacceptably slow.

There are two principal approaches to compressing files and they vary in how much data is lost in order to reduce file sizes.

Key term

Compression: Reduction in file size to reduce download times and storage requirements

Lossy compression

Lossy compression involves removing some of the data from a file in order to reduce its size. For photographs, it is the only method that can achieve significant file reductions because the sequence of pixels is unpredictable. Lossy compression relies on the removal of data which is the least likely to be noticed by the human senses. A file that has been compressed using lossy compression cannot be restored to its original condition.

Figure 6.18 shows a photograph that started out as being about 4 MB in size. It has been compressed to 1 MB and then compressed more to 67 KB. A certain degree of compression is hardly noticeable on a web page, but there comes a point where too much makes for very poor quality.

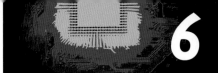

A 1 MB image

The same image compressed to 67 KB

Figure 6.18 Lossy compression

Lossless compression

Sometimes it is important not to lose any of the information in a file. For example, if anything were removed from a computer program, then it would not run correctly. Likewise, a text file must have all the letters transmitted accurately or else it might not be understood.

Sometimes it is possible to compress a file without losing any information. This involves storing enough information about a file so that it can be recreated later exactly as it was before. For example, consider the sentence:

ask not what your country can do for you, ask what you can do for your country

This could be stored as follows:

Index	Word
1	ask
2	not
3	what
4	your
5	country
6	can
7	do
8	for
9	you

1 2 3 4 5 6 7 8 9 , 1 3 9 6 7 8 4 5

Here we have a table where each word is added in the order that it occurs and is given a code number. The text is then represented by code numbers. If a word is repeated, there is an opportunity to make savings, by giving the code number instead of the word.

There is enough information here to recreate the original sentence.

Other common web standards

JPG or JPEG – Joint Photographic Experts Group

This is a compressed bitmap image file format commonly used for photographs. You can usually choose how much compression you want, so for a small image on a web page it is often acceptable to choose a large compression factor.

GIF – Graphics Interchange Format

This is a lossless bitmap image compression standard but it is only suitable for small images such as logos with a limited number of colours. A sequence of GIF images can be displayed so as to produce animations.

PDF – Portable Document Format

This is an open standard for exchanging documents. Text and graphics are displayed exactly as in the original, with no need to have the software that created the document. Many applications are capable of reading or creating PDF documents.

MPEG – Moving Pictures Expert Group

This is a set of standards designed to encode audio visual information. It uses lossy compression for both the sound and visual components. Various versions of MPEG are used for digital transmissions via cable and satellite as well as for terrestrial digital channels. It is used to encode DVD movies as well and can be decoded by most domestic audio visual equipment.

MP3 – Moving Pictures Expert Group Audio Layer 3

This has become the *de facto* standard for distributing digital music files on the internet. It uses lossy compression to reduce file sizes to about a tenth of the original. The compression algorithm is intended to remove sounds that are generally beyond the limits of most people's hearing although some claim that the loss in quality is noticeable.

Summary

The internet is the biggest WAN of all and it has changed all our lives. It depends upon the common adoption of many standard protocols and file types in order to connect users reliably.

Questions

❶ What is file compression?

❷ Explain the purpose of DNS servers.

❸ What is a cascading style sheet?

❹ What is an HTML tag?

Extension tasks

1 Find out the public IP address of the computer you are using. There are many websites that can do this.

2 Use Traceroute (also known as tracert) in order to view the IP addresses of the routers through which data passes between your computer and a website of your choice. Use the command such as tracert bbc.co.uk.

3 Calculate how many nodes can be uniquely coded by one 32-bit IP address.

4 Find out the IP address of a website and then access it from your browser by typing in its numeric IP address.

5 Look at the HTML code on pages 141–143 and answer these questions:

   a How is a link produced?

   b How is a picture inserted?

   c How is a table row produced?

   d If you uploaded the web page to a website, the links would not work. Why is that?

Exam style questions

1 Explain why compression must be lossless when sending a computer program as an email attachment. [2 marks]

2 Explain what is meant by IP addressing. [2 marks]

3 Here are three file formats: [3 marks]

Format	Use
MPEG	
PDF	
JPG	

For each file format, write down the purpose it serves on a website.
Choose from:

a moving pictures

b still pictures

c sound files

d documents

e web pages

4 Describe what HTML is. [3 marks]

5 Explain the purpose of HTML in the creation of web pages. [3 marks]

6 Describe one advantage and one disadvantage of storing music as MP3 files. [4 marks]

## Chapter 7

Programming

In this chapter you will learn about the main types of programming language and the main features and structures used in imperative programming. You will learn about the use of algorithms to describe solutions and the use of pseudocode to express a coded solution in a generic form. The examples given will be in a generic pseudocode typical of that used in the examination paper.

Computers work by following sets of rules and programming is the process of using sets of rules to solve problems. Evidence of programming activities date back to ancient Greece, where they used a mechanical device, the Antikythera mechanism, to calculate the positions of the stars.

Throughout history people have designed and built mechanical devices that can follow a pre-programmed set of instructions to solve a problem. Among the most notable are Joseph Marie Jacquard who used punched cards to control weaving looms and Charles Babbage who used punched cards to control his analytical engine, the first fully working computer design. It had a memory capable of storing 1000 40-digit decimal numbers and an arithmetic unit capable of several different functions. Construction of the device was never completed due to lack of money but part of the machine can be seen in the Science Museum in London. It is particularly noteworthy because the mathematician, Ada Lovelace, who is generally regarded as the first computer programmer, in 1843 wrote a program that would be used by Charles Babbage's analytical machine to calculate a series of numbers.

It was the work by John von Neumann that led to designs for computers that were able to store programs. Early electronic computers were programmed by using switches and patch leads to make connections. Since every computer was built individually the set of instructions for each system was unique and every system would have a different set of instructions to complete the same task. This is called machine code and it is specific to the computer.

The increase in computer programming activities led to the development of assembly languages. Assembly languages are basically a more memorable set of commands that could be converted directly to a specific machine code instruction without the programmer needing to enter the actual machine code. But one command was equivalent to a specific machine code command and each machine

Key terms

Algorithm: A series of steps designed to solve a mathematical or other problem

Pseudocode: A method of describing an algorithm using structured English close to programming language

Figure 7.1 The original Antikythera mechanism

Figure 7.2 John von Neumann (right) with programming panel on EDVAC

had its own assembly language. In 1954 the first general purpose high-level language was developed, Fortran. Fortran had instructions that were translated into the required machine code enabling the programmer to code for any computer with a suitable translator. In the following years the availability of electronic computers and the development of computer programming languages led to the development of the high-level, general purpose languages in common use today.

Algorithms

Computer programming is all about solving problems using a set of rules that a computer can follow. These rules are called algorithms. Devising a set of algorithms to solve a problem is the most important part of developing a solution to a problem and well-defined algorithms will lead to well-constructed and effective programs.

Algorithms are simply sets of rules and can be defined in many ways including program **flow charts** or pseudocode. We often apply simple sets of rules when making decisions.

Example

A central heating system will try to keep the temperature between two values, say 19 °C and 21 °C, such that:

- if the temperature falls below 19 °C it will turn on the heating
- if the temperature goes above 21 °C it will turn off the heating.

A flow chart to show this is:

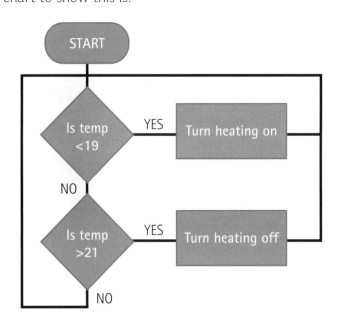

Specification content

(a) Understand algorithms (written in pseudocode or flow diagram), explain what they do and correct or complete them

(b) Produce algorithms in pseudocode or flow diagrams to solve problems

Key term

Flow chart (flow diagram): A diagrammatic method of showing the structure and data flow to define a problem and its solution

Flow charts are one method of describing **processes** and there are a number of standard shapes that represent specific functions. Some of the standard shapes are shown in Figure 7.3.

Key terms

Process: A flow chart symbol that defines any processing to be completed at that stage

Decision: A flow diagram symbol used to show a decision stage, may be 'yes' or 'no' or multiple values

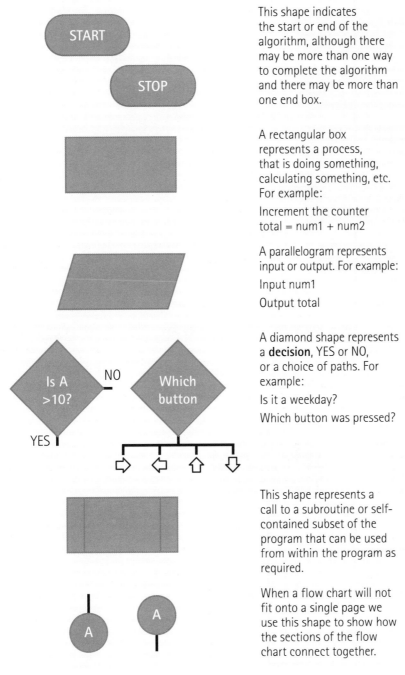

This shape indicates the start or end of the algorithm, although there may be more than one way to complete the algorithm and there may be more than one end box.

A rectangular box represents a process, that is doing something, calculating something, etc. For example:

Increment the counter
total = num1 + num2

A parallelogram represents input or output. For example:

Input num1

Output total

A diamond shape represents a **decision**, YES or NO, or a choice of paths. For example:

Is it a weekday?

Which button was pressed?

This shape represents a call to a subroutine or self-contained subset of the program that can be used from within the program as required.

When a flow chart will not fit onto a single page we use this shape to show how the sections of the flow chart connect together.

Figure 7.3 Typical flow chart notation

Example

If we want to calculate the area of a rectangle we can input the height and width then multiply these together and output the area.

A flow chart to show this process is:

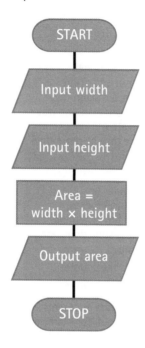

The decision symbol can have two or more options. For example, if we want to check that an input value is within a certain range, say 1 to 10, then we can use the following algorithm:

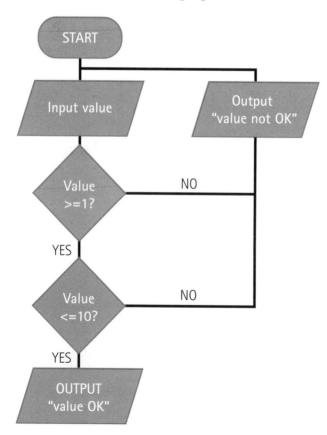

If we are describing a character moving around in a game, however, it is likely we will have more than two options. We can use the decision symbol differently in this case.

For example in a game we control the movement of a character using the arrow keys:

The flow chart for this is:

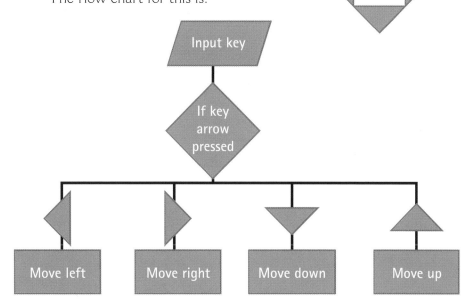

Once the outline of the process has been identified it is possible to identify the coding that will be required to implement the solution. This is often done by writing in a structured form of English known as pseudocode. It uses the concepts and structures from the language but not the detail.

The examples above, for example, could be written in pseudocode as:

```
Input value                          Press key
If value >= 1 THEN                   If key = right arrow THEN move right
    If value <= 10 THEN              Else
        Output "value OK"                If key = left arrow THEN move left
    ELSE                             Else
        Output "value not OK"            If key = up arrow THEN move up
    ENDIF                            Else
ENDIF                                    If key = down arrow THEN move down
Return to Input                      Else
                                         ENDIF
                                        ENDIF
                                       ENDIF
                                   ENDIF
```

This is not program code but is in an English style similar to a programming language that is easy to convert into code when required.

We use flow charts to establish the flow of data through a program and to show how data is used at each stage of the process based on the rules we have to apply.

Once we have established the data flow and rules using the flow chart we can start to organise the structure of the program that will solve the problem.

We use flow charts and pseudocode to organise our thinking and help us with a logical problem solving exercise.

Example

Consider the following problem:

A garden centre has a loyalty card scheme that gives members a 10% discount if they spend more than £50. If any customer spends more than £100, then they get a 5% discount on top of any discounts they may already have. Write a program to calculate how much a customer pays for their goods at the checkout based on these rules.

What are the rules? Let's summarise them in a flow chart:

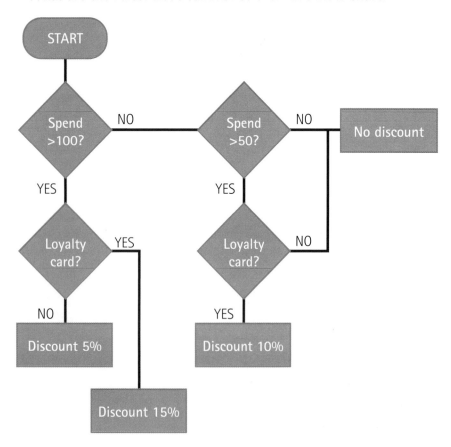

We now have a better idea of how the rules apply. Now we can **trace** through various values to check that the flow chart works as expected.

The values to use are those that check all the possibilities.

Key term

Trace: A method of using data to check that a flow chart covers all possibilities correctly

Loyalty card	Spend >£100	Spend >£50 but <£100	Test values Loyalty card/spend	Result of trace
NO	NO	NO	NO/£35	No discount ✓
NO	NO	YES	NO/£65	No discount ✓
NO	YES	–	NO/£115	Discount 5% ✓
YES	NO	NO	YES/£35	No discount ✓
YES	NO	YES	YES/£65	Discount 10% ✓
YES	YES	–	YES/£115	Discount 15% ✓

Once the flow chart is traced to show it covers all possibilities we can try to turn this into pseudocode that will form the basis for our computer program:

```
INPUT spend
INPUT loyaltycard
IF spend > 100 THEN
    IF loyaltycard = YES THEN Discount = 15%
    ELSE IF loyaltycard = NO THEN Discount = 5%
    ENDIF
ENDIF
IF spend < 100 THEN
    IF spend > 50 THEN
        IF loyaltycard = YES THEN Discount = 10%
    ELSE
        IF loyaltycard = NO THEN No Discount
        ENDIF
    ENDIF
ENDIF
IF spend < 50 THEN No Discount
ENDIF
```

We indent the bits inside the IF to ENDIF to show a block of code inside another block.

This gives us the basic outline of how the solution will work so that we can apply suitable coding techniques to generate the code to make this program work.

Computing in context

In reality most significant programming projects are too large for one individual to complete. It is often difficult for an individual to conceive the full complexity of a problem when it is looked at in its entirety. For this reason most computer programming projects are broken down into several layers. The concepts are simplified at each stage until it is possible to appreciate how each individual part of the problem can be solved. This is often referred to as a top down approach or problem decomposition.

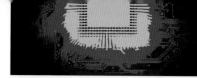

Summary

We use flow charts and pseudocode as problem solving tools to identify data flows and structures that are needed to define the problem logically so that it can be coded. We use a standard set of flow chart symbols to make it easier to see what each element of the flow chart does. Pseudocode is a structured version of English that is close to a programming language and is used to define the steps needed to solve a problem. We indent blocks of code that belong together, inside other blocks, so that we can see clearly the structure of the process.

Questions

❶ Draw a flow chart to describe the process of taking two input values for height and base of a triangle and outputting the area of the triangle.

❷ Draw a flow chart to describe the process of taking in five numbers and outputting:

   a the largest value

   b the smallest value.

❸ Draw a flow chart to describe the process of the user entering a set of values and the computer outputting the average. (You will need to know how many values are input by either counting them or asking for the number to be input. You could try drawing flow charts for both situations.)

   a Trace the flow chart using suitable values to check that it is complete.

❹ Write the pseudocode for each of the above situations.

Extension tasks

1 Heron's formula for finding the area of a triangle is $\sqrt{(s(s-a)(s-b)(s-c))}$ where $s = (a+b+c)/2$ and a, b and c are the lengths of the sides of a triangle. Write the definition for this problem as a flow chart or in pseudocode (or both).

2 Scratch is a simple block based language that can be used to create games, animations and much more. Define, using flow charts, a simple maze game where a character is moved around the screen using key presses to avoid the walls of the maze and the edge of the screen.

Programming languages

In the introduction to the chapter we mentioned briefly the origins of computer programming languages. Initially computers were programmed by using switches and patch leads. Early computers were programmed directly in binary based on the specific instruction set for each computer device. To make it easier for programmers,

sets of mnemonics (simple memory aids) were used to define the instruction set rather than the binary, so instead of perhaps 1011 and 1001 the commands ADD and SUB were used. These early assembly language instructions had a one-to-one correspondence with the actual **machine code** and merely helped make the code easier to understand. Machine code is the code the CPU uses when it decodes an instruction and is specific to the processor. Machine code is in binary, the list of commands available in mnemonic form is called the assembly language and the program to convert the mnemonics to machine code is called an assembler.

To implement these **assembly language** commands the computer uses a lookup table to find the mnemonic and substitutes it with the equivalent binary code so the binary string 01101101 00110101 becomes ADD 00110101 (meaning add the contents of 00110101 to the accumulator).

This is better but the programmer still has to remember the address in binary. However, this was resolved by setting up another lookup table that could contain these binary locations mapped against a label, for example num1.

Now instead of typing 01101101 00110101, the programmer can simply type ADD num1.

The mnemonic ADD is called the operator and the data, num1, is called the operand.

This is an example of a **translator** being used to convert words and symbols the programmer can remember and understand into the binary the computer needs to work with. The computer is simply keeping a list of what the codes are and labels for memory locations rather than the programmer having to do this themself.

For example, the simple program to add two numbers in an assembly language is:

```
INP
STA FIRST
INP
ADD FIRST
OUT
HALT
FIRST DAT
```

When entered into the assembler it is compiled into memory and memory locations are reserved for the data, labelled FIRST.

Key terms

Machine code: Instructions in binary used by the CPU

Assembly language: A low-level programming language that uses more memorable mnemonic codes and labels to represent machine-level code. Each instruction corresponds to just one machine operation

Translator: A program to convert high-level or assembly-level commands into machine code

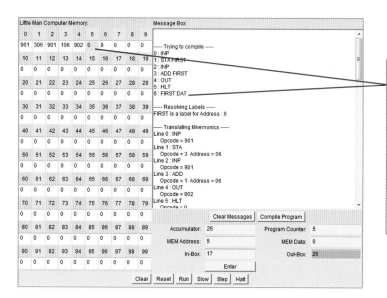

The memory location 6 has been reserved for the data labelled FIRST.

The other instructions have been stored in the first 5 locations.

STORE mnemonic code is STA, machine code is 3, so STA FIRST becomes 306 (store data in memory location 6).

ADD mnemonic code is ADD, machine code is 1, so ADD FIRST becomes 106.

In 1954 the first of the **high-level languages**, Fortran, was developed, quickly followed by many more high-level languages. These languages do not have a one-to-one correspondence between the commands and the machine code and one high-level command may represent many machine code commands. For example, some CPU's machine code does not have a multiply function, so when we ask the computer to do a simple sum such as 5*6 it will use repeated addition and add 5 lots of 6 together to get the result. These high-level commands cannot be executed directly by the computer and have to be translated into the machine code before they can be run.

In a high-level language the assembler above becomes simply:

```
INPUT a
INPUT b
OUTPUT a+b
```

A translator is a program that is able to convert high-level language commands into a set of machine code commands. This means that the high-level language is no longer tied to a specific machine and, providing there is a translator that can convert the high-level commands to the specific machine code required, the computer can execute the program. The translator converts the high-level commands, or **source code**, into machine code.

There are two basic ways to translate high-level code to machine code:

- By taking the whole code and converting it to machine code before running it.
- By taking the high-level code and converting it one instruction at a time then running each instruction before translating the next.

Key terms

High-level language: A programming language that resembles a natural language. Each instruction translates to many machine instructions. It is problem based rather than machine based

Source code: The program written by the end user in a high-level language before it is converted to machine code

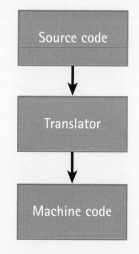

Figure 7.4 Translator converts source code to machine code

7

The **compiler** converts all of the high-level source code to machine-level **object code** before attempting to run the object code produced. The object code can be saved and will run independently of the source code and translator.

The **interpreter** converts the source code one instruction at a time into machine code then runs it before translating the next instruction. It does not produce any object code and must be translated from the source code every time it is run.

There are advantages and disadvantages to both of these approaches:

- If when compiling the code there are several errors they are all reported at once and need to be fixed before the code can be executed.
- Once all errors are fixed the code is turned into object code that will generally run much faster and does not need the translator to be present, taking up much less memory.
- If the code is interpreted it will translate each instruction until it comes across an error before stopping. This makes interpreted code much more use when developing programs.
- Code segments can be run and tested independently from the rest of the code and errors dealt with as they occur.
- An interpreter does not generate any object code so requires the translator to be present whenever it is run.
- An interpreter must translate each instruction before running it. This means it is generally slower and takes up more memory.

The third type of translator has already been mentioned – the assembler. This is the translator that converts the mnemonic assembly language instructions into machine code. In this case there is often a one-to-one correspondence between assembly language instructions and machine code instructions.

Key terms

Compiler: Translation software that converts high-level source code into machine (object) code

Object code: The machine code produced by a compiler

Interpreter: Translation software that converts source code or user input into machine code which is immediately executed one instruction at a time

Translator	Advantages	Disadvantages
Assembler	■ Gives precise and direct access to the computer hardware	■ Difficult to code ■ Few commands available
Compiler	■ Compiler is not needed on the target machine ■ The code runs quickly once compiled ■ The code is difficult for other people to modify without access to the source code	■ Initial compilation is slow ■ Errors generated for all the code at compilation can be difficult to debug
Interpreter	■ Executes one statement at a time so easy to debug code ■ Code can be developed and tested in stages with no lengthy compile time ■ Can be more portable since code will run if an interpreter is available	■ Interpreter is needed on the target machine ■ This also occupies some of the memory ■ Code executes more slowly ■ Easy for other people to modify the code since the source code is available

One disadvantage listed for a compiler is the generation of errors at the compilation stage but modern translators include a range of facilities to aid the programmer including:

■ source code editor

■ translator (compiler, interpreter)

■ automation tools (for example, wizards to autocomplete code as it is typed)

■ debugger

■ run time environment

■ auto documentation.

This is the **integrated development environment (IDE)** from Visual Studio 10 showing some of the features available when editing code:

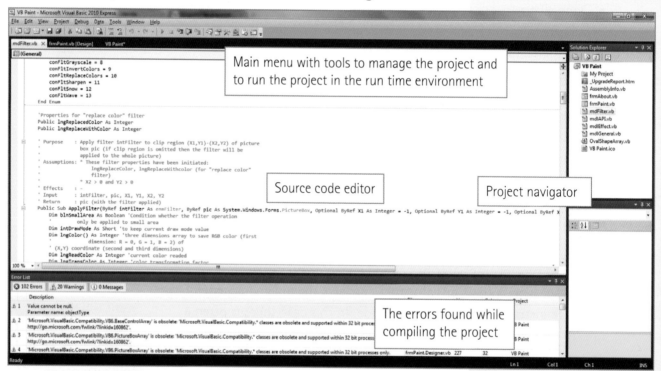

Main menu with tools to manage the project and to run the project in the run time environment

Source code editor

Project navigator

The errors found while compiling the project

This shows the autocomplete wizard suggesting possible inputs based on what has been typed already. This helps avoid syntax errors by showing the correct format for the statements

7

This is the IDE from Visual Studio 10 for editing forms:

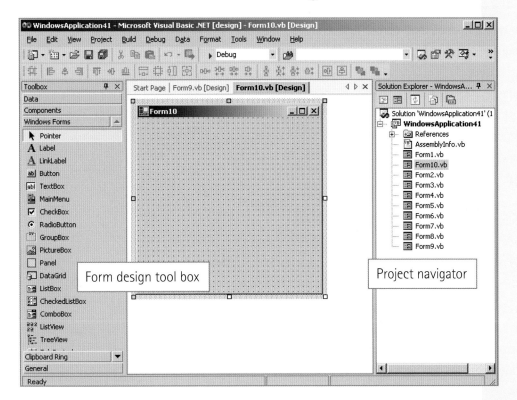

The **code editor** provides a text editing area that helps to organise the code by managing the layout, including: indenting structures and colour coding the command words, variables and comments so that they can be easily identified. Some include other features such as autocomplete wizards.

Error diagnostics include an errors and warnings list to identify any problems in the code.

The **run time environment** allows the developer to run the code during development. This can be used to check for logical errors or that the code does what it is expected to do.

The **translator** compiles or interprets the source code into suitable machine code instructions that can be run on the computer.

The **auto documentation** feature takes a note of all the variables, modules, subroutines and comments as the project is developed and tidies this up into a text file that can be used during any maintenance of the program.

Key terms

Code editor: Text area used to enter code in an IDE

Error diagnostics: System to warn of errors in the code and potential problems

Run time environment: Software to support the execution of programs

Translator: A program to convert high-level or assembly-level commands into machine code

Auto documentation: System that tracks variables, modules and comments for maintenance purposes

Summary

High-level languages use commands that represent several machine code instructions and a language closer to English than the binary of machine code and the mnemonics of assemblers.

- High-level languages:
    - → Commands close to English
    - → Machine independent
    - → Easier to read and write
    - → Easier to maintain.
- Machine code:
    - → Commands in binary
    - → Machine dependent
    - → Difficult to read and write.
- Translators are used to convert high-level and assembly-level languages into machine code that the computer can understand and execute.
- Interpreters convert the high-level language instructions one at a time executing them before moving on. This is useful when developing a program since individual code segments can be tested independently from the rest of the program.
- Compilers convert all of the source code into object code that is executable and can run independently of the translator. This is useful because it makes the code harder to modify, run faster than interpreted code and will take up less memory because it does not need the translator to be present.
- Translators often have integrated development environments (IDEs) that can help identify errors in code as it is being developed.

Questions

❶ Describe the differences between a high-level language and an assembly language.

❷ What are the advantages of compiling a program for commercial distribution?

❸ What are the features of an IDE?

❹ What are the advantages of writing in high-level code compared with machine code?

Extension task

Do some research into how assembly languages are used now, what they are used for and why.

Control flow in imperative languages

The simplest form of program that can be written consists of a list of instructions to be carried out in **sequence**. For example, input two numbers and output their total, as shown in the following flow chart:

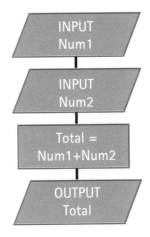

It would be very limiting if all a computer program could do was to follow a sequence of instructions. In order to make computer programs more useful they have a number of standard control features that will allow the program to repeat a sequence or branch to another set of commands if a condition is met. The following section explains different ways in which the execution of commands can be controlled to allow for various pathways through the program.

Selection

The path through a program can be decided by looking at a condition and then taking one of a set of alternative paths based on the result. For example, the IF – THEN – ELSE construct decides which set of commands to follow based on a condition:

```
IF 'this condition is true' THEN
    'do this' (what to do if the condition is true)
ELSE
    'do that' (what to do if the condition is false)
ENDIF
```

Example

A system to check if someone can go into a cinema to see a 15-rated film can be written using an IF – THEN structure.

Specification content

(a) Understand and use sequence in an algorithm

(b) Understand and use selection in an algorithm (IF and CASE statements)

(c) Understand and use iteration in an algorithm (FOR, WHILE and REPEAT loops)

Key terms

Sequence: A list of instructions to be carried out in order, one after the other

Selection: The pathway through a program is selected by using a condition to decide on what instructions to execute next

```
Get age
IF age >= 15 THEN
    Allow into cinema
ELSE
    Do not allow into cinema
ENDIF
```

We indent the commands inside the IF – THEN structure to make it easier to see what is done inside each section of the coding. In order to show that the IF – THEN structure is completed we identify the end of the statement with the command ENDIF. This is particularly useful if we need to check on more than one condition and put an IF – THEN inside another IF – THEN.

Example

In the heating control system mentioned on page 150, the system switched on if the temperature was less than 19 °C and off if the temperature was greater than 21 °C.

The pseudocode using IF – THEN for this situation is:

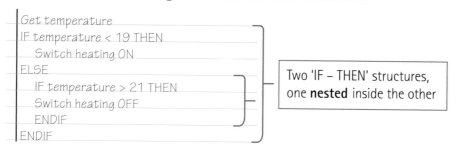

```
Get temperature
IF temperature < 19 THEN
    Switch heating ON
ELSE
    IF temperature > 21 THEN
    Switch heating OFF
    ENDIF
ENDIF
```

Two 'IF – THEN' structures, one **nested** inside the other

By indenting like this we can see that there are two IF –THEN structures, one inside the other, which are described as nested structures.

If the number of decisions required is large the use of IF – THEN could result in quite complex nesting and make the structure very difficult to follow. In this circumstance the CASE command provides a much neater solution.

The CASE command lists a range of alternative paths based on the value of a variable. For example, a multiple choice quiz with five answers would result in a complex set of nested IF – THEN statements, but is quite clear if the CASE structure is used.

Example

To check the input for a question about capital cities:

What is the capital of France?

A Madrid

B Berlin

C Paris

D Lyon

E Brussels

The response would be a single letter, A to E.

The CASE command would have a structure similar to the following pseudocode:

```
INPUT Response
SELECT CASE Response OF
    A:          OUTPUT "No that is the capital of Spain"
    B:          OUTPUT "No that is the capital of Germany"
    C:          OUTPUT "Correct, well done"
    D:          OUTPUT "No that is in France, but is not the capital"
    E:          OUTPUT "No that is the capital of Belgium"
OTHERWISE       OUTPUT "Invalid choice"
END SELECT
```

Iteration

In both of these structures the program is making a decision about which section of code to run, but is only deciding on which branch of the structure to follow.

If we need to repeat a process until a condition is met we need another type of control structure – **iteration**.

There are two ways of deciding if we have repeated a **loop** of instructions enough times:

- By counting a set number of loops.
- Or by setting a condition to be met that will end the loop.

The FOR – NEXT structure allows the program to repeat the set of commands between the FOR and the NEXT a set number of times. For example, the following program will output the traditional multiplication table for seven from 1 up to 12 'times',

```
FOR k = 1 TO 12
    OUTPUT k "times 7 is" k*7
NEXT k
```

In this example, the FOR – NEXT structure uses the index value, k, and each time it reaches NEXT it adds 1 to k and repeats the loop until it has done it with the maximum value for k in the FOR statement, in this case 12. Note, when the loop is finished the value of k is increased once more so at the end of this process k will be equal to 13.

The structure assumes that the value will go up in 1's but this need not be the case, if we need it to count down from 10 to 1, for example to print out a number of lives left in a game, then we can use:

```
FOR lives = 10 TO 1 STEP -1
```

Key term

Iteration or repetition: A group of instructions is executed repeatedly until a condition is met (a **loop**)

This loop will count down from 10 to 1.

It need not count in whole units either – it can count in decimal values such as 0.5, or in larger units such as 2 or 3 or 50, etc.

So the structure of the FOR – NEXT loop is:

```
FOR index = start TO finish STEP step
    <instructions to follow>
NEXT index
```

Further information

In theory it is possible to set up a FOR – NEXT loop that will never stop.

For example, FOR index = 5 TO 10 STEP -1 will generate index values of 5, 4, 3, 2, 1, etc., never reaching 10 and potentially carrying on indefinitely. However, most programming languages will trap this and prevent it from happening by comparing the end point with the current value of the index. In this case it will note that the step is negative and halt the loop once the value of index is lower than the end point. It will always execute the first iteration with the starting value of index.

If the number of iterations is not known or the loop needs to continue until a condition is met there are two other choices. The loop can repeat until a condition is met or can follow a set of instructions while a condition is true. These two structures are REPEAT – UNTIL and WHILE – ENDWHILE.

The REPEAT loop executes the code that follows up to the UNTIL statement until the condition is met. It must execute at least once.

The WHILE loop executes the code that follows while a condition is true. The condition is therefore checked before the code is executed and may not be executed at all.

For example, a program to collect numbers from the user, total them, count how many numbers have been entered and then output the total and average for the set of numbers.

```
count = 0
total = 0
REPEAT
    INPUT "enter number" value
    count = count + 1
    total = total + value
    INPUT "more numbers ?" more
UNTIL more <>"yes"
OUTPUT total, total/count
```

```
count = 0
total = 0
more = "yes"
WHILE more = "yes"
    INPUT "enter number" value
    count = count + 1
    total = total + value
    INPUT "more numbers ?" more
ENDWHILE
OUTPUT total, total/count
```

Notice that the condition in the REPEAT structure is checked at the end of the first pass through the loop, in the WHILE structure it is checked before the first pass. The choice of loop structure depends upon what it is being used for; some languages do not support both of these but through careful planning this is not an issue and either can be used to solve the same problem by making adjustments to the algorithms.

Summary

There are three main control structures used in imperative programming. Sequence is the simplest of these with instructions being carried out in a fixed order one after the other. Selection allows the program to branch through different sets of instructions depending upon a condition. Iteration allows the program to repeat a sequence of instructions a fixed number of times or until a condition is met.

The main selection structures are IF – THEN – ELSE and CASE.

The main iteration structures are FOR – NEXT, REPEAT – UNTIL and WHILE – ENDWHILE.

Questions

❶ Write in pseudocode a program to take five input values and output:
   a the highest value
   b the lowest value
   c the average.

❷ Write in pseudocode a program to allow a user to input any number of values they require and output the average of these values.

❸ A garden centre loyalty card discount scheme gives 10% discount to members if they spend £50 or more and an additional 5% if they spend over £100. The centre also gives a discount of 5% to all customers who spend over £100. Write the pseudocode to describe this system.

❹ Using a FOR – NEXT structure write a pseudocode program to calculate the sum of the first five odd numbers.

❺ Write the pseudocode to take an input value and output the whole numbers from 1 to that value and the squares of those whole numbers using a FOR – NEXT structure.
   a Rewrite this using a REPEAT – UNTIL structure.
   b Rewrite this using a WHILE – ENDWHILE structure.

Extension task

The factorial of a number is calculated by multiplying together all the whole numbers from 1 to the number. For example, 4! (! is the symbol for factorial) is $4 \times 3 \times 2 \times 1 = 24$. Write a pseudocode program to calculate the factorial of a value input by the user.

Handling data in algorithms

Types of data

In order for the computer to prepare memory locations for data in a program it needs to know what type of data it is so that it can reserve the correct amount of space. The basic data types we need to deal with include:

Integer

Integers are whole number values, positive or negative, used to store data which will never have a decimal (or fractional) value such as found in quantities.

Real

Real numbers will store decimal (or fractional) values such as prices.

Boolean

Named after the English mathematician, George Boole, **Boolean** variables store just two values, TRUE or FALSE, and these are often used as flags to indicate the result of a condition.

Character

This data type stores a single **character** (digit or letter) such as A, g, 6 or &.

String

This is a data type used to store a string of characters such as names, telephone numbers, etc.

In the examples of algorithms above we have used various references to values, such as k, index, value or count, etc. The names we have used to represent values are simply labels and the computer would allocate a location in memory for the values these labels represent. If the value represented by the label can change then it is called a **variable**, if it is fixed then it is called a **constant**. Whichever of these it is, it needs to be identified in the program by a label and its type identified so that the space in memory can be allocated and labelled accordingly. Variables and constants are used in the following example.

Example

A program to return the circumference and area of a circle based on the radius input by the user has an example of a variable (the input radius) and a constant (the value of pi).

```
pi = 3.14159
radius = 0
INPUT "Enter the radius for the circle ", radius
OUTPUT "The circumference is ", 2*pi*radius
OUTPUT "The area is ", pi*radius*radius
```

Declaring a name for a variable or constant identifies a storage location in memory in which the values associated with that variable or constant name can be found by the program. We initialise the variables at the start of the program so that we clear the associated memory location of any data already stored in there by other programs that may have used the same memory location in the past. If we did not initialise the values then we may find the variables take the values left behind by other programs and our program may not work as expected.

Some programming languages insist that variables are declared before being used, others do not and simply take the first **assignment** of a value to that variable as a declaration. However, a variable will not be available until it has been declared or assigned an initial value.

The amount of space required to store a Boolean variable is not the same as that required for a real number. In fact variables require varying amounts of space. Typical reservations are:

- Integers usually require either 2 or 4 bytes of memory but it can be other values (for example, 1 or 8 bytes, etc.).
- Real numbers require 4 or 8 bytes.
- A character requires 1 byte.
- Strings require as many bytes as the number of characters they contain.
- A Boolean requires just 1 bit.

Key terms

Declaration: Identifying a variable or constant or array to a program so that memory space can be allocated
Assignment: Setting the value of a variable

Further information

To produce reliable and maintainable software, programmers need to apply a systematic and consistent approach to its development. The application of standard practice means code can be more readily understood and maintained. Declaring variables and constants at the start is just one example of good practice. Another example we have already met is indenting of control structures to clarify the structure of the program. It is also good practice to: use meaningful variable names that identify what data they represent; annotate the code to explain what each section does; and structure the code into blocks or procedures/subroutines that have a specific identifiable purpose.

It is important to select the most appropriate type of variable for the purpose when coding a solution. While a string variable will be able to store prices for items in a shop, it will not be easy to use these values in calculations. For example, telephone numbers contain just the numeric digits 0–9, but these are not numbers in the sense we would perform any arithmetic on them, so we store these as strings.

Consider an online shop that needs to keep customer order details. They store the following information:

- Customer account number (C followed by 5 digits then 2-digit country code, UK, IE, FR, etc.)
- Item code for the item purchased (3-letter department code followed by 4-digit number)
- Quantity of item purchased
- Cost of item purchased
- Item despatched (yes or no).

Variable	Typical value	Type	Size
CustomerAccount	C31245UK	String	8 bytes
ItemCode	ARG3456	String	7 bytes
Quantity	2	Integer	4 bytes
Cost	35.99	Real	8 bytes
Despatched	Yes or No	Boolean	1 bit

In choosing names for the variables it is good practice to capitalise the first letter of the words used to make up the variable name and to not include any spaces. For example, to store the customer's first name we might choose the variable name, FirstName, for postal code, PostCode, etc. Following this convention makes code much more readable and maintainable.

Operations

There are several standard operations that can be performed on numerical data types. The results of calculations are usually **assigned** to a variable. Depending upon the language being used the assignment **operator** is =, := or ::=, but these all mean the same. The result of the operation is to be stored in the variable on the left-hand side of the assignment. For example, with the standard operators:

Operator	Name	Example	Comment
+	Add	total=num1+num2	Adds the values represented by the variables num1 and num2 and stores the result in the variable total
-	Subtract	value=num1-num2	Subtracts the value represented by num2 from the value represented by num1 and stores the result as value

Key terms

Assign: Set the value of a variable

Operator: A logical, arithmetic or comparison operator used by the program

Operator	Name	Example	Comment
*	Multiply	value=num1*num2	Multiplies the value represented by num1 by the value represented by num2 and stores the result as value
/	Divide	value=num1/num2	Divides the value represented by num1 by the value represented by num2 and stores the result as value

Note

num1 and num2 could be integers and the results of addition, subtraction and multiplication will then also be integers. BUT after division it is possible that the result will be a real number. If num1 and num2 are real numbers then the result could be either real or integer.

Some operations only apply to integers:

Operator	Name	Example	Comment
MOD	Modulus (or remainder)	value=num1 MOD num2 For example: num1 = 14, num2 = 3 num1 = 28, num2 = 7 num1 = 11, num2 = 17	14 MOD 3 = 2 This returns the remainder or modulus of 14 divided by 3. Similarly: 28 MOD 7 = 0 11 MOD 17 = 11
DIV	Quotient (or whole number part)	value=num1 DIV num2 For example: num1 = 14, num2 = 3 num1 = 28, num2 = 7 num1 = 11, num2 = 17	14 DIV 3 = 4 This returns the whole number part or quotient of 14 divided by 3. Similarly: 28 DIV 7 = 4 11 DIV 17 = 0

When using variables in conditional structures the computer has to make decisions by comparing values.

Example

In a multiple choice quiz with five answers, the user has to select the correct answer by typing in a number. If the correct answer is 4, the computer has to compare what the user inputs with 4 to see if they are equal or not. If they are, then the program follows one set of commands, if not another:

```
INPUT Answer
IF Answer = 4 THEN
    OUTPUT Correct
ELSE
    OUTPUT Wrong
ENDIF
```

This is a simple **comparison** and the IF statement returns a TRUE or FALSE after the comparison 'Answer = 4'. In this case the = sign is not being used as an assignment. We are not asking the computer to make the value of Answer 4, but to decide if the value of Answer is 4. It is important to distinguish between these two different uses of the = sign.

Key term

Comparison: Comparing the values of two items and returning TRUE or FALSE depending upon the result of that comparison

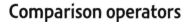

Comparison operators

Num1 = 4 is using = as an assignment and asking the computer to make Num1 equal to 4.

IF Num1 = 4 THEN is using = as a comparison operator to ask if Num1 = 4 and then the outcome, TRUE or FALSE.

The basic list of comparison operators is:

Comparison operator	Meaning
=	Is equal to
>	Is greater than
<	Is less than
<>	Is not equal to
>=	Is greater than or equal to
<=	Is less than or equal to

Some examples

Variables	Condition	Comment	Value returned
num1 = 5, num2 = 7	num1>num2	5 is less than 7, so num1>num2 is	FALSE
num1 = 1, num2 = 2	num1<>num2	num1 and num2 are different, so num1<>num2 is	TRUE
num1 = 3, num2 = 4	num1<=num2	3 is less than 4, so num1<=num2 is	TRUE
num1 = 3, num2 = 3	num1>=num2	num1 and num2 are the same, so num1>=num2 is	TRUE
num1 = 3, num2 = 3	num1<>num2	num1 and num2 are the same, so num1<>num2 is	FALSE

These can be combined into more complex comparisons as necessary using AND, OR and NOT.

For example, if we have a password program that needs to decide if a password length is between 6 and 12 characters then the if statement might be:

```
IF PasswordLength >= 6 AND PasswordLength <= 12 THEN
    OUTPUT "Password OK"
```

PasswordLength	PasswordLength >= 6	PasswordLength <= 12	Value returned by PasswordLength >= 6 AND PasswordLength <= 12
5	FALSE	TRUE	FALSE
7	TRUE	TRUE	TRUE
13	TRUE	FALSE	FALSE

When using arithmetic or comparison operators we need to make sure that the operations are applied in the order we intend. For example:

3*5-2 means 15 − 2 = 13

But:

3*(5-2) means 3 × 3 = 9

The multiply operator takes priority over the subtract operator.

The order in which operators are applied is:

Operations inside brackets are dealt with first	( )
Unary operations are next	- (negative sign, e.g. -5), NOT
Multiplication and division	*, /, DIV, MOD
Addition and subtraction	+, – (e.g. 6-3)
Comparison operators	<, >, <=, >=, = (equals), <>
Boolean operators	AND, OR
Assignment	:= or = (e.g. x := 3+5 or x = 3 + 5)

Arrays

When we discussed variables we explained the need to name these using meaningful variable names to make the program easy to understand and maintain. When the program requires a large number of items all with the same basic description, such as a list of players and their scores for a high score table then we use an array.

An array uses an identifier (or variable name) with an index value to provide a set of variables. For example, if our high score table needs to hold 20 names then our game players' names and scores could be declared as arrays using:

```
PlayerName(20)
HighScore(20)
```

This then reserves 20 spaces in memory for each variable labelled.

```
PlayerName(1)
PlayerName(2)
...
PlayerName(20)
```

And similarly for HighScore(1) to HighScore(20).

Further information

- -

Arrays are declared at the start of the program to reserve the appropriate number of spaces.

In Visual Basic .Net (VB.NET) the command to declare an array for 20 integers is:

Dim num(20) As Integer

In BBC BASIC the command is:

DIM num%(20) {The % sign is used in BBC BASIC to indicate that the value is an integer}

For example, a program to allow the user to input 20 values into memory for names and high scores:

```
DIM Name(20) As String
DIM Score(20) As Integer
FOR j = 1 TO 20
  INPUT Name(j)
  INPUT Score(j)
NEXT j
```

The arrays are just a set of indexed variables and when the program is closed the values will be lost. If the values are to be kept then they need to be written into a **file** and stored.

In order to use a data file the program must identify the name of the file including its location, whether the file is to be read from or written to, and a communication channel. The commands to do this vary between programming languages.

There will be commands to:

- open for write access (this will often allow a new file to be created if the file does not exist)
- open for read access
- close
- identify the end of the file.

For example, to save the data in the arrays for name and score we would need to:

```
OPEN for write access file highscores.dat
FOR i = 1 TO 20
  WRITE to file name(i), score(i)
NEXT i
CLOSE file highscores.dat
```

To read these back

```
OPEN for read access file highscores.dat
j = 1
REPEAT
  READ from file name(j), score(j)
  j = j + 1
UNTIL End Of File highscores.dat
CLOSE file highscores.dat
```

Key term

File: Stored data on suitable media

Further information

In VB.NET there are various ways to create files, and write and read data from files, including:

Createfile, Writefile and Readfile API's

In BBC BASIC the commands follow a pattern:

OPENIN, OPENOUT and CLOSE. For example:

```
chan1 = OPENIN "c:\data.dat"
INPUT#chan1,data
CLOSE#chan1
```

This opens a channel for input from the file data.dat on the C drive, reads an item of data in the variable data then closes the file.

Summary

- Variables are labels attached to locations in memory that contain values that can be accessed and modified by a program. Constant labels refer to values stored in memory locations that do not change during the execution of a program. The variable type has to be specified so that the correct amount of space can be reserved. The main types of variables are integer, real, Boolean, string and character.
- There are various operations that can be carried out on numeric variables including +, -, * and / and these will be completed in order of precedence.
- The = sign is used as an assignment to allocate a value and as a comparison to compare two values. If used as a comparison it returns TRUE or FALSE. There are various other numerical comparison operators including <, > and combinations of these. Comparisons can be combined into more complex conditions using AND, OR and NOT, with the resulting outputs of TRUE or FALSE based on the rules from Boolean algebra.
- When a number of identical variables are required we can use an array to create a set of variables with the same name and an index value.
- To store data outside a program, programming languages have facilities to create, write to and read from data files.

Questions

1. What is a variable?
2. Why do we use constants in programs?

❸ A shop keeps track of stock using a program. The data kept includes:
  - ID – two letters followed by 3 digits
  - The number of items in stock
  - Price
  - Order placed for new stock.

  Define suitable variable names for each of these and state the type and size for each.

❹ What value will be assigned to the variable x? If:
  a x = 11–3*5
  b x = 8/(3–1)
  c x = 8*2/4
  d x = 8/2–1
  e x = 19 MOD 3
  f x = 21 DIV 6
  g x = 19 MOD 5*2
  h x = 28/7 DIV 3

❺ What will be returned by the following comparisons?
  a Num1<>Num2   if Num1 = 6 and Num2 = 3
  b Num1>=Num2   if Num1 = 3 and Num2 = 3
  c Num1<Num2 OR Num1=Num3   if Num1 = 4, Num2 = 3 and Num3 = 4
  d Num1>=Num2 AND Num1<Num3 if Num1 = 3, Num2 = 3 and Num3 = 5

Extension tasks

1 Write a program to check the values you get for Questions 4 and 5 above.

2 Create a program to collect and store data for names and highscores using an array and a data file.

Testing

Good program design with properly constructed and checked algorithms will eliminate most errors in a program, and the integrated development environment provides features that help to reduce them. Despite these features errors do still occur because the commands have not been used correctly or because the initial logic in the design is flawed and the system does not work as anticipated.

Programming languages require very precise instructions and unless the correct language rules (syntax) are used the program will generate an error message.

In the simple example shown in Figure 7.5 the variable num1 is declared but without a suitable type.

Specification content

(a) Describe syntax errors and logic errors which may occur while developing a program

(b) Understand and identify syntax and logic errors

(c) Select and justify test data for a program, stating the expected outcome of each test

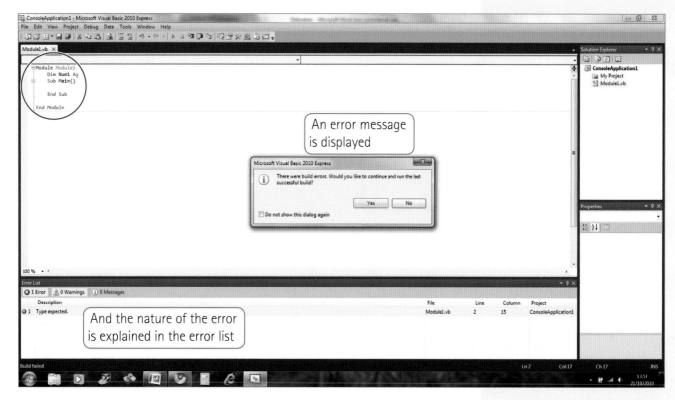

Figure 7.5 Visual Studio 10 IDE showing error message

The language has not been used properly and this is a **syntax error**.
Examples of syntax errors include:

- variables not declared before use
- using an assignment incorrectly, for example $3 + 4 = x$ instead of $x = 3 + 4$
- variable names incorrect, for example incorrect spelling or formatting.

If syntax errors are eliminated errors in the logic of the program can still lead to the program failing to work as expected. These errors are called **logic errors** and can be generated by values in variables not being as expected and division by zero.

For example, this code produces the output to the right:

```
y = 100
x = 10
REPEAT
t = y/x
x = x - 1
OUTPUT t
UNTIL x = 0
```

Key terms

Syntax error: The rules of a language are broken by the program
Logic error: The logical structure of the program produces unexpected results

But if one of the lines is typed in the wrong order then the output is different:

```
y = 100
x = 10
REPEAT
x = x - 1
t = y/x
OUTPUT t
UNTIL x = 0
```

```
(untitled)                      x
11.1111111
       12.5
14.2857143
16.6666667
         20
         25
33.3333333
         50
        100

Division by zero
>_
```

There is now an error message because x was altered before the division instead of after the division. The syntax is correct but the logic is not.

Logical errors can generate a range of problems such as:

- division by zero
- programs that do not complete
- the memory is filled with data and we get a stack overflow message
- incorrect output.

Or the program will simply crash.

The main causes of logical errors are:

- division by zero
- conditions that cannot be met in conditional statements
- infinite loops (looping so that the condition is not met)
- incorrect algorithms (the algorithm does not do what it is meant to)
- incorrect expressions (calculations that are incorrect or have missing brackets).

It is important when coding to try to eliminate the possibility of errors and careful validation of input values is an essential component of good programming practice. Typical validation will include ensuring the variable is of the correct type or within a suitable range. Checking data at the input stage for validity will minimise run time errors.

These errors are often only found at run time with certain data, so to minimise these it is usual to test the program with a range of data covering normal and abnormal situations. To test a program it is necessary to identify suitable test data and the expected outcome from using that data.

Test data

Suitable test data should cover the following situations:

Valid

Test data that represents typical input into the system.

Valid extreme

Test data that is valid but at the **extreme** end of the range of acceptable input.

Invalid

Test data that is out of range and should be rejected.

Invalid extreme

Test data that is **invalid** but only just at the limit of being unacceptable.

Erroneous

Test data that should be rejected because it is the wrong type of input.

For example, to test a system to calculate the cost of making a mobile phone call, if the call is entered in whole seconds but charged per minute or part of a minute at 5p per minute.

There are many combinations to check but some suitable values include:

Test	Data	Reason	Expected
Valid whole minutes	120 seconds	Whole minutes only	10p
Valid < whole minute	35 seconds	To see if rounded up	5p
Extreme value in range	60 seconds	To check boundary condition	5p
Extreme value in range	59 seconds	To check boundary condition	5p
Extreme value in range	61 seconds	To check boundary condition	10p
Invalid data	35.76 seconds	To check value not in whole seconds	Error
Invalid data non-numeric	hat	To check only numbers accepted	Error

It is important to check boundary or extreme conditions because it is here the use of < rather than <=, for example, will bring unexpected results. While it may seem strange to include non-numeric values these will often be interpreted as zero if they are not suitably validated on entry or the wrong variable type has been chosen.

Key terms

Valid: Data used in testing that represents normal data that could be expected

Extreme: Data that is at the extreme limit of valid or invalid to check boundary conditions

Invalid: Data used to test a program that should be rejected because it is 'out of range'

Erroneous: Data that would not normally be expected such as the wrong data type

Summary

Errors in programs can be errors in syntax or logic. The IDE helps to minimise the syntax errors but logical errors cannot be detected in this way and must be found through testing. Testing should look at valid, invalid, extreme (boundary) and erroneous data. The purpose of testing is not to show that a program works, but to try and break it and hence to fix it. Test plans should include the test data, the reason for the test and the expected outcome. It is important to check the validity of any input data at the input stage to minimise run time errors introduced by values that are not of the right type or unacceptable values.

Questions

❶ What is meant by a syntax error? Give an example of a syntax error.

❷ What is meant by a logical error? Give an example of a logical error.

❸ The following code segment will produce an error:

```
Avalue = 0

Anothervalue = 12

OUTPUT Anothervalue/Avalue
```

What is the error and what type of error is this?

❹ The expression A + B := C is incorrect.
Explain the error and how this expression should be written to remove this error.

❺ A system used at an ATM (automated teller machine) uses the PIN and available credit to decide whether to dispense cash or not. Draw a test table to check that the code for this works, giving the reason for the test, the test data used and the expected outcome for the test.

Extension task

1 The program to collect high scores in the previous section should validate the data at input. Include the validation to make sure data is acceptable.

2 When writing a program to calculate the area of a triangle using Heron's formula, what validation on input is required? Heron's formula is $\sqrt{(s(s-a)(s-b)(s-c))}$ where $s = (a + b + c)/2$ and a, b and c are the lengths of the sides of a triangle.

Manipulating strings

String variables consist of a string of alphanumeric characters of any length. All programming languages include commands to manipulate these strings of characters in various ways.

If we use the string variable 'word' where word = "Computing is good" then we can use a range of string commands to manipulate the string word in various ways:

LENGTH

The **LENGTH** of the string variable can be returned as an integer value.

Example

LENGTH(word) = 17 (note the spaces are counted in the length of the variable word)

1	2	3	4	5	6	7	8	9	10	11	12	13	14	15	16	17
C	o	m	p	u	t	i	n	g		i	s		g	o	o	d

LEFT and RIGHT

The **LEFT** and **RIGHT** string commands are used to return the left-hand or right-hand portions of a string. The format of the command is usually:

LEFT('string to be manipulated',<number of characters to return>)

Example

LEFT(word,5) = "Compu" (the first 5 characters of the variable word)

1	2	3	4	5	6	7	8	9	10	11	12	13	14	15	16	17
C	o	m	p	u	t	i	n	g		i	s		g	o	o	d

RIGHT('string to be manipulated',<number of characters to return>)

Example

RIGHT(word,7) = "is good" (the last 7 characters of the variable word)

1	2	3	4	5	6	7	8	9	10	11	12	13	14	15	16	17
C	o	m	p	u	t	i	n	g		i	s		g	o	o	d

MID

It is also possible to return a set of characters from the middle of a string using the **MID** string command. The format of this command is typically:

MID('string to be manipulated',<start point>,<number of characters to return>)

Example

MID(word,7,5) = "ing i" (the 5 characters starting from the seventh character of the variable word)

1	2	3	4	5	6	7	8	9	10	11	12	13	14	15	16	17
C	o	m	p	u	t	i	n	g		i	s		g	o	o	d

INSTRING

The **INSTRING** command is used to return the first time a particular string or character appears within another string. Typically the command format is:

INSTRING('string to be manipulated','string to be found')

Example

INSTRING(word,"in") = 7 (in starts at the seventh character of the variable word).

This command can be used to find strings or single characters and returns 0 if the search string is not found.

1	2	3	4	5	6	7	8	9	10	11	12	13	14	15	16	17
C	o	m	p	u	t	i	n	g		i	s		g	o	o	d

Sorting strings

Characters are stored using binary code and have a numeric value (an **ASCII** value). If strings are sorted this is done so using their ASCII values. 'A' has the ASCII value 65, 'a' has the ASCII value 97 which explains why the list 'Banana, apple, Pear, Orange' would be sorted into the order:

Banana, Orange, Pear, apple

even though alphabetically 'a' precedes 'B'.

ASC and CHR

We can convert characters into their numeric ASCII value and back using:

ASC(character) and **CHR**(integer)

Key terms

ASCII (American Standard Code for Information Interchange): 7-bi system to code the character set of a computer

CHR: Uses the ASCII value to look up the character associated with a particular number

Example

```
ASC("B") = 66
(The ASCII value of the character B is 66)
CHR(67) = "C"
(C has the ASCII value 67)
```

There are also usually features to combine or **concatenate** two or more strings together. This is often done by adding the variables together using the + sign.

Example

If Onestring = "Comp" and Twostring = "uter" then
    Onestring+Twostring = "Computer"

Key terms

Concatenation: Combining two strings into a single string

Summary

Programming languages have features to manipulate string variables including commands to return the length of the string, or particular sections, for example the left, right and mid portions. There are features to find the location of strings within strings or to combine two strings together into a single one. ASCII values are used to sort strings of characters and to identify individual characters in the computer's character set.

Questions

❶ If Astring is "John von Neumann" what do the following commands return?
  a LEFT(Astring,4)
  b RIGHT(Astring,4)
  c MID(Astring,6,3)
  d MID(Astring,10,4)
  e INSTRING(Astring,"von")
  f INSTRING(Astring,"Hn")

❷ What is returned by this expression?
CHR(87)+CHR(69)+CHR(76)+CHR(76)+CHR(32)+CHR(68)+CHR(79)+CHR(78)+CHR(69)

Extension tasks

1 Write a program to look at each character in an input string one character at a time and output its ASCII value.

2 Write a program to take two strings and search for the second one inside the first, returning the starting position of the second string within the first.

3 Extend this program to discard the left portion of the first string then search in the remaining part for another occurrence of the second string. For example, search for all the occurrences of 'ra' inside the string 'abracadabra'.

Exam style questions

1 In the following code:

```
CONSTANT rate = 5.5
INPUT B
INPUT C
A = B/C
K = A * rate
OUTPUT K
```

a Identify:

  i a variable [1 mark]

  ii a constant. [1 mark]

b B and C are integers. What variable type should be declared for A?

  Explain your choice. [2 marks]

c What is output if the values input are:

  i B = 2, C = 2 [1 mark]

  ii B = 0, C = 1 [1 mark]

  iii B = 4, C = 2? [1 mark]

d What happens if C is entered as 0? [2 marks]

2 A program includes the following code:

```
INPUT hours
IF hours <= 8 THEN
  pay = hours * 6.00
ELSE
  pay = 8 * 6.00 + (hours - 8) * 9.00
ENDIF
OUTPUT pay
```

a What is output if the hours are input as:

  i 3 [1 mark]

  ii 8 [1 mark]

  iii 10? [1 mark]

b This is a program to calculate how much someone is paid for the hours they work at a basic rate of £6.00 per hour.

    i Describe what the program is doing when hours worked are more than 8. [3 marks]

    ii Modify this program to allow the user to input values for hourly pay rates. [2 marks]

3 A program to calculate the area of a circle uses the constant, pi=3.14 and asks the user to input a value for the radius of the circle in cm. The program rejects values for the radius that are 0 or less and anything over 20 cm. Write an algorithm for this program. (The area of a circle is pi*radius^2.) [5 marks]

4 An electronic point of sale device requires the user to enter a 4-digit PIN to accept payment. If the PIN is entered incorrectly three times the card is rejected and marked as invalid. The correct PIN is 5146 for test purposes. The program displays the following message if the code is accepted:

PIN ACCEPTED

Or displays the following message if the code is entered incorrectly three times:

PIN REJECTED,

CARD NO LONGER VALID

a Complete the table below with four different test cases. For each test case: identify test data, the reason for the test and the expected outcome. [8 marks]

Test case	Test data	Reason for test	Expected outcome
1			
2			
3			
4			

b Write an algorithm to describe this process. [8 marks]

Introduction to controlled assessment

As with many other GCSE specifications, OCR GCSE Computing requires the submission of controlled assessment work. This is the current equivalent of what used to be called coursework. It differs from previous examples of coursework in that specific tasks are set by OCR, with only limited choices made by the candidates. There are clear guidelines about how much help students get with preparing their work. They basically mean that students are expected to get help in preparing for the assessment, but once the actual OCR set task is under way, the student must produce the work with no extra help, as if under exam conditions. The main thing is that what is finally submitted is all the student's own work.

To make sure that you get the best credit for the work that you do, it is essential that you have access to the assessment criteria supplied by OCR during this task-taking phase so that you know how you will be assessed. The evidence you will need to provide is also important and OCR do not want you to spend a long time at the end of the process writing a long report on what you did.

The philosophy behind the OCR GCSE Computing controlled assessment

The thinking behind the OCR Computing GCSE is somewhat different from many previous IT related specifications. Computing has become the exciting, vibrant activity that it is because of clever people thinking differently and breaking the rules. New uses for computers do not always come from working through a checklist although clearly a system being made for a paying client must at least fulfil its design specification. The iPad wasn't dreamed up purely from a set of attainment descriptors laid down by a committee. It may have started from a few basic requirements, but it developed into what it is because of inspiration, creative flair and risk taking.

It is not expected that students will 'jump through hoops' in order to do well. On the contrary, the assignments have been designed to open up the possibilities for students and teachers to produce interesting and innovative work. This is not to say that the assessments are a free for all. Students who do well show that they have a solid understanding of computing principles which include those in the A451 specification, but also go beyond them. So, the controlled assessments do not always have one expected pre-planned solution and neither do they have to be of a certain length. Sometimes a problem can be solved by a clever but brief short cut. That sort of approach will be rewarded and it is not always necessary to slavishly follow the obvious pathway. So, if you see a clever but brief solution to a problem, there is no need to worry that you have not written enough, as long as the problem is actually attempted and preferably solved effectively.

For these reasons, the mark schemes for the controlled assessments are deliberately rather vague. You will notice that firstly there are not very many criteria. Then, within each marking criterion, there are only three levels. These levels make it quite easy to categorise a piece of work very roughly as excellent, good or poor. To refine the marks further, it is necessary to look at the descriptors and you will notice that the higher the mark band, the more things there are in it. These things are not a check list. They are just a guide to the sort of characteristics that work at that level will have. So, if a piece of work fits most of the descriptors at a certain level, then that is probably the mark that it will get.

However, there is a further important point to watch. The controlled assessments are made from separate tasks. The A452 assignments contain a list of tasks to do and questions to answer. The A453 programming tasks always have three problems to solve. However clever you are and however you impress with your computing knowledge, you cannot get full marks unless all the required work is done. So the components of each assessment should all be completed if at all possible.

Unit A452 Practical investigation

In this chapter, you will learn what Unit A452 is for, and how to approach and present it in order to get the best possible marks. This chapter will be based on a scenario that is typical of some of the assignments already set and those that may be set in the future.

What is Unit A452?

The OCR GCSE Computing specification sets out a body of knowledge that forms the basis of computer science as a subject. Much of what is set out has quite a long history – the underlying principles of computing have been with us at least since the 1940s. Likewise, the basic model of a computer with its memory store and processor has been successfully used in many machines for a quite a long time. The principle of representing data as binary codes also has not changed since the 1940s and 1950s even though the range of data stored has grown.

But, the number of applications of computers is still racing ahead, with new developments appearing all the time. New uses for computing devices are continually being thought of and developed. This is because the basic ideas behind computing science and the cheap availability of technology to exploit them have allowed a huge flowering of human creativity which is still continuing. Computing remains a vibrant and exciting part of human endeavour and a rewarding career choice.

Unit A452 goes beyond the basic facts in the specification and provides opportunities to:
- look at some practical uses of computing
- investigate real-world examples of computer use
- show some creativity by solving problems with a computer.

The assessment is designed to require some investigation by the student. Normally, this will involve quite a lot of web-based enquiry, but it doesn't all have to be like that. In some cases, you can find out what you need by talking to IT professionals, reading and using books, or consulting the computing press. This stage is important because part of the assessment takes into account whether the student has a broader knowledge of computing than can be demonstrated in a practical assessment.

Some of the assignments involve programming. This is deliberate because each of them leads along a path that might not have been covered in the basic specification. Some assignments require knowledge of a particular programming language or approach. For example, one looks at assembly language and another requires students to understand the link between a client-side scripting language and web forms. Other assignments do not require programming.

Unit A452 differs from the programming unit (Unit A453) in a number of ways. Firstly, it may in some cases specify a language, whereas Unit A453 does not. Unit A453 leaves the decision on how to produce code to the individual. Secondly, Unit A452 requires the demonstration of a wider understanding of computing in context – how computing has an impact in some other part of life. This book has a number of 'computing in context' features which suggest the sort of topics that students should be showing an interest in as they work through the course.

Unit A452 assignments are made up from a set of tasks and questions. They variously require research, practice, practical activities, evaluation and wider comments. The last question in each set suggests a specific issue that should be commented on.

Presentation

There is no requirement to present your work in a particular way. This is deliberate so that students can choose their own way to provide the evidence that they have completed the tasks. Some might like to present their work as a PowerPoint presentation. Some might like to produce animated screen captures to show what happens in their solutions. Movie clips are acceptable too. Some students have made movie clips where they demonstrate what they have done and provide a spoken commentary. Many still prefer to word process their work and illustrate it with screenshots.

But, having said that, it is important that, whatever medium is chosen, thought must go into presenting the work logically and attractively. Whoever is marking or moderating the work needs to find a way through it quickly and easily. An obvious point is that the numbered tasks in Unit A452 should be presented, clearly numbered and in order. There is always a danger that careless presentation might lead to some of the essential evidence getting 'lost' in unexpected places resulting in you losing credit. So, you should always make sure that you understand what each task is looking for and that your work is presented in a full and plain fashion.

Less is more

GCSE and A-level coursework has often tended to take up a lot of time. Many students spend a lot of effort in writing huge amounts of text and not enough in actually developing their solutions. This sort of hard labour is not required or wanted. What matters is that the work is completed and that it does exactly what is asked for. In many cases, this can be achieved in a very short space. Lengthy reports can often get in the way of showing the essentials.

Example assignment

The rest of this chapter will look at an example assignment and how it could be approached.

The scenario

Python

Many schools and colleges are now introducing GCSE Computing. Among other things, GCSE Computing requires students to learn and demonstrate programming skills. With many programming languages already in existence, deciding on a language to use in class can be a difficult decision. Some considerations when making this choice are:

■ Does the teacher already have a preferred language?
■ Is the language easy to learn?
■ Is the language easily and economically available?
■ Will the language work adequately on the school network?
■ Does the language cover the constructs required by the specification?
■ Does the language support graphical interfaces?

Many teachers have decided to use the programming language Python. This assignment looks at whether Python is a good choice for teaching and learning programming.

Your assignment

1 Many books and courses about programming start with the traditional 'Hello World!' program. It just outputs those words – nothing else.

   a Show how a Python program would be written to achieve this.

   b Show how the 'Hello World!' program would be written in any two other languages.

2 A Fibonacci sequence is a set of integers where the first two are 0 and 1, and each subsequent number is the sum of the previous two. The first few numbers are 0, 1, 1, 2, 3. Here is some Python code that produces a set of Fibonacci numbers.

```python
def fib(n):     # write Fibonacci series up to n
   """Print a Fibonacci series up to n."""
   a, b = 0, 1
   while a < n:
      print (a),
      a, b = b, a + b


fib(2000)
```

   a Enter this code into a suitable editor, save it and run it in the Python shell. Show the output.

   b Explain what each line of the code does.

   c Identify the two functions in this program.

   d State the purpose of the # sign in this program.

3 a Write a program to produce a Fibonacci sequence in another language of your choice.

   b Comment on which of the two programs would be easier to demonstrate to someone learning to program.

4 Here is some Python code that can be used to store details of a music collection.

```python
# program to write music details to file
f = open("my _ music.txt","a")
print (f)
print ("Enter the details")


ok=True
```

```
while ok==True:
    serial_number = (input("Enter serial number: "))
    f.write(serial_number+"\n")
    genre = (input("Enter genre: "))
    f.write(genre+"\n")
    artist = (input("Enter artist: "))
    f.write(artist+"\n")
    title = (input("Enter title: "))
    f.write(title+"\n")
    ask=(input("Another? "))
    if ask in ('y', 'ye', 'yes', 'Y'):
        ok=True
    else:
        ok=False

f.close()

input("press enter to finish")
```

Enter this code into a Python shell and run it. You will find it easier if you save it as a Python file first using a suitable editor such as Idle. Test it with at least three records. Use a text editor such as Notepad to demonstrate what the program has done.

5 Write a Python program that will read back and display the data that you have entered.

Produce evidence to show that you have planned, written and tested your code.

6 Write a Python program that will search for a particular record by serial number and display the details.

Produce evidence to show that you have planned, written and tested your code.

7 Combine the three Python programs together and add a menu so that the user can choose whether to write new records, read the whole file or search for a particular record.

Produce evidence to show that you have planned, written and tested your code.

8 Write a conclusion about the effectiveness of your solutions.

9 To what extent would you recommend Python as a language for learning how to program?

Extension tasks

1 Look up the range of programming languages that are available. There are hundreds, but try to identify the main categories that there are.

2 Which languages are most popular in the professional IT world? You can get some idea of this by looking up computer programmer job advertisements.

3 Find out why Fibonacci sequences are important in understanding the natural world. You could write a program to generate a shape using values from a Fibonacci sequence.

How to do the example assignment

We shall look through each part of the assignment and see how best to tackle it in order to get the best possible marks.

Right from the outset, it is important to look at the marking criteria. Some of the things you are credited for are here in the Mark Scheme, rather than in the details of the questions. Look through the Mark Scheme and in particular look at the descriptions in the right-hand column. These are the characteristics of a top grade answer and you may want to be aiming for them. There is no need to treat this as a check list. In some cases not all of the descriptions will be appropriate, but most of them will.

The Mark Scheme headings

A. Practical activity   0–15 marks

Most Unit A452 assignments will require some research in order to find out things that are not in the Unit A451 specification. Your work should show some evidence that you have given some thought to what you need to find out and how you will do this. Normally the first few questions lead naturally to doing this, but you might need to do further research as you go along. Typically, somewhere there will be mention of websites visited, books and people consulted, and the things you hope to learn from them. Successfully solving the problems can be evidence itself that you have investigated the topic.

B. Effectiveness and efficiency   0–10 marks

This section highlights first that you have done ALL the required work and second that it has been done in an efficient way. For work that involves programming, the code should be efficient – that usually means that it is the minimum to achieve what is needed. For example, long repeated sections of code should be avoided where loops are more efficient.

C. Technical understanding   0–10 marks

This refers to a general feeling that you really know what you are talking about. To score well here, the work submitted should include relevant references to computing principles and, in particular, should use appropriate technical language. For example, when describing code, you should refer to terms correctly (when relevant) such as functions, parameters, variables and loops. For high marks in this section, the work should look as if it has been produced by someone who has a secure understanding of the scenario and its implications.

D. Testing, evaluation and conclusions   0–10 marks

The solution to all parts of the problem should work and evidence should be supplied that demonstrates this. It is also important to comment on your work. Comments about how much you learned or how much you enjoyed or hated it are no use to anyone. If your solution worked fine and you think it is effective, then say so. There is no need to go on about it. If parts are less good than you think they could be then make a few remarks about that too. Maybe you produced a 'kludge' – a crude solution – instead of an efficient one. Say what you think.

This section will usually require evidence that the scenario has been understood in a wider context. There will usually be a final question that asks for specific comments.

This section of the Mark Scheme also relates to how well you communicate your work. It doesn't matter whether you use slides, videos or printed work, the standard of English should be good, with no spelling mistakes or bad grammar. In the real world of computing, it is not enough to be just a good technical person. It is important to be able to communicate with colleagues and customers in a way that they can understand.

The sample assignment, step by step

1 Many books and courses about programming start with the traditional 'Hello World!' program. It just outputs those words – nothing else.

   a   Show how a Python program would be written to achieve this.

   b   Show how the 'Hello World!' program would be written in any two other languages.

Specimen answer

The Hello World! program is so well known that it is easy to find it in any language by doing a quick Google search. Here it is in Python, C++ and Java.

a Python

```
print ("Hello, World!")
```

b i C++

```
#include <iostream>
using namespace std;

int main ()
{
  cout << "Hello, World!";
  return 0;
}
```

ii Java

```
public class HelloWorld {

  public static void main(String[] args) {
    System.out.println("Hello, World!");
  }

}
```

Examiner's comment

All that is asked for here is to show the methods in different languages. There is no need to do anything else, although a mention of how the answers were found can help to provide evidence of the planning. Already, the simplicity of Python is becoming apparent.

Remember that this could perhaps be presented as a slide, which would be one way of separating each part of the answer.

2 A Fibonacci sequence is a set of integers where the first two are 0 and 1, and each subsequent number is the sum of the previous two. The first few numbers are 0, 1, 1, 2, 3. Here is some Python code that produces a set of Fibonacci numbers.

```
def fib(n):     # write Fibonacci series up to n
    """Print a Fibonacci series up to n."""
    a, b = 0, 1
    while a < n:
        print (a),
        a, b = b, a + b

fib(2000)
```

a   Enter this code into a suitable editor, save it and run it in the Python shell. Show the output.

b   Explain what each line of the code does.

c   Identify the two functions in this program.

d   State the purpose of the # sign in this program.

Specimen answer

a   The output from the code supplied.

```
>>>
0
1
1
2
3
5
8
13
21
34
55
89
144
233
377
610
987
1597
>>>
```

b

```
def fib(n):    # write Fibonacci series up to n
```

This line defines a function called Fib. It requires a parameter n to be passed to it so that it knows how many times to iterate.

```
"""Print a Fibonacci series up to n."""
```

This is a "docstring". It is an optional description that goes in triple quotes and must be the second line of the function. It helps us to remember what the function was for and it can also pop up as interactive help when editing code in Idle.

```
a, b = 0, 1
```

This is initialising variables. You can assign more than one variable in one line. a takes the value 0 and b takes the value 1.

```
while a < n:
```

The start of the loop. What follows is repeated as long as a is less than n. n was passed to the function on the declaration line. The loop includes all code below until the next unindent.

```
print (a),
```

The current value of a is output.

```
a, b = b, a + b
```

Again, we have multiple assignments here. a takes the value of b (the next number in the series) and then b takes the value of a + b which will produce the next Fibonacci number. Incidentally, the next line of the code is unindented, so the loop stops here.

```
fib(2000)
```

This is in fact the start of the program. It calls the function fib and hands it the parameter 2000. So the function will produce all the Fibonacci numbers below 2000.

c The two functions are `fib(n)` (which was written by the programmer) and `print()`, which is a built in Python function.

d The # sign is for a comment. Anything written after this is ignored by the interpreter – it is just to help understand what is going on.

Examiner's comment
- -
This section could be presented in alternative ways. A voice over in a video clip would be another possibility.

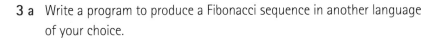

3 a Write a program to produce a Fibonacci sequence in another language of your choice.

Specimen answer

Here is a program written in JavaScript that generates a Fibonacci sequence.

```html
<html>
<body>
<script type="text/javascript">
var a=0
var b=1
var temp=0
while (a<2000)
  {
  document.write(a);
  document.write("<br />");
  temp=a
  a=b;
  b=temp+b;
  }
</script>
</body>
</html>
```

b Comment on which of the two programs would be easier to demonstrate to someone learning to program.

Specimen answer

The Python program is much shorter and it would be easier to get someone to understand the logic than in the JavaScript program. The JavaScript program uses a temporary variable when swapping the values and that is an extra concept that the person learning would have to grasp.

Examiner's comment

- -

The approach is a little different in the JavaScript example. A function is not used, but the question only requires a sequence to be generated and the code does this.

4 Here is some Python code that can be used to store details of a music collection.

```python
# program to write music details to file
f = open("my _ music.txt","a")
print (f)
print ("Enter the details")


ok=True


while ok==True:
  serial _ number = (input("Enter serial number: "))
  f.write(serial _ number+"\n")
  genre = (input("Enter genre: "))
  f.write(genre+"\n")
  artist = (input("Enter artist: "))
  f.write(artist+"\n")
  title = (input("Enter title: "))
  f.write(title+"\n")
  ask=(input("Another? "))
  if ask in ('y', 'ye', 'yes', 'Y'):
    ok=True
  else:
    ok=False


f.close()


input("press enter to finish")
```

Enter this code into a Python shell and run it. You will find it easier if you save it as a Python file first using a suitable editor such as Idle. Test it with at least three records. Use a text editor such as Notepad to demonstrate what the program has done.

Specimen answer

Here is a screenshot of the program running in a Python shell, with the first record being entered.

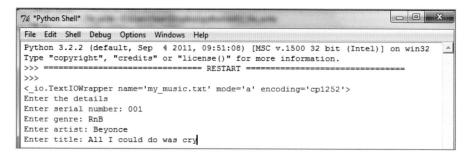

The program created the file my_music.txt. This can be read by any text editor. Here is the file displayed in Notepad. Each field is on a separate line, because the program wrote the "\n" new line character to file after each response.

The file is opened with the line:

```
f = open("my _ music.txt","a")
```

This assigns a file variable f to the file "my_music.txt" and opens it for 'appending' (the "a" parameter). This means that if the file does not exist, the program will create it. If the file does already exist, new records will be added to the end.

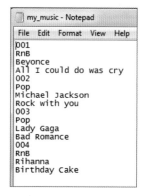

Examiner's comment

It is always a good idea to add a few comments in order to demonstrate a wider understanding. This can help boost the marks in the Technical understanding section of the Mark Scheme. Screenshots of what is happening are useful too, but avoid too much repetition of similar screens.

5 Write a Python program that will read back and display the data that you have entered.

Produce evidence to show that you have planned, written and tested your code.

Specimen answer

This program demonstrates one of several Python file read methods. The "r" in the file open function means 'read'. The readlines method takes in all of the file until the end of the file and stores it in a list. The code here assigns the list to the variable lines, prints out the list with print(lines), then using the len function, it prints the number of elements in the list. We entered four records, so the number of elements is 16.

In order to have finer control, we then loop through the list, printing one element (line) at a time. This will be useful when we come to do a search later.

The algorithm for this is:

```
open the file for reading
display confirmation message
read the entire file into a list variable
(display the result – for test purposes – can be removed later)
repeat
output each line of the list
until end of list
close file
```

Here is the code that will read back the file:

```python
# program to read music details from file
f = open("my_music.txt","r")
print ("Reading file..")


# read into list


lines=f.readlines()
print(lines)
print(len(lines))
for line in lines:
  print(line)


f.close()
```

Here is the output from the file read program.

```
>>>
Reading file..
['001\n', 'RnB\n', 'Beyonce\n', 'All I could do was cry\n', '002\n',
'Pop\n', 'Michael Jackson\n', 'Rock with you\n', '003\n', 'Pop\n', 'Lady
Gaga\n', 'Bad Romance\n', '004\n', 'RnB\n', 'Rihanna\n', 'Birthday Cake\n']
16
001

RnB

Beyonce

All I could do was cry

002

Pop

Michael Jackson

Rock with you

003

Pop

Lady Gaga

Bad Romance

004

RnB

Rihanna

Birthday Cake

>>>
```

Examiner's comment

The initial file dump is not strictly necessary for the purposes of the assignment, but it was included in order to show the thinking behind the next stage of the program development and how easy it is to manipulate the data once it is read in.

6 Write a Python program that will search for a particular record by serial number and display the details.

Produce evidence to show that you have planned, written and tested your code.

Specimen answer

This program again uses the **readlines** method to take in the whole file and then examines the lines one by one to find the serial number asked for. Python has a useful list operator **in** that detects if an item is a member of a list. As the record details are always the next three lines in the list, it is easy to extract them and display them.

The process is as follows:

```
get the serial number required
open the file for reading
read the file into a list
iterate through the list
examine each line
check for the required serial number
if found print this and the next three lines
close file
```

Here is the code to do this.

```python
# search by serial number then display all details of song found
target=(input("What serial number do you want? "))
f=open("my _ music.txt","r")
lines=f.readlines()
for i in range(0, len(lines)):
  line=lines[i]
  if target in (line):
    found=True
    print("Found " + line)
    print(lines[i+1])
    print(lines[i+2])
    print(lines[i+3])
    break

f.close()
```

Here is a test run of this program, searching for record number 003.

```
>>>
What serial number do you want? 003
Found 003

Pop

Lady Gaga

Bad Romance

>>> |
```

Further tests were made on invalid data.

- The number 6 was input – which does not exist in the file.
- The letters rrr were input which is not a serial number.

In any case of invalid data, the input is ignored and the program terminates. We can make this more user friendly when we create a menu in the next section.

Here is the raw output at this stage:

```
>>> ================================ RESTART ================================
>>>
What serial number do you want? 6
>>> ================================ RESTART ================================
>>>
What serial number do you want? rrr
>>>
```

Examiner's comment

The technique is explained and an algorithm presented. Some test runs are included. Reference is made to what is planned for the next stage, which shows that the assignment is being treated as a whole.

7 Combine the three Python programs together and add a menu so that the user can choose whether to write new records, read the whole file or search for a particular record.

Produce evidence to show that you have planned, written and tested your code.

Specimen answer

The easiest way to combine these programs is to make each of them a function. A menu is then written which gets a choice from the user and directs the program to the correct function.

The functions are declared by using the **def** statement. The menu makes use of a simple input function and checks the response. The list operator **in** is used to allow some variation of input from the user – upper or lower case response is acceptable.

   In this section of the code, the loop is iterated as long as the condition is TRUE, in other words, the response is one of the acceptable ones. If the response is acceptable, the appropriate function is called, otherwise an error message is displayed.

```python
print("The music program\n")
print("What do you want to do?\n\n")
print("Add new data\n")
print("Read the file\n")
print("Find record\n")
print("Quit")


# valid_response="True"
while True:
  answer=(input("Press A, R, F or Q: "))
  if answer in("A", "a"):
    write_file()
  elif answer in ("R", "r"):
    read_file()
  elif answer in ("F", "f"):
    find_rec()
  elif answer in ("Q", "q"):
    break


  else:
    print("Invalid response")
```

Here is the complete program.

```python
# function to write music details to file
def write_file():
  """Write details to file"""


# create a new file or add to an existing file
  f = open("my_music.txt","a")
  print ("Enter the details")

  ok=True
```

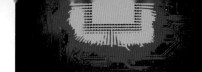

```
# loop through user inputs, writing to file at the same time
  while ok==True:
    serial_number = (input("Enter serial number: "))
    f.write(serial_number+"\n")
    genre = (input("Enter genre: "))
    f.write(genre+"\n")
    artist = (input("Enter artist: "))
    f.write(artist+"\n")
    title = (input("Enter title: "))
    f.write(title+"\n")
    ask=(input("Another? "))
    if ask in ('y', 'ye', 'yes', 'Y'):
      ok=True
    else:
      ok=False

    f.close()


# function to read music details from file
def read_file():
  """Read the details back from the file"""

# open file for reading then read and display entire file
  f = open("my_music.txt","r")
  print ("Reading file..")

  # read into list
  lines=f.readlines()
  print(lines)
  print(len(lines))
  for line in lines:
    print(line)

  f.close()

# function to find a record
def find_rec():
  """Find a record input by user"""
```

```
# search by serial number then display all details of song found
  target=(input("What serial number do you want? "))
  f=open("my_music.txt","r")
  lines=f.readlines()
  for i in range(0, len(lines)):
    line=lines[i]
    if target in (line):
      found=True
      print("Found " + line)
      print(lines[i+1])
      print(lines[i+2])
      print(lines[i+3])
      break


    f.close()



print("The music program\n")
print("What do you want to do?\n\n")
print("Add new data\n")
print("Read the file\n")
print("Find record\n")
print("Quit")

# valid_response="True"
while True:
  answer=(input("Press A, R, F or Q: "))
  if answer in("A", "a"):
    write_file()
  elif answer in ("R", "r"):
    read_file()
  elif answer in ("F", "f"):
    find_rec()
  elif answer in ("Q", "q"):
    break


  else:
    print("Invalid response")
```

Testing the complete program

Test 1 An invalid response is given: the letter d is input.

```
The music program

What do you want to do?


Add new data

Read the file

Find record

Quit
Press A, R, F or Q: d
Invalid response
Press A, R, F or Q: |
```

Result The program asks again for a response.

Test 2 q is input to terminate the program.

```
The music program

What do you want to do?


Add new data

Read the file

Find record

Quit
Press A, R, F or Q: q
>>> |
```

Result The program terminates.

Test 3 f is input to call up the 'Find' function.

```
The music program

What do you want to do?


Add new data

Read the file

Find record

Quit
Press A, R, F or Q: f
What serial number do you want? 001
Found 001

RnB

Beyonce

All I could do was cry

Press A, R, F or Q: |
```

Result The Find function appears and 001 is searched for and found.

Test 4 a is input to append a new record.

```
Press A, R, F or Q: a
Enter the details
Enter serial number: 005
Enter genre: Pop
Enter artist: Mariah Carey
Enter title: One Sweet Day
Another? n
Press A, R, F or Q: q
>>> |
```

Result The details are asked for, then quit is selected to terminate the program.

Test 5 r is input to read the file. This will show if the last record was appended correctly.

```
005

Pop

Mariah Carey

One Sweet Day

Press A, R, F or Q:
```

Result The screenshot shows the end of the output with the new record in place.

Examiner's comment

Sufficient examples have been demonstrated to show that the program works well with expected and some unexpected data.

8 Write a conclusion about the effectiveness of your solutions.

Specimen answer

The solutions all produce the results asked for. The code makes effective use of some of Python's capabilities that allow coding to be shorter than in some other languages. The user interface is primitive but it does the job required of it.

To make the program more attractive, a modern graphical user interface could easily be set up using the Python toolkit, Tkinter, or one of many others that exist. The underlying code would be largely the same.

9 To what extent would you recommend Python as a language for learning how to program?

Specimen answer

There is much to recommend Python as a teaching and learning language. Much depends upon the preferences and past experiences of the teacher but here are some possible considerations:

Advantages of using Python

- Available on most platforms
- Free of charge
- Simple to learn
- Beginners get results quickly
- Because it is easy to code quickly, fewer mistakes are made
- Less emphasis on variable typing so the student can concentrate on algorithms
- No need to declare variables so the code is shorter
- Variables can change their data type during run time, allowing flexibility
- Errors show up immediately – there is no need to keep recompiling
- Strings, lists and tuples make it easy to handle data collections
- It is easy to write clean uncluttered code
- There are many helpful editors that present the code logically as it is typed
- It encourages experimentation
- Many libraries are available to make most jobs easier
- Large companies such as Google use it
- It's fun to write

Disadvantages of using Python

- It is an interpreted language – compiling it is a separate issue so students don't get to work with compilation from the start
- Slow execution compared with a compiled language
- Not suited to memory intensive tasks
- The language changes quite regularly

In conclusion, Python looks like a great choice for a first teaching language or a quick and elegant way to produce solutions.

Examiner's comment

Enough has been said here to demonstrate that the student has investigated the issue and formed some opinions. Above all, there is use of technically assured language which shows that the student has done some good investigation and has a secure understanding of the issues.

Extension task

Python is sometimes described as a 'batteries included' language. What does this mean and is it helpful to someone learning to program for the first time?

Unit A453 Programming project

As part of the OCR GCSE Computing course you are expected to produce working coded solutions to some problems using a suitable programming language. The choice of language is not specified and it is best to work in the language you have most experience with. The tasks are set so that they can be completed in many different ways, and providing these produce coded solutions, all are acceptable. In this chapter we will look at the processes involved in analysing, designing, developing, testing and evaluating these coded solutions.

This chapter will be based on a set of tasks that is typical of those already available and are likely to be set in the future.

What is Unit A453?

The OCR GCSE Computing specification includes a significant section on programming using an imperative language. An imperative language is one that basically instructs the computer about what to do and in what order to reach a result. Imperative languages are derived from the assembly languages used by the pioneers of digital binary computing but with significant variations in the features and techniques that each of these languages make available to the programmer. Most languages will include facilities for subroutines or procedures that make the programming task much more organised and efficient, but the elements used within these subroutines remain imperative and understanding basic imperative programming provides a solid basis for learning to code in a wide variety of languages. The code samples included in the chapter have been written in BBC BASIC because of the similarity of BBC BASIC to pseudocode which therefore makes it easier to translate the logic into other programming languages.

The Unit A453 tasks provide an opportunity to develop working code segments that could be used as part of larger programs. The purpose of the unit is for you to demonstrate logical thinking and problem solving skills using a suitable programming language. The tasks will generally consist of three sub-tasks often within the same context but the sub-tasks are meant to be treated as stand-alone programming exercises and not as a single project. The assessment of these tasks by the teacher is, however, based on the work produced for all three sub-tasks and not on individual solutions, so opportunities to demonstrate specific skills may not arise in every sub-task.

The assessment of your work is based on:

- an analysis of the tasks
- development of suitable designs including algorithms that describe the solution
- evidence of development
- testing and an evaluation of the solution.

The Mark Scheme headings

The assessments are based on descriptors provided by OCR and the following Mark Scheme headings:

A. Use of programming techniques   0–18 marks

There are a lot of marks for the use of programming techniques which reinforces the practical nature of this unit. Marks are awarded for the use of a suitable range of programming techniques to solve all three sub-tasks and for the effective and efficient use of these techniques. For example, using a loop where this is more efficient than a long sequence of commands. If you are using a procedural language then the use of procedures for frequently used code segments would also provide an opportunity to demonstrate efficient code.

B. Design   0–9 marks

In order to design an effective solution to a problem, careful analysis of the problem and identification of the end user requirements is essential. These requirements can then be turned into a set of success criteria to be used when assessing the program using a suitable test strategy. Designs must include suitable algorithms that describe in detail the proposed solution. Detailed, precise algorithms describing the solution will inevitably lead to effective working code and therefore provide an opportunity to improve the mark achieved for section A.

C. Development   0–9 marks

The development of a solution should be cyclic in nature. Using the algorithms write the first section of code and test it using the data identified in the test strategy. When that section of code is working, code the next element and test it. Repeat this cyclic development until all the code for the sub-task is completed and tested. This section is assessed against evidence for this process and the sensible use of variable names, and the explanation of the purpose for each section of code.

D. Testing and evaluation

0–9 marks

For this section the testing carried out during development and any extra testing following completion of the code should be cross-referenced against the success criteria to show the success or otherwise of the developed solution. The purpose of testing is to try and break the code to identify faults and flaws. Since these are code segments you should expect the solutions to have some faults after completion and the fact that these exist should not be hidden or ignored. Identifying these flaws is part of the process and knowing what they are and suggesting how they might be fixed is a positive feature of the work.

The report

There is no specific requirement for the way you present your solution. This is quite deliberate so that students can make a choice based on the way they have completed the task. For those who have coded in console mode, that is text-based interfaces, annotated screenshots of the testing and annotated code segments may suggest a word processed document or PowerPoint report. For those who have created a more visual interface the inclusion of screen capture video may be more appropriate. The report should explain the process followed by the students and can be regarded as a commentary.

It is a good idea to start the report at the research phase with an analysis of the end user requirements, adding success criteria, algorithms, test strategies, evidence of development and testing as it is produced to tell the story of the process. This approach will record the process from start to finish alongside the practical activity, leaving only the evaluation to complete at the end of the process. Lengthy explanations and screenshots of every key press are not required. It should be a report on the development of a coded solution and not a description of how each technique was used in the process. It is also important to keep track of the code as it is developed and to save versions of the code at various key stages in its development. These code segments are used to assess the work, and have the added bonus of being available as a backup if changes to the code cause problems that cannot be resolved and you need to return to a previous working version.

Example assignment

The following example assignment is going to be used to illustrate the various elements of the solution:

Task A

Design, code and test a program to calculate the body mass index (BMI) for an adult.

The program should work in metric units (kg and cm) or imperial units (stones and pounds, and feet and inches). The user should be asked to choose which units. The system should output the BMI and the appropriate category from:

- *Less than 18.5 – Underweight*
- *Between 18.5 and 25 – Normal*
- *Between 25 and 30 – Overweight*
- *Greater than 30 – Obese*

The formulae are:

Metric units: BMI = weight in kg/(height in cm)^2

Imperial units: BMI = (weight in pounds × 703)/(height in inches)^2

Task B

Alan is trying to lose weight and weighs himself every few days. He wants to keep track of these weights and the days they were taken in a file on his computer. Design, code, test and evaluate a system that allows Alan to input a date and a weight and record this in a suitable file on his computer. The system should automatically output previous data when the program is run. The program should advise if there is a weight loss or weight gain since last time and should output the weight loss (or gain) with a suitable message. It should also output the overall weight change since the first entry in the file.

Task C

The EAN-13 system is used with barcodes and multiplies the digits in the product code alternately by 1 then 3, etc. These results are added together and subtracted from the next multiple of 10 above the sum to give the check digit that is added to the end of the product code.

For example, the product code 978034096789

9	7	8	0	3	4	0	9	6	7	8	9	
1	3	1	3	1	3	1	3	1	3	1	3	
9	21	8	0	3	12	0	27	6	21	8	27	= 142

The next multiple of 10 greater than 142 is 150, so 150 − 142 = 8, which is the check digit.

The first three digits of a barcode are used to identify the country in which the business is registered, the next 9 identify the business and the product, and the final digit is the check digit calculated as above.

Analyse, design, develop, test and evaluate a system that asks for the following data to be input:

- *A three-digit country code*
- *A three-digit business code*
- *A six-digit product code.*

The system should be able to output a valid EAN-13 number and to validate EAN-13 numbers input into the system. It should also be able to identify the country and manufacturer codes from an EAN-13 number.

The assessment – Research phase

OCR provides sets of tasks for the Unit A453 controlled assessment and once a set has been selected all three tasks in that set should be completed. The three tasks will be set so as to cover a range of the programming techniques identified in the specification, but they will not require all techniques to be used so there is no need for a tick list to check off the techniques.

The controlled assessment is split into two sections – research and task taking. The first of these involves some group activity to discuss what the tasks are asking you to do and how they might be approached. It is an opportunity to research suitable programming techniques and to discuss with others, including the teacher, what you will need to do during the task taking phase. At the end of the research phase you should be clear about what you have to do and have a good idea of how to proceed. The research phase should be used to clarify what needs to be done and what evidence will be required at the end of the controlled assessment.

The controlled assessment will start with a relatively straightforward coding task and progress through more complex situations. A typical starter task might be something like the body mass index (BMI) calculator shown on page 216.

Design, code and test a program to calculate the body mass index (BMI) for an adult.

  The program should work in metric units (kg and cm) or imperial units (stones and pounds, and feet and inches). The user should be asked to choose which units. The system should output the BMI and the appropriate category from:

- *Less than 18.5 – Underweight*
- *Between 18.5 and 25 – Normal*
- *Between 25 and 30 – Overweight*
- *Greater than 30 – Obese*

The formulae are:

Metric units: $\quad BMI = weight\ in\ kg/(height\ in\ m)^2$

Imperial units: $\quad BMI = (weight\ in\ pounds \times 703)/(height\ in\ inches)^2$

During the research phase you need to decide what needs to be done and what the other tasks require you to do. Highlight the key points and record them:

- The program must work in metric units (kg and m) or imperial units (stones and pounds, and feet and inches).
- The user should be asked to choose which units.
- The system should output the BMI.
- The system should output the correct category – underweight, normal, overweight or obese.
- The formula for metric units is:
  - → $BMI = weight\ in\ kg/(height\ in\ m)^2$

  and for imperial units is:
  - → $BMI = weight\ in\ pounds*703/(height\ in\ inches)^2$
- This means the input in feet and inches must be turned into inches, so:
  - → height = feet*12 + inches
- And the weight input in stones and pounds must be turned into pounds, so:
  - → weight = stones*14 + pounds

This gives you a set of criteria for the finished system that you can use to check if you have been successful or not.

The assessment – Task-taking phase

In the task-taking phase you will need to design, code and test your solution to this problem. This phase of the controlled assessment must be completed in controlled conditions so you will not be able to ask for help or feedback from your teachers or other students. Record your progress after each session in a diary or commentary illustrating each session's work with evidence from the development process. Keeping versions of the program at key stages is a good idea because it means you can return to a known working version if you make a mistake, but it also provides evidence for the teacher and moderator of how you developed the solution.

The tasks are intended to produce code segments that would form part of a larger program and are not intended to produce complete programs in themselves. The tasks are also designed so that they can be completed in a variety of programming languages and the choice of language will be based on your coding experience. The tasks will, however, require coding and should not be completed by using applications such as database or spreadsheet software. A significant number of marks are awarded for the use of a range of programming techniques.

Programming techniques

Many of these concepts have been covered in Chapter 7 and you should, by the time you start the controlled assessment, have had some experience using these techniques within programming tasks.

It may be that your chosen language deals with some of the techniques differently to that described in Chapter 7. This is not an issue and the main aim is to use suitable techniques to solve the problems set.

In the assessment for Unit A453 the first category is 'Use of programming techniques' worth 6 marks. This is used to assess if an appropriate range of techniques has been used in solving the three problems. The second category is 'Efficient use of programming techniques' worth 12 marks. This is used to award marks for the appropriate and effective use of those techniques, so here the assessor is looking for efficient coding. For example, in a menu with five choices it is possible to code this with nested IF – THEN structures:

Specification content

(a) Identify and use variables, operators, inputs, outputs and assignments

(b) Understand and use the three basic programming constructs used to control the flow of a easily navigable program: sequence, conditionals, iteration

(c) Understand and use suitable loops including count and condition controlled loops

(d) Use different types of data including Boolean, String, Integer and Real appropriately in solutions to problems

(e) Understand and use basic string manipulation

(f) Understand and use basic file handling operations: open, read, write and close

(g) Define and use arrays as appropriate when solving problems

```
INPUT MenuChoice
IF MenuChoice = 1 THEN
  Option1
  ELSE
  IF MenuChoice = 2 THEN
    Option2
    ELSE
    IF MenuChoice = 3 THEN
      Option3
      ELSE
      IF MenuChoice = 4 THEN
        Option4
        ELSE
        Option5
      ENDIF
    ENDIF
  ENDIF
ENDIF
```

While this works, a more efficient approach, if the feature is available, might be the use of CASE – ENDCASE.

```
INPUT MenuChoice
CASE MenuChoice OF
  WHEN 1: DO Option1
  WHEN 2: DO Option2
  WHEN 3: DO Option3
  WHEN 4: DO Option4
  OTHERWISE DO Option5
ENDCASE
```

The efficiency of the final coding will be improved by careful design and through developing efficient and effective algorithms to describe the solutions.

Design

In the research phase the tasks were discussed and the user requirements identified. These user requirements can be classified into what you know and what you need to find out. In the example of the BMI calculator

Specification content

(a) Analyse and identify the requirements for a solution to the problem

(b) Design suitable algorithms to represent the solution to a problem

(c) Design suitable input and output formats and navigation methods for their system

(d) Identify the data requirements for their system

(e) Identify suitable variables and structures with appropriate validation for their system

(f) Identify test procedures to be used during and after development to check their system against the success criteria

research might have been required to find out that there were 12 inches in a foot and that there were 14 pounds in a stone before the calculations to convert to inches and pounds could be identified. In the more complex tasks that follow, significantly more research may be required and it is not safe to assume that all the information necessary to complete a task is given in the task. Researching the task is part of the assessment and you will need to identify the requirements for a solution from the information given and any further information you will require. For example, in a task relating to European Article Numbers (EAN) the outline method may be stated but the details will have to be researched in order to fully understand what is required:

The EAN-13 system is used with barcodes and multiplies the digits in the product code alternately by 1 then 3, etc. These results are added together and subtracted from the next multiple of 10 above the sum to give the check digit that is added to the end of the product code.
For example, the product code 978034096789

9	7	8	0	3	4	0	9	6	7	8	9	
1	3	1	3	1	3	1	3	1	3	1	3	
9	21	8	0	3	12	0	27	6	21	8	27	= 142

The next multiple of 10 greater than 142 is 150, so 150 − 142 = 8, which is the check digit.
   The full EAN-13 for this product is 9780340967898

9	7	8	0	3	4	0	9	6	7	8	9	8	
1	3	1	3	1	3	1	3	1	3	1	3	1	
9	21	8	0	3	12	0	27	6	21	8	27	8	= 150

150 is a multiple of 10 so this EAN-13 is valid.
   The first three digits are used to identify the country in which the business is registered, the next 9 identify the business and the product, and the final digit is the check digit calculated as above.
   Analyse, design, develop, test and evaluate a system that asks for the following data to be input:
- *A three-digit country code*
- *A three-digit business code*
- *A six-digit product code.*

The system should be able to output a valid EAN-13 number and to validate EAN-13 numbers input into the system. It should also be able to identify the country and manufacturer codes from an EAN-13 number.

It would be useful to research this topic in more depth in order to understand how this works and to identify suitable data for testing.

How to do the example assignment

Research the EAN-13 system and how it works. Identify the data you would need to be able to test this system during development. List the data and the reason for its inclusion and the expected result/output.

   The analysis for this task should identify the following end user requirements which can be divided into three main sub-tasks:

Sub-task 1 Calculate a valid EAN-13 number given:

- Country code
- Manufacturer code
- Product code

Sub-task 2 Check that an EAN-13 number is valid

Sub-task 3 From a valid EAN-13 number identify:

- Country code
- Manufacturer code

Using the information in the scenario and any further research a solution can be designed using suitable algorithms.

1 Calculate a valid EAN-13 number

- Inputs required are:
    - → Country code (3 digits)
    - → Manufacturer code (3 digits)
    - → Product code (6 digits)
- Processing required to combine the three inputs into a single item
- Use EAN-13 method to multiply each digit by 1 then 3 alternately
- Add the products of the multiplications
- Round to nearest multiple of 10 above the total
- Subtract the total from this value
- Append the result of the subtraction to the EAN-13 number

2 Check that an EAN-13 number is valid

- Input required:
    - → EAN-13 number
- Use EAN-13 method to multiply each digit by 1 then 3 alternately
- Add the products of the multiplications
- Check that total divides by 10 exactly

3 From a valid EAN-13 number identify country and manufacturer codes

- Input required:
  - → EAN-13 number
- Find first three digits of EAN-13 – these are the country code
- Find second group of three digits (digits 4 to 6) – these are the manufacturer code

This program does not require the EAN-13 to be treated as a number but simply requires each digit in the number to be used individually. There are a number of ways this can be done including:

- Use an array to store the individual digits
- Store the EAN-13 number as a string

The algorithms to describe these can be expressed in any suitable form – as flow charts or in pseudocode. For example, sub-task 1 is shown below as a flow chart and as pseudocode:

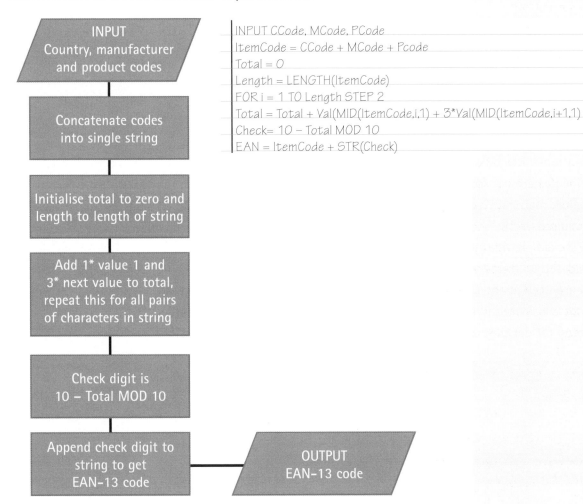

```
INPUT CCode, MCode, PCode
ItemCode = CCode + MCode + Pcode
Total = 0
Length = LENGTH(ItemCode)
FOR i = 1 TO Length STEP 2
Total = Total + Val(MID(ItemCode,i,1) + 3*Val(MID(ItemCode,i+1,1)
Check= 10 – Total MOD 10
EAN = ItemCode + STR(Check)
```

Flow chart boxes:
- INPUT Country, manufacturer and product codes
- Concatenate codes into single string
- Initialise total to zero and length to length of string
- Add 1* value 1 and 3* next value to total, repeat this for all pairs of characters in string
- Check digit is 10 – Total MOD 10
- Append check digit to string to get EAN-13 code
- OUTPUT EAN-13 code

The process shown in the flow chart needs some more detail before it can be coded and by referring to reference materials you will be able to identify that you need to use:

- string variables for input of country, manufacturer and product codes
- a string variable for the item code without check digit and for EAN with check digit
- the total initialised to zero to add up the individual calculations of the numbers in the item code
- string concatenation
- the LENGTH function for a string
- a FOR – NEXT loop with a step of two to process the pairs of characters in the string
- the MIDSTRING function to extract the single characters
- the VAL function to turn the characters into numeric values
- the MOD operator to calculate the reminder when the total is divided by 10.

You are allowed to refer to support materials, manuals and online support to find out about these functions during the task-taking phase of the controlled assessment, but you will need to use your research time to be aware of their existence.

During the development phase you will have to use suitable data to check the solution works as expected and it is important to decide upon the data to be used at this stage, making sure all reasonable possibilities are considered. For this sub-task a suitable country code (3 digits), manufacturer code (3 digits) and product code (6 digits) will be required. In the scenario there is a worked example and using this data should provide typical data. Other possibilities should also be considered: extreme values including 0s which might cause issues if they are used at the start of a code; and alphabetic characters should also be considered, with and without numeric values. This gives a test strategy for development.

Type of test	Data	Reason	Expected result
Typical data	978, 034, 096789	To test that the final version calculates the correct check digit	Check digit 8
Typical data	123, 456, 123456	To check for code concatenation	Output 123456123456
Typical data	123	To test code length validation	Accepted
Invalid data	awe	To check alphabetic characters are not accepted	Wait for new input
Invalid data	12a	To check combinations starting with numbers not accepted	Wait for new input
Invalid data	31	To check numeric values less than acceptable code length not accepted	Wait for new input
Invalid data	1234	To check numeric values larger than code length not accepted	Wait for new input
Invalid data	0012	To check leading 0s with out of range data do not get accepted	Wait for new input
Valid data	010	To check leading 0s with acceptable code length are accepted	Accepted

Extension task

Design a solution for the BMI calculator using flow charts and pseudocode.

Describe the variables to be used and identify suitable test data giving reasons for the data and the expected result.

Development

Using the design so far for the EAN-13 activity there is now enough information to produce the first version of the code for the first of the three sub-tasks.

Initially just the input and concatenation are checked using the code:

```
INPUT "Country Code" CC$
INPUT "manufacturer Code" MN$
INPUT "Product code" PR$

ItemCode$=CC$+MN$+PR$

PRINT ItemCode$
```

This step-by-step approach ensures mistakes are identified easily and can be rectified before moving on.

Specification content

(a) Develop a solution to the identified problem using a suitable programming language

(b) Demonstrate testing and refinement of the code during development

(c) Explain the solution using suitable annotation and evidence of development

Once working the PRINT can be removed and the next section of code written and tested:

```
Total = 0
  length = LEN(ItemCode$)


  FOR i = 1 TO length STEP 2
    Total = Total + VAL(MID$(ItemCode$,i,1)) + 3*VAL(MID$(ItemCode$,i+1,1))
    PRINT Total
  NEXT i
```

Notice the value of Total is being printed at each stage so that it can be checked against test data. In this case it is being tested against the data in the scenario.

Finally the PRINT is removed, the final bits of the code inserted and the full segment checked.

The final code for this version is:

```
ean version 1.bbc - BBC BASIC for Windows 5.91a
File   Edit   Utilities   Options   Run   Help

    INPUT "Country Code" CC$
    INPUT "manufacturer Code" MN$
    INPUT "Product code" PR$

    ItemCode$=CC$+MN$+PR$

    Total=0
    length=LEN(ItemCode$)

    FOR i = 1 TO length STEP 2
      Total= Total+  VAL(MID$(ItemCode$,i,1))+ 3*VAL(MID$(ItemCode$,i+1,1))
    NEXT i

    Check=10-Total MOD 10
    EAN$= ItemCode$+STR$(Check)
    PRINT EAN$

Press F1 for Help                                          308   57,16                    NUM
```

Testing this with the same data to see if it gives the result calculated in the scenario gives the output:

This is the correct result and the code appears to work. This is the first version of the code which should be kept as evidence of the development.

Now this segment works there is more design to complete:

Further information

Important point: Design, development and testing should form a cyclic process leading to a final working version of the program based on a series of intermediate versions. It is important you show this process has taken place by keeping records of each stage in the development showing evidence of the design, development and testing. Use a diary or log to keep track of this and keep versions of the program at each stage.

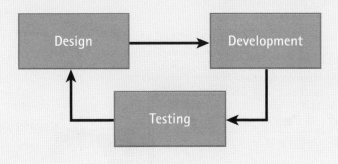

The LEN function will help check the length of the string but we also need to ensure each character in the string is numeric. One approach to this, although there are others, is to use the ASCII value of the characters. The ASCII value of 0 is 48 and the ASCII values of 1–9 are 49–57 respectively.

This gives us the validation of the input into the program.

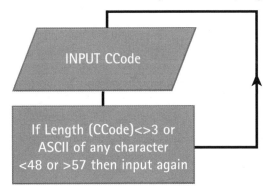

To check if any of the characters is not 0–9 we can use a flag to signal that we have found one that is not acceptable. To do this we set a flag to false before we start and if we find an unacceptable value we reset the flag to true. The loop keeps asking for input values until they are the right length **AND** the flag has not been set to true.

For the flag use a Boolean variable that will allow for just the two states, TRUE or FALSE.

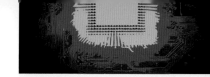

```
REPEAT
INPUT CCode
Flag = FALSE
FOR j = 1 TO LENGTH(CCode)
IF MIDSTRING(CCode,j,1)<48 OR MIDSTRING(CCode,j,1)>57 THEN
Flag = TRUE
UNTIL Flag = FALSE AND LENGTH(CCode) = 3
```

This will simply keep asking for CCode to be input until the value is entirely numeric and three characters long.

This code can now be modified and used with the main program to validate all the inputs. Apart from some tidying up, we now have a working version of the program to test with suitable data. The next step will be to design, code and test the remaining sub-tasks and combine these into a single code segment, perhaps, with a simple menu.

Summary

Design, development and testing should be completed in a cyclic manner – designing, coding and testing each segment of the program before moving on to the next one. The designs should include algorithms that describe the process in a suitable form and simply supplying working code is not evidence of good design. Use flow charts to outline the process and pseudocode to describe the detail. Identify suitable test data and use the results of testing to inform further design.

Extension task

The code above used variables CCode, PCode, etc. These are not particularly helpful names. Choose more meaningful names for the variables in this program.

Evidence requirements

The evidence should be shown in the diary or commentary supplied with the work. Keep a detailed log of all the processes and link this to the evidence supplied. It is a good idea to start and maintain a document that is updated at key stages in the process, perhaps a presentation or a word processed document. The commentary should:

- contain analysis of the problem identifying the end user requirements
- contain designs for the solution including suitable algorithms as flow charts and/or pseudocode (remember pseudocode should not simply be a copy of the coded solution)
- contain any input–output formatting or navigation requirements identified by the scenario
- include, if any data is being used, what type of data is used and how it will be used, processed, stored or manipulated
- identify the variables, their type, range and any validation required
- identify how the system will be tested giving a test strategy and suitable test data.

Extension tasks

1 Design the solutions for the EAN-13 activity sub-tasks 2 and 3 using algorithms and pseudocode.

   Describe the techniques required and identify suitable test data to use during development.

2 Using the language you intend to use for Unit A453 create the code for the three sub-tasks in this scenario and test using the data identified above.

Testing and evaluation

Much of the testing will be completed during development and should be recorded in the commentary along with any basic evaluation of the programs as they are developed. It is good practice to do this and, in the real world, programmers will keep full notes of testing, the results of testing and comments on each section of their code. This is done so that other programmers will be able to understand what was done and why it was done when they need to modify or maintain the program at a later date.

Specification content

(a) Use a suitable test plan and data to test the function of the system

(b) Test the system against the success criteria

(c) Provide good evidence of test procedures

(d) Modify the system, if required, to meet success criteria where these are not met

(e) Evaluate the system against the success criteria to establish how successful, or otherwise, their implementation has been

In the design stage the programmer will use the end user requirements to create a set of success criteria on which to judge the success or otherwise of the solution. The success criteria should be something that can be measured or checked and not vague subjective concepts such as 'a friendly user interface'.

For the BMI calculator task the success criteria identified were:

- The program must work in metric units (kg and m) or imperial units (stones and pounds, and feet and inches).
- The user should be asked to choose which units.
- The system should output the BMI.
- The system should output the correct category – underweight, normal, overweight or obese.
- The formula for metric units is:
  - → $BMI = $ weight in $kg/($height in $m)^2$

  and for imperial units is:
  - → $BMI = $ weight in pounds$*703/($height in inches$)^2$
- This means the input in feet and inches must be turned into inches, so:
  - → height = feet$*12 + $inches
- And the weight input in stones and pounds must be turned into pounds, so:
  - → weight = stones$*14 + $pounds

Typical test data to be used as part of the test strategy for this could include the following categories:

- The choice – only allows metric or imperial (m or i)
- Asks for height in appropriate units
- Asks for matching weight in appropriate units
- Is able to convert height in feet and inches to inches
- Is able to convert weight in stones and pounds to pounds
- Can calculate BMI
- Can convert BMI to category – underweight, normal, overweight or obese

Many of these will have been tested during the development of the code. For example, to test that the system only allows 'm' or 'i' for choice of units, the following code could be tested with m, I, M, a, 5, i.

```
PRINT "Choose units"
PRINT "Metric, Kg and m .... m"
PRINT "Imperial Stones/pounds and feet/inches .... i"
REPEAT
INPUT "Units" Unit$
UNTIL Unit$ = "m" OR Unit$ = "i"
```

The results of this testing will appear in the commentary and these should be referenced in the evaluation of the system to show that the program met the first of the success criteria created at the design stage.

It is good practice to list these success criteria and to show that they have been met by referring to specific evidence in the report.

Success criteria	Success?	Evidence	Comment
The choice – only allows metric or imperial (m or i)	Yes	Test with m, l, M , a, 5 and i	See development section slide 3 (for example)
Asks for height in appropriate units	Yes	Tested with metric then imperial	See development section slide 4 (for example)
--- and so on for all the success criteria ---			

Below is a sample from the report submitted for task 1 referred to in the evaluation.

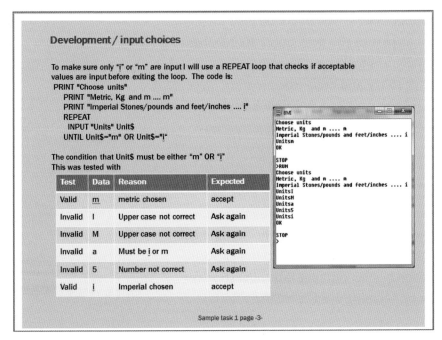

Development / input choices

To make sure only "i" or "m" are input I will use a REPEAT loop that checks if acceptable values are input before exiting the loop. The code is:

```
PRINT "Choose units"
   PRINT "Metric, Kg and m .... m"
   PRINT "Imperial Stones/pounds and feet/inches .... i"
   REPEAT
     INPUT "Units" Unit$
   UNTIL Unit$="m" OR Unit$="i"
```

The condition that Unit$ must be either "m" OR "i"
This was tested with

Test	Data	Reason	Expected
Valid	m	metric chosen	accept
Invalid	l	Upper case not correct	Ask again
Invalid	M	Upper case not correct	Ask again
Invalid	a	Must be i or m	Ask again
Invalid	5	Number not correct	Ask again
Valid	i	Imperial chosen	accept

```
BMI
Choose units
Metric, Kg  and m .... m
Imperial Stones/pounds and feet/inches .... i
Unitsm
OK

STOP
>RUN
Choose units
Metric, Kg  and m .... m
Imperial Stones/pounds and feet/inches .... i
Unitsl
UnitsM
Unitsa
Units5
Unitsi
OK

STOP
>
```

Sample task 1 page -3-

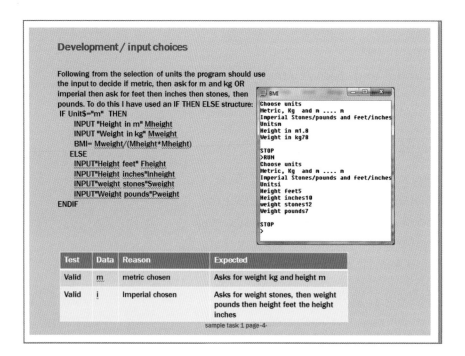

Development / input choices

Following from the selection of units the program should use the input to decide if metric, then ask for m and kg OR imperial then ask for feet then inches then stones, then pounds. To do this I have used an IF THEN ELSE structure:

```
IF Unit$="m"  THEN
      INPUT "Height in m" Mheight
      INPUT "Weight in kg" Mweight
      BMI= Mweight/(Mheight*Mheight)
   ELSE
      INPUT"Height feet" Fheight
      INPUT"Height inches"Inheight
      INPUT"weight stones"Sweight
      INPUT"Weight pounds"Pweight
ENDIF
```

```
Choose units
Metric, Kg  and m .... m
Imperial Stones/pounds and feet/inches
Unitsm
Height in m1.8
Weight in kg78

STOP
>RUN
Choose units
Metric, Kg  and m .... m
Imperial Stones/pounds and feet/inches
Unitsi
Height feet5
Height inches10
weight stones12
Weight pounds7

STOP
>
```

Test	Data	Reason	Expected
Valid	m	metric chosen	Asks for weight kg and height m
Valid	i	Imperial chosen	Asks for weight stones, then weight pounds then height feet the height inches

sample task 1 page -4-

It is also necessary to test that all the code segments work together when finished. Some extra end-product testing might be necessary, but remember it is part of the assessment to get others to check the final work and provide some feedback under controlled conditions in the classroom. All that is required is that those you worked with in the research phase spend a few minutes trying your programs and making any comments. These comments and your responses to them should be included in your report. If one of the beta testers finds something that doesn't work properly, you might be able to suggest how this could be fixed as part of the evaluation. Remember, the purpose of testing is not simply to show that the program works under strict conditions but to try and break the program. Finding issues need not necessarily be seen as a negative but as an opportunity to demonstrate problem-solving skills in suggesting how these can be fixed.

Evidence

The report should be a commentary recording progress as you proceed with the tasks. You need to show the assessor how you went about solving the problem and comment on why you did things. Using task B as an example the following highlighted text is a suggestion for some of the content that might be submitted in the report:

> *Alan is trying to lose weight and weighs himself every few days. He wants to keep track of these weights and the days they were taken in a file on his computer. Design, code, test and evaluate a system that allows Alan to input a date and a weight and record this in a suitable file on his computer. The system should automatically output previous data when the program is run. The program should advise if there is a weight loss or weight gain since last time and should output the weight loss (or gain) with a suitable message. It should also output the overall weight loss since the first entry in the file.*

Analysis

By highlighting the key elements in the task it is possible to identify the basic end user requirements for this task. Further analysis of the problem should identify that there are other issues that need to be taken into account.

If the data entered is not in the right format then it will not be possible to make the system work as required,. For example, weights entered in the wrong format will mean it is not possible to calculate the weight changes. The analysis should therefore identify that some validation of input data is required to make the system work.

Initial values are important because there will be no previous figures to base any changes or comments on, so these need to be entered separately to any subsequent data.

This analysis should be recorded and summarised. For example, as a bulleted list:

- Initialise system with first date and weight input
- Input date and weight
- Validate date and weight inputs
- Store date and weight in a file
- Recover and output dates and weights so far
- Add new data
- If weight gain, message with weight gain and overall gain/loss to date
- If weight loss, message with weight loss and overall gain/loss to date

The analysis of the task is a group activity and your teacher and other students will all have some input. What you take away from this and record in your own analysis is your own work and it is possible you will identify other elements that should or could be included once the research phase is complete. You should take your notes from the research phase and produce your own analysis of the problem based on that research and any other ideas you wish to include.

The remaining part of the process is task taking and you will be working independently with no further direct support from the teacher or others.

Design

In the design, the end user requirements should be used to create a set of success criteria. These will be quite similar to the end user requirements you identified but you need to make sure they can be tested and show they have been achieved. In the design there should be a set of success criteria or system objectives. These can be recorded as a bulleted list. For example:

- Check if file already exists
- If not, create:
  - Input and validate initial data for date and weight
  - Write to file
  - If it already exists then:
    - read data from file into an array
    - request input for date and weight
    - validate input data
    - append data to array
    - write date from array back to file
    - compare weight with previous weight in array
- If larger:
  - Calculate weight gain
  - Message "Oops weight gain of" (calculated weight gain)
- If smaller:
  - Calculate weight loss
  - Message "Well done loss of" (calculated weight loss)
- Calculate overall weight loss from array item 1 to current item
- Output message "Your weight change since start is" (calculated weight change)

The design should also include a detailed description of the processes involved in solving the problem. Flow charts should be drawn that describe the problem accurately. Using the traditionally shaped flow chart symbols is useful but not essential – the logic of the description is what is being assessed.

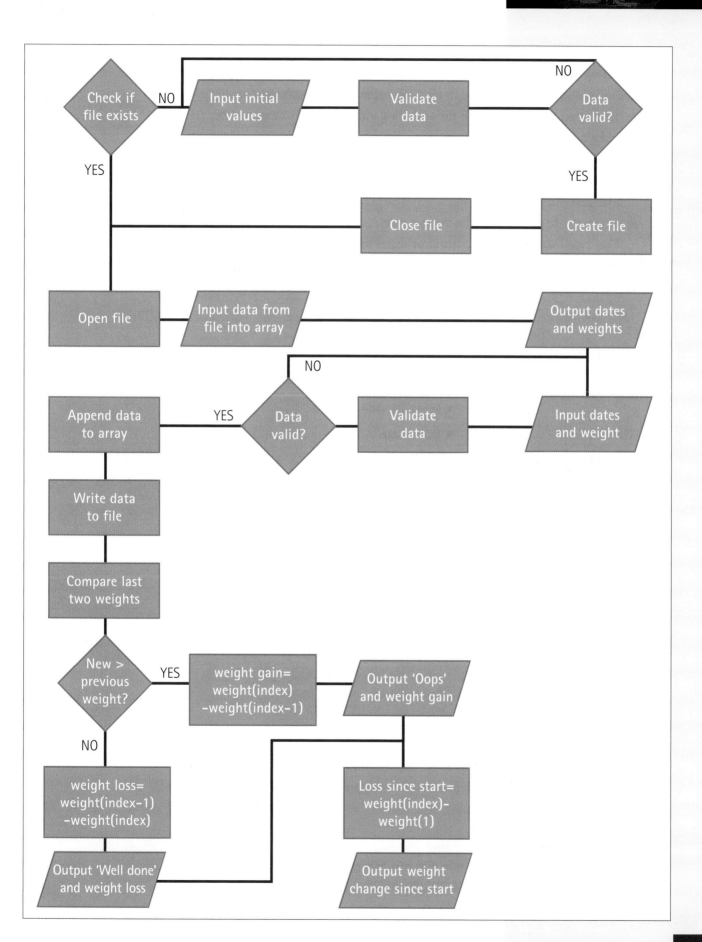

It is clear from this flow chart that the problem is not one that can be solved with just a few lines of code and that there are various aspects to the solution that should be dealt with separately. The code should be developed one section at a time, testing each section to make sure it works before moving on to the next. In order to test how it works you will need some test data and the final part of the design should be a test strategy.

The test strategy should show what data will be used during development to check that the code works.

The initial values should consist of dates and weights:

Test	Data	Reason	Expected result
Initial date (erroneous data)	▪ 35/02/12 ▪ 1/1/12 01/2/5	▪ Does not exist ▪ Incorrect formats (should be dd/mm/yy)	Rejected
Correct date	▪ 12/01/12	▪ Typical value	Accepted
Initial weight (erroneous data)	▪ hat ▪ 0 ▪ -20	▪ Not a number ▪ Impossible value ▪ Impossible value	Rejected
Correct weight	▪ 90	▪ Typical value	Accepted

For subsequent values the same test data can be used for erroneous data but some typical data to check that weight gains and losses are properly dealt with are also required:

Test	Data	Reason	Expected result
Weight loss	05/02/12, 87	Weight less than previous	Message "Well done weight loss of 2kg, overall weight loss 3kg"
Weight gain	12/02/12, 88	Weight greater than previous	Message "Oops weight gain of 1kg, overall weight loss 2kg"
Overall weight gain	19/02/12, 91	Weight greater than initial value	Message "Oops weight gain of 3kg, overall weight loss -1kg"

This allows the system to be tested as it is developed, but other test data may be required as issues arise that have not been foreseen which can be added to the evidence of development with a suitable comment.

Extension task

What other data might be required to test this system during development?

Development

Development should record how you went about solving the problem and include evidence of the code, the testing and any 'evaluation' of the test results that requires you to make any changes to your solution.

The report will follow on from the analysis and design and should show how the program was built and tested in stages. For example, the first task is to check if the file exists and if it doesn't to create it.

One approach to this is to try to open the channel to the file – if it returns 0 it does not exist so an empty file can be created.

The data arrays need to be declared before this can be done and the index for the arrays must be set to 0. Some pseudocode will explain the logic:

```
DIM date(20) string
DIM weight(20) integer
Initialise index to 0
Attempt to open file for read access and check channel value returned
If the value is 0 create the file
Close the file channel
```

This logic is then turned into code and the code tested:

```
index = 0
IF OPENIN "c:\users\george\weightwatch.txt" = 0 THEN
  chan1 = OPENOUT "c:\users\george\weightwatch.txt"
  CLOSE#chan1
ENDIF
```

Evidence of the file being created can be shown with before and after screenshots:

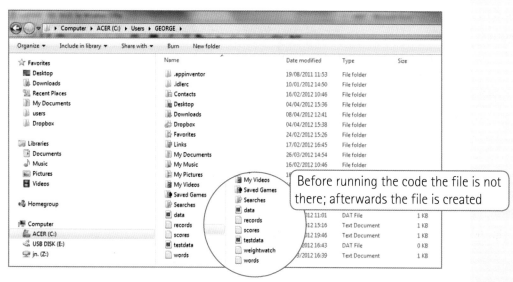

Before running the code the file is not there; afterwards the file is created

That part of the process is shown to work and the next section of the code can then be developed.

The next section of the code will be:

- Collect initial values if new file.
- Write these values to the file.
- End the program.

The code is extended to include these new features and tested with typical data from the test strategy – date 21/01/12 and weight 90kg.

```
REM initialise arrays and index variable
DIM date$(20)
DIM weight(20)
index = 1
REM check if file exists, if not create it
IF OPENIN "c:\users\george\weightwatch.txt" = 0 THEN
  INPUT "date for first weight measurement "; date$
  INPUT "initial weight measurement in kg "; weight
  chan1 = OPENOUT "c:\users\george\weightwatch.txt"
  PRINT#chan1, date$,weight
  CLOSE#chan1
  END
ENDIF
```

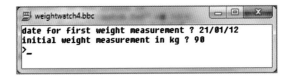

Now that the file is created and you can enter the initial data the next step is to add more data to the file and to extend the code to incorporate a request for new values and to write this data to file.

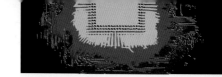

The additional code required is:

```
chan1 = OPENIN "c:\users\george\weightwatch.txt"          Open the file to read data
REPEAT
    INPUT#chan1,date$(index)
    INPUT#chan1,weight(index)                   Input date and weight into array
                                                until the end of the data file
    PRINT date$(index),weight(index)
    index = index + 1
UNTIL EOF#chan1
REM close the file
CLOSE#chan1
REM prompt for input data
INPUT "Date of reading" newdate$
                                    Get new data input
INPUT "Weight" newweight
REM update the array with new data
date$(index) = newdate$
weight(index) = newweight
REM write the data in the array over the existing data file
chan2 = OPENOUT "c:\users\george\weightwatch.txt"      Write to next array elements
FOR count = 1 TO index
    PRINT#chan2,date$(count),weight(count)       Write data in array over existing file
NEXT count
CLOSE#chan2
ENDIF
```

Running the program again should output the initial value and request new data:

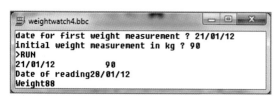

The code has been written and tested to show that the file is created and that the data can be retrieved and output. It is now a good time to annotate this code, as shown above, using remark statements to identify what each piece of code does. The use of meaningful variable names is also good practice and makes the code more readable and maintainable.

```
REM initialise arrays and index variable
DIM date$(20)
DIM weight(20)
index=1
REM check if file exists, if not create it
IF OPENIN "c:\users\george\weightwatch.txt" =0 THEN
  INPUT "date for first weight measurement ";date$
  INPUT "initial weight measurement in kg "; weight
  chan1 = OPENOUT "c:\users\george\weightwatch.txt"
  PRINT#chan1, date$,weight
  CLOSE#chan1
  END
ENDIF
REM read in data from file and display, repeat until the end of file is reached
chan1=OPENIN "c:\users\george\weightwatch.txt"

REPEAT
  INPUT#chan1,date$(index)
  INPUT#chan1,weight(index)
  PRINT date$(index),weight(index)
  index=index+1
UNTIL EOF#chan1
REM close the file
CLOSE#chan1

REM prompt for input data
INPUT "Date of reading" newdate$
INPUT "Weight" newweight
REM update the array with new data

date$(index)= newdate$
weight(index)= newweight

REM write the data in the array over the existing data file
chan2=OPENOUT "c:\users\george\weightwatch.txt"
FOR count=1 TO index
  PRINT#chan2,date$(count),weight(count)
NEXT count
CLOSE#chan2
ENDIF
```

Now that the data can be collected and stored we can add the feature that checks the data and reports progress to the user. Some explanation of how this is to be done should be included.

The current weight value is weight(index), the previous one is weight(index-1). To check if the weight has increased you need to compare these two array values.

To show a weight gain, the weight change will be:

$$weight(index)-weight(index-1)$$

To show a weight loss, the weight change will be:

$$weight(index-1)-weight(index)$$

The overall weight loss will be weight(1)-weight(index)

The revised code should be included and tested.

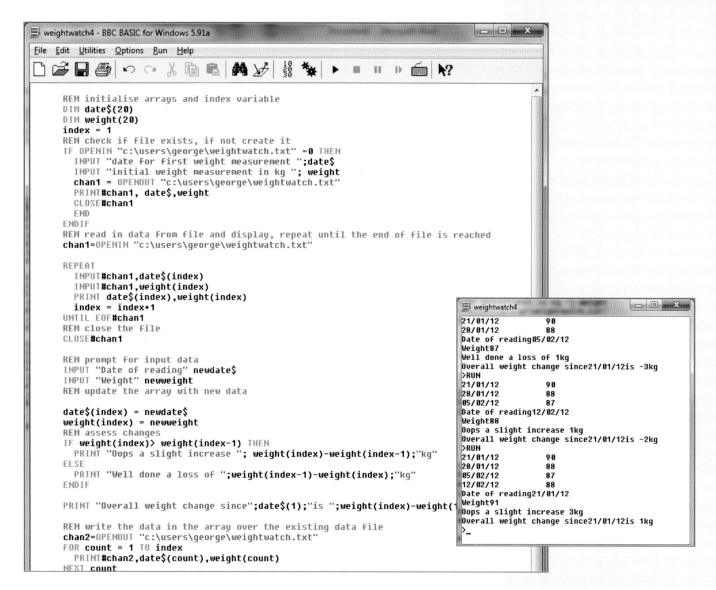

Now the validation can be dealt with. The process used in this example sets up a REPEAT – UNTIL loop around the input until the values conform to the requirements. For example, the initial weight should be numeric and positive so the following code will provide a reasonable validation for this value:

```
REPEAT
  INPUT "initial weight measurement in kg "; weight
UNTIL weight > 0
```

Dates are a little more troublesome in BBC BASIC and there is a library routine that can be found using the help feature that will provide some suitable validation. It is perfectly acceptable to use the help features supplied with the programming language in order to solve problems. It is also a good idea to indicate that these have been used rather than to try and explain a section of code that works but may be quite complex and beyond your understanding.

The following code segment will validate most dates to ensure they are in the form dd/mm/yy and will reject impossible dates such as 35/01/12.

```
INSTALL @lib$+"DATELIB"
REPEAT
  INPUT date$
  what = FN _ readdate(date$,"dmy",2000)
  what$ = FN _ date$(what, "dd")+"/"+FN _ date$(what,"MM")+"/"+FN _ date$(what,"yy")
UNTIL what <>&80000000 AND date$=what$
```

If you find such a code segment that does what you want then use it but make sure you reference the source in your work. If you write such a segment of code make sure you explain how it works.

This code is tested with the data from the test strategy and works, as shown below:

```
weightwatch5                                    _ □ X
date for first weight measurement ? 35/02/12
date for first weight measurement ? 1/1/12
date for first weight measurement ? 01/2/5
date for first weight measurement ? 12/01/12
initial weight measurement in kg ? hat
initial weight measurement in kg ? 0
initial weight measurement in kg ? -20
initial weight measurement in kg ? 90
>_
```

This code segment is inserted into the main program to give a final version of the program.

But you might well decide that some of the validation could be improved. For example:

The initial weight values are unlikely to be less than 20 kg or more than 200 kg, so a modified validation routine might be:

```
REPEAT
  INPUT "initial weight measurement in kg "; weight
UNTIL weight >20 AND weight <200
```

The weights entered subsequently are unlikely to change by more than 10 kg and the validation routine might be:

```
REPEAT
  INPUT "Weight" newweight
UNTIL newweight > weight(index-1)-10 AND newweight < weight(index-1)+10
```

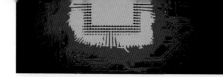

Further information

In computer programs dates are stored as a number of days since a fixed point in time. By converting the input date$ string to the modified Julian calendar you can check for valid date formats entered in the dd/mm/yy style. This returns a number if the format is correct and it represents a modified Julian date. However, the input 35/01/12 is in a valid format and is converted to a number in the modified Julian calendar representing 04/02/12. The process will therefore check for the correct format, but not a valid date. However, other values not in the correct format will be rejected and the function returns &80000000.

If we use the function to convert to the modified Julian calendar then convert back to a date string and compare the values we can check that the date is valid.

```
INSTALL @lib$+"DATELIB"
REPEAT
  INPUT date$
  what = FN_readdate(date$,"dmy",2000)
  what$ = FN_date$(what, "dd")+"/"+FN_date$(what,"MM")+"/"+FN_date$(what,"yy")
UNTIL what <>&80000000 AND date$=what$
```

This routine loads the library functions and requests a string input for the date.

If the string is in the form dd/mm/yy then it will convert it to a number representing the number of days since 2000, if not it will return &80000000.

The value is then converted back to the day+month+year using string concatenation and compared with the original input value.

This loop repeats until the date entered is in the correct format and when converted to the modified Julian calendar then back matches the original input.

Extension task

Consider the frequency that data is submitted (weekly or monthly) and the starting values for the weight – might these have an effect on the values that were realistic? Checking with the user when data is out of range might be a better approach, by asking 'Are you sure?' Add this feature to the code or pseudocode.

> These additional features can always be included even though not identified in the analysis. The assessment does not expect you to have a completely finished design that cannot be improved before coding. Any changes that occur during the development and testing process can be incorporated into the final product by simply commenting on why in the report.

Testing should now be carried out on the final version of the code, using classmates as end users as well as yourself, the developer. The purpose of testing is not simply to show that a system works, but to try and break the code. Identifying any problems with the code should be considered good testing, and these code segments are likely to contain some unresolved issues. If this example program is fully tested you will find that inputting something such as 'hat' in the date field will cause the program to stop and print out the error message:

This should be found and considered; the solution might not be identified but the existence of the problem should be acknowledged in the evaluation.

Extension task

Dates are handled more effectively in other programming languages; look at how two other languages deal with date types and try to work out how the date could be validated effectively in these languages. Will these languages deal with the input 'hat' or would extra code be needed to reject this input as in BBC BASIC?

```
INSTALL @lib$+"DATELIB"
  REM initialise arrays and index variable
  DIM date$(20)
  DIM weight(20)
  index = 1
  REM check if file exists, if not create it
  IF OPENIN "c:\users\george\weightwatch.txt" = 0 THEN
    REPEAT
      INPUT "date for first weight measurement ";date$
      what = FN _ readdate(date$,"dmy",2000)
      what$ = FN _ date$(what,"dd")+"/"+FN _ date$(what,"MM")+"/"+FN _ date$(what,"yy")
    UNTIL what <>&80000000 AND date$ = what$
    REPEAT
      INPUT "initial weight measurement in kg "; weight
    UNTIL weight >20 AND weight <200
    chan1 = OPENOUT "c:\users\george\weightwatch.txt"
    PRINT#chan1, date$,weight
    CLOSE#chan1
```

To make the code easier to understand REM (REMARK) statements, meaningful variable names, line breaks and indented printing are used.

```
      END
    ENDIF
REM read in data from file and display, repeat until the end of file is reached
chan1 = OPENIN "c:\users\george\weightwatch.txt"
REPEAT
   INPUT#chan1,date$(index)
   INPUT#chan1,weight(index)
   PRINT date$(index),weight(index)
   index = index + 1
UNTIL EOF#chan1
REM close the file
CLOSE#chan1
REM prompt for input data
REPEAT
   INPUT "Date of reading" newdate$
   what = FN _ readdate(newdate$,"dmy",2000)
   what$ = FN _ date$(what,"dd")+"/"+FN _ date$(what,"MM")+"/"+FN _ date$(what,"yy")
UNTIL what <>&80000000 AND newdate$ = what$
REPEAT
   INPUT "Weight" newweight
UNTIL newweight > weight(index-1)-10 AND newweight < weight(index-1)+10
REM update the array with new data
date$(index) = newdate$
weight(index) = newweight
REM assess changes
IF weight(index) > weight(index-1) THEN
   PRINT "Oops a slight increase "; weight(index)-weight(index-1);"kg"
ELSE
   PRINT "Well done a loss of ";weight(index-1)-weight(index);"kg"
ENDIF

PRINT "Overall weight change since";date$(1);"is ";weight(index)-weight(1);"kg"

REM write the data in the array over the existing data file
chan2 = OPENOUT "c:\users\george\weightwatch.txt"
FOR count = 1 TO index
   PRINT#chan2,date$(count),weight(count)
NEXT count
CLOSE#chan2
ENDIF
```

Evaluation

The purpose of the evaluation is to assess how well the solution addresses the original problem. In the design you identified a set of success criteria and a test strategy. Cross-reference the success criteria against the evidence from testing to show how well or otherwise the solution solves the problem.

Success criteria	Success?	Evidence	Comment
Check if file already exists, if not create it	Yes	Created file 'weightwatch'	See development page...
Input and validate initial data for weight	Yes	Tested with hat, 0 and -20	
Input and validate initial data for date	Yes	Tested with 35/02/12, 1/1/12, 01/5/5 and 12/02/12	

```
weightwatch5
date for first weight measurement ? 35/02/12
date for first weight measurement ? 1/1/12
date for first weight measurement ? 01/2/5
date for first weight measurement ? 12/01/12
initial weight measurement in kg ? hat
initial weight measurement in kg ? 0
initial weight measurement in kg ? -20
initial weight measurement in kg ? 90
>_
```

Repeat this for the remaining success criteria and include any modifications to the system made during development.

Extension tasks

1 This chapter includes some evidence to support the development of the solution. Complete this evaluation using the success criteria identified in the design and references to the evidence provided in the chapter.

2 Comment on any further testing needed, how effective this solution is and any suggested improvements.

The evaluation should also take into account any feedback from end-user testing carried out by classmates and include comments on problems identified and how these might be dealt with. It is also an opportunity for you to tell the assessor how smart you have been by pointing out the best bits of the system or the clever stuff you have done.

In the evaluation, the assessor will also be looking to see if you have used technical language correctly and at the quality of your written communication.

Summary

The report should be written as a commentary on the whole process supported by screenshots and electronic versions of the program at various stages.

The report should include:

- Analysis of the problem including:
  - → end-user requirements
  - → the proposed approach to the problem
  - → any resources identified.
- Design including:
  - → success criteria
  - → test strategy
  - → algorithms that describe the solution.
- Development including:
  - → evidence of the 'thinking' behind the approach
  - → evidence of the code being developed in stages
  - → evidence of testing and (if required) modifications at each stage
  - → annotated code with meaningful variable names.
- Testing and evaluation including:
  - → final product test evidence
  - → test evidence cross-referenced to the success criteria
  - → comments on the feedback from potential users
  - → a summary of the good points
  - → the not so good points
  - → any issues and suggestions of how these issues might be dealt with
  - → overall summary of the effectiveness of the solutions and any suggestions for improvement.

Glossary

Accumulator: A register in the CPU that stores data currently being used by the CPU

ACID: A set of rules that protects a database from errors during a transaction

Actuator: A device to produce physical movement based on output from a computer system

Address: A location in main memory used to store data or instructions

Algorithm: A series of steps designed to solve a mathematical or other problem

ALU: The ALU performs all the arithmetic and logical operations within the CPU

Analogue: Refers to continuously changing values

Applet: A small application that performs one specific task

Application: Software designed to carry out a useful real-world task

ASCII (American Standard Code for Information Interchange): 7-bit system to code the character set of a computer

Assembler: Software that translates assembly language code into machine code

Assembly language: A low-level programming language that uses more memorable mnemonic codes and labels to represent machine-level code. Each instruction corresponds to just one machine operation

Assignment: Setting the value of a variable

Attribute: A characteristic of an entity. It becomes a field in a data table

Auto documentation: System that tracks variables, modules and comments for maintenance purposes

Bar code: A pattern of thin and thick lines representing a number that can be scanned by a reader for input into a computer system

Binary: A system of numbers using only two digits, 0 and 1 (also called the base-2 system), unlike the decimal (or denary) system in everyday use that uses ten digits (base-10)

Bit: Binary digit 1 or 0

Bit rate: The bit rate is the space available for each sample, measured in kilobits per second (kbits/s). (128 kbits/s is 128 kilobits per second of sampled sound)

Boolean: A value that can only be true or false

Boolean algebra: A method for expressing mathematically a logic circuit

Bus: A part of the computer architecture that transfers data and signals between the components of the computer

Byte: 8 bits

Cache memory: Special high speed memory used by a computer

Camera: A device to capture still or moving images

CD: A type of optical device with a capacity of 700 MB

Character: A single alphabetic or numeric character

Character set: The characters available to a computer

CHR: Uses the ASCII value to look up the character associated with a particular number

Client: Software or hardware that requests services from a server

Clock chip: The electronic device in a computer that controls the timing of signals

Code editor: Text area used to enter code in an IDE

Colour depth (or bit depth): The number of bits used for each pixel or dot. The more bits the more colours that can be represented

Command line: The place where typed commands are given to the operating system

Comparison: Comparing the values of two items and returning TRUE or FALSE depending upon the result of that comparison

Compiler: A translator that converts all of the source code to machine code in one go to produce the object code

Compression: Reduction in file size to reduce download times and storage requirements

Computer architecture: The internal, logical structure and organisation of the computer hardware

Concatenation: Combining two strings into a single string

Constant: A label referring to a location in memory containing a value that can be accessed but not changed by a program

Control unit: The control unit works with the CPU to control the flow of data within the system

CPU: Central processing unit of the computer containing the control unit, ALU and cache memory

Custom written: Software developed specially for one or a few customers

Data dictionary: The stored schema of a database

Data integrity: The state of data being as it should be, reflecting reality

Data redundancy: The unnecessary repetition of data

Debugger: Software that helps a programmer track down faults in a program

Decision: A flow diagram symbol used to show a decision stage, may be 'yes' or 'no' or multiple values

Declaration: Identifying a variable or constant or array to a program so that memory space can be allocated

Decode: An instruction is decoded by the CPU into two parts – the operator and the operand

Dedicated: Something which is designed for one particular purpose

Defragmenter: A utility that brings together file fragments on a disk and collects all the free space in one area

Denary: A system of numbers using ten digits, 0 and 1–9 (also called the base-10 system)

Device driver: A program that enables communication between a computer and a peripheral

Disk organisation: The process of arranging files and data bytes on a secondary storage device

Domain name: A human readable name for a resource on a network. It is changed to a numerical IP address by a DNS server

Dual-core/quad-core: A CPU with multiple processors (a dual-core has two, a quad-core has four)

DVD: A type of optical device with a capacity of 4.7 GB

Editor: Software used for entering source code when writing a program

Embedded system: A computer system that forms part of an electronic device

Entity: Something that we store data about in a database

Entity relationship diagram: A diagram that shows how different entities used in a database are connected

Erroneous: Data that would not normally be expected such as the wrong data type

Error diagnostics: System to warn of errors in the code and potential problems

Extreme: Data that is at the extreme limit of valid or invalid to check boundary conditions

Failover: Automatic switching to a backup computer system in the event of system failure

Fetch–execute cycle: This is the process of fetching the instructions from memory, decoding them and then executing them so that the CPU performs continuously

Field: A characteristic of something stored in a database

File: Stored data on suitable media

Firewall: Software and/or hardware that limits access to and from a computer system

Firmware: Software that is stored permanently in a device, such as control programs for devices

Flash memory: Solid-state memory used as low cost secondary storage in portable devices and as removable memory

Flat file database: Database consisting of only one table

Flow chart (flow diagram): A diagrammatic method of showing the structure and data flow to define a problem and its solution

Gigabyte: 1024 megabytes

Graphical user interface: A user interface that makes use of icons for interacting with the user

Hexadecimal: The base-16 number system

High-level language: A programming language that resembles a natural language. Each instruction translates to many machine instructions. It is problem based rather than machine based

HTML: Hypertext mark up language – a text based system for defining web pages

Hub: A device for connecting multiple network devices in one segment

Hyperlink: An item on a web page that directs the user to another location when clicked

Icon: A picture on screen that represents a file, a program or an action

Indexed sequential file: A sequential file that is accessed using an index, which is a separate file

Input device: A hardware device used to input data into a computer system for processing

Instructions: A set of commands that a processor can recognise and act upon

Integer: Whole number, positive or negative, with no decimal or fractional part

Integrated development environment (IDE): Resources supplied with high-level languages to help the programmer

Interface: The boundary between systems or between systems and humans

Interpreter: Translation software that converts source code or user input into machine code which is immediately executed one instruction at a time

Interrupt: A signal to the operating system to stop what it is doing and perform a different task instead

Intranet: A private data resource using the same technology as the internet, such as browsers and protocols

Invalid: Data used to test a program that should be rejected because it is 'out of range'

IP address: A number that identifies a device on a TCP/IP network

Iteration or repetition: A group of instructions is executed repeatedly until a condition is met (a **loop**)

Kernel: The lowest level of an operating system that controls the hardware

Keyboard: A device that uses labelled keys to enable data input into a computer

Kilobyte: 1024 bytes

LAN: Local area network – confined to one location

Linker: Software that combines together a number of separate object code files

Logic circuit: A circuit made by combining a sequence of logic gates

Logic error: The logical structure of the program produces unexpected results

Logic gates: A circuit that produces an output based on the inputs:

> **NOT:** A logic gate that outputs the opposite value to the input
>
> **AND:** A logic gate that outputs 1 if both inputs are 1
>
> **OR:** A logic gate that outputs 1 if either, or both, of the two inputs are 1

Low-level language: A programming language that is directed at controlling each machine operation.

Machine code: Instructions in binary used by the CPU

Magnetic hard disk: Secondary storage device using magnetised platters to store data and files

Megabyte: 1024 kilobytes

Metadata: Information about the image data that allows the computer to recreate the image from the binary data in the file. This must contain the height and width in pixels and the colour depth in bpp (bits per pixel)

Microphone: A device for capturing sound

Monitor: A device that can display images and text

Motherboard: The central printed circuit board (PCB) that holds the crucial components of the system

Mouse: A device that controls the movement of a pointer on screen, based on its own movement, and allows the user to select an object by pressing a button

Nesting: Structures inside other structures

Nibble: 4 bits or half a byte

Non-volatile: Data retained even when power is turned off

Object code: The machine code produced by a compiler

Off the shelf: Software that is aimed at many users and sold 'as is'

One to many: A relationship where one record in a table may have links to many records in another table

Operand: This is the part of the instruction that tells the CPU what to apply the operation to

Operating system: The software that controls the hardware. It acts as an interface between the user and the hardware and also between applications and the hardware

Operator (arithmetic and logic): A logical, arithmetic or comparison operator used by the program

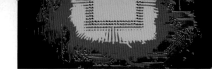

Operator (assembly language): This is the part of the instruction that tells the CPU what to do

Optical disk: Secondary storage device using lasers to read (and write) data to a reflective surface. For storing files to be distributed or transferred or for backup of important files.

Overflow: When a number becomes too large to fit into the number of bits allocated it is said to 'overflow' and some bits are 'lost' leaving an incorrect value

PDF: Portable document format – a file standard that displays a document accurately on any computer platform

Peer-to-peer: A network arrangement where all computers are equal

Pixel: The smallest element of an image. Pixels are the dots that make the image on screen

Platform: A combination of hardware and operating system that supports the running of particular applications

Pretty printer: An editor that automatically sets out program code in an easy to read way

Printer: A device to produce physical copies of output from a computer system

Process (flow chart): A flow chart symbol that defines any processing to be completed at that stage

Process (program): A program currently being executed

Program: A stored set of instructions for a computer to execute

Program counter: A register in the CPU that keeps the address of the next instruction

Programming language: A way of writing instructions for a computer to execute

Protocol: A set of rules or standards that control communication between devices

Pseudocode: A method of describing an algorithm using structured English close to programming language

Random access memory (RAM): Main memory of a computer that stores data, applications and the operating system whilst in use. When the power is turned off RAM loses its data

Raster: Graphics format consisting of a matrix of dots

Read only memory (ROM): A store for data in a computer that cannot be overwritten. Data in ROM is always available and is not lost when the computer is turned off

Real: A number that can have decimal or fractional parts

Record: All the data about one item in a database

Register: Special fast access part of the CPU that stores data in use by the CPU

Resolution: The number of pixels or dots per unit, for example ppi (pixels per inch), often referred to as dpi (dots per inch)

RFID: Radio frequency identification uses radio frequencies to represent a number that can be scanned for input into a computer system

Run time environment: Software to support the execution of programs

Sample rate: The number of times the sound is sampled per second, measured in Hz (100 Hz is 100 samples per second)

Schema: Definition of a database

Secondary storage: Non-volatile storage used to store programs and files that need to be kept even when the power is not on

Selection: The pathway through a program is selected by using a condition to decide on what instructions to execute next

Self-booting: The ability of a program to load itself. Some small devices load their applications directly without the need for a conventional operating system

Sensor: A device that can detect physical conditions such as temperature, weight, light, sound, etc.

Sequence: A list of instructions to be carried out in order, one after the other

Sequential file: A serial file in order

Serial file: A file of items one after another

Server: Software that provides services to a client, or the hardware that is running it

Shell: Software that provides a traditional text based interface to an operating system

Software: The programs that run on a computer

Software engineering: Formal methods to guide the writing of software

Solid state: Technology based on electronics with no moving parts, for example transistors and capacitors as used in memory chips

Source code: The program written by the end user in a high-level language before it is converted to machine code

Speaker: A device to output sound

Spyware: Malicious software that detects what a user is doing and sends the details back to the originator

String: A string of alphabetic and/or numeric characters

Switch: A device for connecting multiple network devices and multiple segments

Syntax error: The rules of a language are broken by the program

TCP/IP: Transmission control protocol/internet protocol – a set of standards that control how data is sent across networks including the internet

Terabyte: 1024 gigabytes

Touch screen: A touch sensitive surface that allows the user to select, control or move objects by touching icons and symbols using fingers

Trace: A method of using data to check that a flow chart covers all possibilities correctly

Translator: A program to convert high-level or assembly-level commands into machine code

Trojan: Harmful software that is disguised as something useful

Truth table: A method for recording all the possible input combinations and determining the output for each

Unicode: Up to 32-bit system to code the character set of a computer (usually 16-bit or 32-bit versions)

User interface: The boundary between the computer and the user

Utility: A small program designed to carry out a limited maintenance task

Valid: Data used in testing that represents normal data that could be expected

Validation: The process of checking data as it is input to ensure that it is reasonable

Variable: A label referring to a location in memory containing a value that can be accessed or changed by a program

Verification: The process of checking that data is true or correct

Virtual memory: A section of the hard disk used as if it were RAM to supplement the amount of main memory available to the computer. Used when there is not enough main memory to run the programs required

Virus detection: The process of discovering possibly harmful viruses in a computer system

Volatile: Data lost when there is no power

WAN: Wide areas network – covers large geographical area

Web server: A server that handles requests to a website

Index

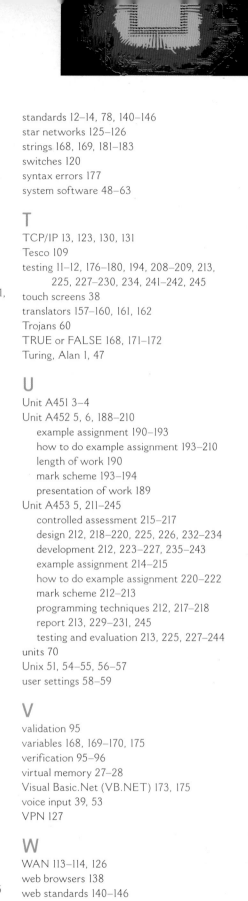